READERS' GUIDES TO ESSENTIAL CRITICISM

CONSULTANT EDITOR: NICOLAS TREDELL

Published

Susie Thomas	Hanif Kureishi
Nicolas Tredell	F. Scott Fitzgerald: *The Great Gatsby*
Nicolas Tredell	Joseph Conrad: *Heart of Darkness*
Nicolas Tredell	Charles Dickens: *Great Expectations*
Nicolas Tredell	William Faulkner *The Sound and the Fury – As I Lay Dying*
Nicolas Tredell	The Fiction of Martin Amis
Nicolas Tredell	Shakespeare: *Macbeth*

Forthcoming

Paul Baines	Daniel Defoe: *Robinson Crusoe – Moll Flanders*
Sandie Byrne	Contemporary British Poetry
Peter Dempsey	The Fiction of Don Delillo
Jodi-Anne George	*Beowulf*
William Hughes	Bram Stoker: *Dracula*
Matthew Jordan	Milton: *Paradise Lost*
Jago Morrison	The Fiction of Chinua Achebe
Nicholas Potter	Shakespeare: *Antony and Cleopatra*
Stephen Regan	The Poetry of Philip Larkin
Gina Wisker	The Fiction of Margaret Atwood
Angela Wright	Gothic Fiction

Palgrave Readers' Guides to Essential Criticism
Series Standing Order
ISBN 1–4390–0108–2
(*outside North America only*)

You can receive future titles in this series as they are published by placing a standing order. Please contact your bookseller or, in the case of difficulty, write to us at the address below with your name and address, the title of the series and the ISBN quoted above.

Customer Services Department, Palgrave Macmillan Ltd
Houndmills, Basingstoke, Hampshire RG21 6XS, England

Shakespeare
Macbeth

NICOLAS TREDELL

Consultant editor: Nicolas Tredell

First published in 2006 by
PALGRAVE MACMILLAN
Houndmills, Basingstoke, Hampshire RG21 6XS and
175 Fifth Avenue, New York, N.Y. 10010
Companies and representatives throughout the world.

PALGRAVE MACMILLAN is the global academic imprint of the Palgrave Macmillan division of St. Martin's Press, LLC and of Palgrave Macmillan Ltd. Macmillan® is a registered trademark in the United States, United Kingdom and other countries. Palgrave is a registered trademark in the European Union and other countries.

ISBN-13: 978–1–4039–9924–5 hardback
ISBN-10: 1–4039–9924–4 hardback
ISBN-13: 978–1–4039–9925–2 paperback
ISBN-10: 1–4039–9925–2 paperback

This book is printed on paper suitable for recycling and made from fully managed and sustained forest sources.

A catalogue record for this book is available from the British Library.

A catalog record for this book is available from the Library of Congress.

10 9 8 7 6 5 4 3 2 1
15 14 13 12 11 10 09 08 07 06

Printed and bound in China.

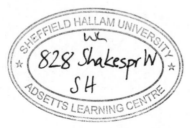

For Angela

CONTENTS

CHAPTER THREE   43

The Early Twentieth Century: Tragedy, Psychoanalysis and Imagery

Explores A. C. Bradley's idea of Shakespearean tragedy and key elements of his interpretation of *Macbeth*; Sigmund Freud's reading of *Macbeth* as a play about childlessness; Caroline Spurgeon's widely disseminated analysis of recurrent images in the play; G. Wilson Knight's 'spatial' approach to Shakespeare and his reading of *Macbeth* as a vision of evil; L. C. Knights's famous attack on a character-based approach to Shakespeare, 'How Many Children Had Lady Macbeth?'; and William Empson's ingenious close readings of key passages in the play.

CHAPTER FOUR   68

The Mid-Twentieth Century: History, Nature and Evil

Examines E. M. W. Tillyard's account of *Macbeth* as a history play; Henry N. Paul's consideration of the play's relationship to contemporary historical events; Eugene M. Waith's discussion of masculinity in *Macbeth*; Cleanth Brooks's famous 'New Critical' analysis of the image of the naked babe and the clothed man in the play; the ripostes to Brooks of Oscar James Campbell and Helen Gardner; L. C. Knights's complex interpretation of *Macbeth* in relation to Shakespearean notions of 'nature'; Jan Kott's emphasis on the murderous, nihilistic aspects of the play; and Wilbur Sanders's Nietzschean reading of *Macbeth* as exemplifying the energy of evil.

CHAPTER FIVE   94

The Later Twentieth Century: Politics, Violence and Ideology

Traces Harry Berger Jr's pioneering investigation of the paradoxes of the early scenes of *Macbeth*; Michael Hawkins's thoughtful discussion of the links between the play and the political ideas of the time; Peter Stallybrass's sharp examination of the relationships between witchcraft and political power in *Macbeth* and in society; Stephen Booth's exploration of the indefiniteness of *Macbeth* in relation to a theory of tragedy; James L. Calderwood's analysis of *Macbeth* as a counter-*Hamlet*, a tragedy about the nature of tragedy, and a study of culture and violence; and Alan Sinfield's provocative account of the relationship of *Macbeth* to the contrasting ideologies of James I and George Buchanan.

ACKNOWLEDGEMENTS

I am most grateful to my wife Angela for her help and support during the writing of this Guide.

NOTES ON THE TEXT

A ll Act, scene and line references are keyed to the Oxford and Norton Shakespeares and given in Arabic rather than Roman numerals, e.g. 3.4.74–83 rather than III.iv.74–83.

In older texts, such as those of Samuel Johnson, capitalization, italicization and punctuation have been silently modified to accord with modern usage, except where the older usage seems especially significant.

Definitions are from the *Concise Oxford Dictionary* (COD), 10th edn, unless otherwise stated.

Introduction

*M*acbeth is a play that seems to go to extremes, though not always immediately appealing ones: it has been variously regarded as the most concentrated, most humourless, most rapid, most topical, most tremendous, most vehement and most violent of Shakespeare's tragedies.[1] It is certainly the shortest, and, in theatrical lore, the unluckiest, to be named only indirectly ('the Scottish play') for fear that the utterance of its actual title may bring toil and trouble. While not quite as central to Western culture as *Hamlet*, it offers an apparently inexhaustible store of cultural references, and in one key area it surpasses *Hamlet* – it provides an unparalleled set of images of feminine monstrousness, transgression and remorse: Lady Macbeth has ingrained herself into cultural consciousness in a way that pale Ophelia never can. If *Hamlet* has held up a mirror in which Western man has often seen not wholly unflattering images of himself, *Macbeth* provides a reflection which Western man – and Western woman – find less easy to contemplate steadily; characteristically, it has been turned to an oblique angle to catch, as in a glass darkly, the image of the abhorred other – tyrant, murderer, lethal spouse and mother – in comparison with which our own virtue may shine.

As this Guide to Essential Criticism will show, *Macbeth* can be seen, and has been seen, as a play of metaphysical absolutes, pitting good against evil, light against dark and fruitfulness against barrenness: a play that plumbs the depths, and hints at the heights, of humankind. It can also be seen – and the Guide will explore this view as well – as a highly political play, an intervention in urgent early seventeenth-century debates about kingship, about king-killing, about witchcraft, and about the role and nature of women. The references to 'equivocation' in the Porter scene (2.3) can make the play reverberate with the impact of an explosion which never happened, but which, had it done so, would have had an impact comparable to that of 9/11 – the explosion, planned by the conspirators of the Gunpowder Plot, that would have blown up the House of Lords on State Opening Day, 5 November 1605, when King James I, his queen, his eldest son and members of the Lords and Commons would all be in the chamber.

Macbeth can also resonate alarmingly with our own time. It shows a world in which internal and external threats to the state are met, in terms of the sword-and-dagger technology of the period in which the play is set, with ultimate force and with spectacular, special-effects violence ('unseamed him from the nave to the chops', 1.2.22); in which regime change is brought about by slaughter, perpetrated first by Macbeth, then by Malcolm and Macduff; in which a tyrant wantonly kills men, women and children; in which the invaders weaken their enemy with shock and awe (impossibly, Birnam Wood starts to move) before they unleash full-scale violence; and in which severed heads on poles are the most visible symbols of who's boss. Whether viewed metaphysically or politically, whether related to its own time or our own, it is an urgent, exciting play and it has generated a rich critical response.

This Guide aims to trace the history of that response by examining key commentaries and interpretations from the seventeenth to the early twenty-first century. Chapter 1 begins by discussing the text of *Macbeth* and the likelihood that it is not wholly by Shakespeare, and goes on to consider the account of a 1611 Globe performance by Simon Forman (1552–1611) – the only record we have of a performance of *Macbeth* in Shakespeare's lifetime. It then examines the uneasy relationship of *Macbeth* – and of Shakespeare's plays more generally – to the notions of drama that emerged after the restoration of the monarchy in 1660 and became dominant in the earlier eighteenth century. It discusses the popular 1664 adaptation of *Macbeth* by Sir William D'Avenant (1606–68) and the critical implications of the extensive changes, cuts and additions it makes to the text; considers the attempt by Nicholas Rowe (1674–1718) to acknowledge Shakespeare's vulnerability to neoclassical criticism while seeking terms with which to grasp the power of his drama; and surveys the extensive and characteristically forthright comments by Samuel Johnson (1709–84) on the language, plot and characters of the play. The Guide then considers significant examples, in the later eighteenth century, of character-centred criticism of Shakespeare. It examines the observations of William Richardson (1743–1814) on the character of Macbeth in the light of a more general theory of human nature and psychology and considers key aspects of the debate on Macbeth's character and courage between Thomas Whately (died 1772), John Philip Kemble (1757–1823) and Richard Cumberland (1732–1811).

Chapter 2 of the Guide concentrates on key examples of nineteenth-century criticism of *Macbeth*. To some extent, the Romantic criticism of the early nineteenth century continued and elaborated the emphasis on character which had developed in the later eighteenth century, but it did not focus exclusively on this aspect of the play, and it gave greater scope to its wildness and excess, to those elements of it which seemed to coincide with the aspiring, transgressive and primeval energies which the Romantic imagination valued. The chapter starts with the vigorous attack by William Hazlitt (1778–1830) on what he sees as Samuel

Johnson's inadequacies as a critic of Shakespeare and then considers Hazlitt's discussions of Macbeth's character, of Lady Macbeth, of the witches, and of the structure, themes and language of the play. It moves on to examine the account by Samuel Taylor Coleridge (1772–1834) of *Macbeth* as a pure tragedy, and his penetrating explanation of the reasons for the change from resolve to remorse in Lady Macbeth. After this, the chapter turns to a celebrated essay on *Macbeth* which does not focus on character: the exploration by Thomas de Quincey (1785–1859) of the knocking on the gate as marking the end of the murderous moment in which ordinary life has been suspended. The chapter continues with an examination of a discussion by Anna Jameson (1794–1860) of the character of Lady Macbeth in relation to prevailing ideas of women's nature and to the representations of women in ancient Greek drama, and concludes with the observations on *Macbeth* by the quintessential Victorian critic of Shakespeare, Edward Dowden (1843–1913).

Chapter 3 opens with the famous definition of tragedy offered in 1904 by A. C. Bradley (1851–1935) and examines key aspects of his detailed interpretation of *Macbeth*. It then looks at the founding text of psychoanalytical criticism of *Macbeth*, which appeared as a section of the essay 'Some Character-Types Met With in Psycho-Analytical Work' in 1916 – the interpretation of *Macbeth* as a play about childlessness by the father of psychoanalysis, Sigmund Freud (1856–1939). It goes on to consider three critics who, in their respective ways, revolutionized Shakespeare criticism in the 1930s: Caroline Spurgeon (1886–1942), who pioneered the analysis of recurrent images in Shakespeare's plays and on whose work many subsequent critics have drawn; G. Wilson Knight (1897–1985), who developed an influential 'spatial' approach to Shakespeare and mapped *Macbeth* in terms of oppositions between evil and good; and the analysis of *Macbeth* provided by L. C. Knights (1908–91) to support his famous attack on a character-based approach to Shakespeare, 'How Many Children Had Lady Macbeth?' (1933). The chapter also examines the ingenious close readings of key passages in the play by William Empson (1906–84).

Chapter 4 highlights the opening up of issues of history and historical context in the mid-twentieth century by E. M. W. Tillyard (1889–1962) and Henry N. Paul, and looks at the path-breaking discussion by Eugene M. Waith of ideas of masculinity in the play – a discussion which will later be taken up and pursued further by feminist critics. It then moves on to another especially famous piece of *Macbeth* criticism – the analysis of the imagery of the naked babe and clothed man in the play – by the best-known exponent of American 'New Criticism', Cleanth Brooks (1906–84) – and considers the ripostes of Oscar James Campbell (1897–1970) and Helen Gardner (1906–86). It returns to L. C. Knights to explore the complex interpretation of *Macbeth* in relation to Shakespearean notions of 'nature' which he put forward in 1959, and goes on to examine two especially challenging interpretations of the 1960s: one, by Jan Kott (1914–2001), emphasizes the murderous, nihilistic aspects of *Macbeth*, and the other, by Wilbur Sanders, stresses the ambivalence of the play, in which evil is associated with energy in a way that resembles the 'strong pessimism' discussed by the philosopher Friedrich Nietzsche (1844–1900).

In Chapters 5, 6 and 7 of the Guide, we consider key examples of the provocative new readings of *Macbeth* which emerged in the 1980s and 1990s as part of a larger challenge to the prevailing assumptions of Shakespeare criticism, of Renaissance studies and of literary criticism in general. Chapter 5 begins with a pioneering analysis by Harry Berger Jr., first published in 1980, of the paradoxes and ambiguities of the early scenes of the play. It goes on to discuss the historically based account of *Macbeth*, by Michael Hawkins, which quietly but effectively questions many of the received mid-twentieth-century ideas about the play. This is followed by the sharp analysis by Peter Stallybrass of the relationships between witchcraft and political power in *Macbeth* and in the society in which the play emerged. The chapter then summarizes two important book-length studies of *Macbeth*: King Lear, Macbeth, *Indefinition, and Tragedy* (1983) by Stephen Booth, which emphasizes the indefiniteness of *Macbeth* and relates this to a broader theory of tragedy; and *If It Were Done*: Macbeth *and Tragic Action* (1986) by James L. Calderwood, which considers *Macbeth* as a sort of 'counter-*Hamlet*', as a tragedy about the nature of tragedy, and as a study of the interaction of culture and violence. Chapter 5 ends with Alan Sinfield's influential and provocative account, in 1986, of the relationship of *Macbeth* to the contrasting ideologies of King James I (1566–1625) and the historian and scholar George Buchanan (1506–82).

Chapter 6 engages with the close analysis by Catherine Belsey of the split subjectivity of the soliloquies of *Macbeth*; compares and contrasts Terry Eagleton's playfully serious elevation of the witches to heroic status with the sober account of the play that 'Terence Eagleton' (as he then styled himself) provided in 1967; and looks at Malcolm Evans's vivid account of the equivocal operations of language in the play. Chapter 7 of the Guide considers three key readings of *Macbeth* by feminist critics – all of whom, as it happens, dwell more on the play's exploration of masculinity than of femininity – and two crucial interpretations which consider the play's attitude to women by focusing especially on the witches: Coppélia Kahn sees the play as about the failure to attain a fully individuated masculine identity; Marilyn French argues that it is about the suppression of the feminine principle in an heroic, 'manly' culture; and Janet Adelman regards it as representing the contradictory fantasies of an absolute maternal power and of an absolute escape from such power. Stephen Greenblatt, asking whether *Macbeth* should be seen as evil because it reinforces prejudices against witches and women, mounts a case for the defence, and Stephen Orgel sees the witches as opening up a paradoxical space for women in the play. The Conclusion of the Guide considers possible future directions for *Macbeth* criticism in the twenty-first century.

Macbeth matters: it is Shakespeare's most disturbing play and it sends out multiple shock-waves, metaphysically, philosophically, ethically, historically and politically. The essential criticism explored in this Guide offers us the opportunity to measure and define those shock-waves, to gain a deeper understanding of the play's many meanings, to listen to the most significant *Macbeth* critics of the past and present, and to pursue and develop our own interpretations.

CHAPTER ONE

The Seventeenth and Eighteenth Centuries: The Development of *Macbeth* Criticism

The dates of the composition and first performance of *Macbeth* are uncertain. Most critics and editors suggest that it was composed in 1606 – this is the date given by, for example, the Oxford Shakespeare[1] – but in his introduction to his Arden edition, Kenneth Muir points to earlier dates that have been suggested – 1599 and 1601, for example – though he himself opts for the period 1603 to 1606.[2] The main reason for the 1606 dating is that there are several references in the Porter scene (2.3) to 'equivocation' – a term strongly linked with the Superior of the English Jesuits, Father Henry Garnett (1555–1606), who was hanged, drawn and quartered on 3 May 1606 for alleged complicity in the Gunpowder Plot. Garnett had become notorious for his defence of equivocation – of making a statement that seemed to have one meaning then privately adding further words to it which gave it quite a different meaning (for further discussion of this, see Chapter 4 of this Guide). It is, however, possible that the references to 'equivocation' were a topical insertion into an earlier text.

The first printed text of *Macbeth* was in the 1623 Folio edition of Shakespeare. This version was probably based on a promptbook. Most modern scholars agree, however, that the Folio text is an adapted one that is not wholly by Shakespeare. In contrast to Shakespeare's other tragedies, it is remarkably short, and it contains episodes that Shakespeare may not have written – the *Oxford Shakespeare* editors identify 3.5, and two parts of 4.1: 38–60 and 141–8. The attribution of these episodes to Shakespeare is doubtful on at least three counts: they are the only appearances of Hecate in *Macbeth*; they are in octosyllabic couplets (eight-syllable lines that rhyme *aa, bb, cc*, etc.), and are thus in a markedly different style from the rest of the play, which is mainly in iambic pentameter blank verse (ten-syllable non-rhyming lines); and they include two songs whose opening words also occur in *The Witch* (date uncertain) by Shakespeare's fellow-playwright Thomas Middleton (about 1580–1627).

As well as the Folio text of 1623, we also have one fascinating record, by the astrologer and physician Simon Forman, of a contemporary performance of *Macbeth* at the Globe in 1611.

SIMON FORMAN

Simon Forman wrote accounts of Globe performances of *Macbeth*, *Cymbeline* and *The Winter's Tale* in a manuscript called *The Bocke of Plaies and Notes therof per formane for Common Pollicie* – that is, for practical use in everyday life; for example, Forman draws this moral from the confidence tricks of Autolycus in *The Winter's Tale*: 'Beware of trusting feigned beggars or fawning fellows'.[3] The performance date for *Macbeth* Forman gives – 20 April 1610 – seems wrong, as 20 April did not fall on a Saturday in 1610 (1611 has been suggested as a more likely date[4]), and his account may draw on Holinshed's *Chronicles* as well as on his memory of the performance; he refers to the witches as '3 women feiries or Nimphes', which echoes one of the phrases Holinshed uses in relation to them, 'some nymphes or feiries'.[5] But Forman's record remains important because it is the only contemporary account of a performance of *Macbeth* that we have, and because of its inclusions, omissions and even apparent errors.

For example, Forman seems to make a major error when he claims that Duncan made Macbeth 'Prince of Northumberland'; in the list of characters, Siward is the 'Earl of Northumberland' who joins forces with Macduff and Malcolm to overthrow Macbeth, and he is explicitly referred to as 'Northumberland' only once in the play, as a likely ally of Macduff's, along with Northumberland's son, Young Siward (3.6.31), whom Macbeth will later kill in combat. Forman's remark might be a confused reference to Duncan's bestowal of the title of Prince of Cumberland on his eldest son, Malcolm (1.4.38–9) – a crucial moment in the play because it effectively designates Malcolm as Duncan's successor, since successors named by the king in his lifetime at once received the title of Prince of Cumberland. The Scottish monarchy was not hereditary at the time in which *Macbeth* is set, so it could not be assumed that Malcolm, as the eldest son, would automatically inherit the throne; in principle, Duncan could have named Macbeth as his successor. By bestowing the title on Malcolm, Duncan puts an obstacle in the way of Macbeth's ascension to the throne, as Macbeth himself almost immediately acknowledges in an aside: 'The Prince of Cumberland! – That is a step / On which I must fall down, or else o'erleap / For in my way it lies' (1.4.48–50). It has, however, been argued by Daniel Amneus, in *The Mystery of Macbeth* (1983), that there was an original version of *Macbeth* by Shakespeare, written in 1599, in which Macbeth was in fact made

Prince of Cumberland and thus effectively designated as Duncan's successor so that he at first decided not to murder him, but was later persuaded to collaborate with his wife in doing so. But this argument is not conclusive.[6]

Forman's account goes on to say that Macbeth 'contrived to kill Duncan' and that it was 'through the persuasion of his wife'[7] that he murdered Duncan on the night when the king was a guest in his castle. He notes that 'many prophecies [were] seen that night and the day before', and writes as though Duncan's blood indelibly stained Macbeth's hands as well as Lady Macbeth's: 'And when Macbeth had murdered the King, the blood on his hands could not be washed off by any means, nor from his wife's hands, which handled the bloody daggers in hiding them, by which means they became much amazed and affronted'. Forman then records the flight of Duncan's two sons; the suspicion that falls upon them as a result of their flight; the crowning of Macbeth (which of course takes place offstage in the text that we have); Macbeth's fear of Banquo because of the witches' prophecy that Banquo should beget kings but not be king himself; the murder of Banquo; and the appearance of Banquo's ghost. Forman's description of this seems to indicate that, in the performance he saw, the ghost was played by an actor:

■ The next night [after Banquo's murder], being at supper with his noblemen whom he had bid to a feast to the which also Banquo should have come, he began to speak of Noble Banquo, and to wish that he were there. And as he thus did, standing up to drink a carouse to him, the ghost of Banquo came and sat down in his chair behind him. And he [Macbeth] turning about to sit down again saw the ghost of Banquo, which fronted him so, that he fell into a great passion of fear and fury, uttering many words about his murder, by which, they heard that Banquo was murdered they suspected Macbeth.[8] □

Forman then quickly summarizes Macduff's flight to England to join Malcolm, the killing of Macduff's wife and children, the raising of an army by Macduff and Malcolm, their invasion of Scotland, their defeat of Macbeth at Dunsinane and Macduff's slaying of Macbeth. There is also a last paragraph on the sleepwalking scene (5.1):

■ Observe also how Macbeth's queen did rise in the night in her sleep and walk and talked and confessed all, and the doctor noted her words.[9] □

The 'observe also' which opens this paragraph suggests that this may be the part of the play which seemed to Forman to offer a useful lesson in everyday life – perhaps particularly for his work as a physician. He also picks out other scenes that would have related to his astrological and medical interests: the original prophecies, the 'prodigies' or portents, the apparently indelible bloodstains and, above all, the appearance of Banquo's ghost and its psychological effects on Macbeth. All these scenes will feature prominently in later critical commentaries on the play.

The omissions from Forman's account have provoked speculation about whether the performance he saw differed from the Folio text. Muir, for example, feels that Forman, as an astrologer, might have been expected to mention 4.1, the cauldron scene and its prophecies,[10] and that the fact that he did not do so may mean that this scene was not in the 1611 performance; Kathleen McCluskie points out that Forman makes no reference to the Porter (2.3.1–39) and suggests that by 1611 this character may have been left out because his allusions to the 'equivocation' associated with the 1605 Gunpowder Plot were no longer topical.[11] She also remarks that the absence of the cauldron scene and its prophecies from Forman's account brings home 'how flat the play would be without them', how important they are 'in the narrative and emotional structure of *Macbeth*'.[12] Without other evidence, of course, it is impossible to know whether the omissions in Forman's account indicate omissions in the version of *Macbeth* that he saw.

We have to wait some time for further accounts of *Macbeth*. As the seventeenth century advanced, tension grew between the kind of public theatre Shakespeare had known, the kind of theatre, involving the staging of elaborate masques, centred around the Stuart court, and the anti-theatrical polemics of Puritans such as William Prynne (1600–69). When the English Civil War broke out in 1642, a Parliamentary ordinance closed the theatres, which were seen as potential sites of lawlessness; it was not until the Restoration of the monarchy and the accession of Charles II in 1660 that theatre was rehabilitated, but the theatre which then emerged was of a very different kind to that for which Shakespeare has written. As Brian Vickers points out, in Shakespeare's time there had been between five to eight public theatres in London with weekly audiences of 18,000 to 24,000 people; these theatres, and the years in which they opened, were the Theatre (1576) and the Curtain (1577) in Shoreditch, the Rose (1587), the Swan (1595) and the Globe (1599) on Bankside, Southwark, the Fortune (1600) in the parish of St Giles without [outside] Cripplegate, and the Red Bull (about 1604) and the Hope (1613–14) on Bankside. In the immediate post-Restoration period, however, there were only two theatre companies licensed by Charles II – the Duke's Men, managed by Sir William D'Avenant, and the King's Men, managed by Sir Thomas Killigrew. The theatre buildings were roofed over and smaller than Elizabethan public theatres – they held about 400 people – and the cost of admission was much higher.[13] Perspective scenery designed to create an illusion of depth became far more widespread[14] and professional actresses were used for female parts.[15] Moreover, the critical canons by which plays were judged had changed: neoclassical criteria, derived from the writings of the ancient Greek philosopher Aristotle (384–322 BC) and those of the ancient Roman poet Horace (65–8 BC) via the Italian sixteenth century and the French seventeenth century, had become dominant, and these stipulated that plays should observe the unities of time, place and action and should demonstrate propriety and decorum in their language and action.[16]

Shakespeare's work, however, notoriously failed to accord with these criteria and thus presented critics and theatrical producers with a problem: here was a presence that was too powerful and fecund to be ignored, but that could not easily be accommodated to existing critical principles. One way for theatrical producers to deal with this was to adapt Shakespeare; and the most important and popular adaptation of *Macbeth* in the later seventeenth century was by the manager of the Duke's Men, who was also a playwright and poet: Sir William D'Avenant.

SIR WILLIAM D'AVENANT

D'Avenant's adaptation was probably first performed on 5 November 1664 and it was first published in 1674; it became the version most often seen in London until Garrick's 1744 production. D'Avenant, who claimed to be Shakespeare's illegitimate son – he was, in fact, his godson[17] – played a key part in the revival of interest in Shakespearean drama after the Restoration, but he heavily adapted the versions of Shakespeare that he presented on stage, and his version of *Macbeth* was no exception. Of course, it is not a piece of literary criticism, but it does have significant critical implications; while some of the changes it makes to Shakespeare's text are primarily due to the pressures of performance, others could be taken as an implicit criticism of Shakespeare in terms of the critical criteria which were dominant in D'Avenant's day.

D'Avenant's most notable changes are to the language of *Macbeth*. He removes ambiguities, cuts down imagery by eliminating it entirely or substituting more abstract terms, and tones down violence and excess. Memorable metaphors vanish – for example, Lady Macbeth's vivid 'But screw your courage to the sticking place' (1.7.60), an image drawn from the process by which a screw is turned to tighten a crossbow string in its notch, becomes the more abstract 'But bring your courage to the fatall place'.[18] Passages that will especially interest later critics are simplified or disappear altogether – for instance, D'Avenant excises the 'Pity, like a naked new-born babe' image,[19] which will be the object of close scrutiny and intense discussion by mid-twentieth-century critics such as Cleanth Brooks and Helen Gardner. The intensity and compression of Shakespeare's language is reduced, as we can see if we compare and contrast Macbeth's speech in 3:2 with D'Avenant's version:

■ *Macbeth*:   Come, seeling Night,
Scarf up the tender eye of pitiful day,
And, with thy bloody and invisible hand,
Cancel and tear to pieces that great bond
Which keeps me pale. Light thickens, and the crow
Makes wing to th'rooky wood.
Good things of day begin to droop and drowse,
Whiles night's black agents to their preys do rouse. □   [3:2:47–54]

■ *Macbeth*:   Come, dismal Night
Close up the Eye of the quick-sighted day
With thy invisible and bloody hand.
The Crow makes wing to the thick shady Grove,
Good things of day grow dark and overcast,
Whilst Nights black Agents to their Preys make hast.[20] □

By using the adjective 'dismal', D'Avenant eliminates the metaphor drawn from falconry that Shakespeare employs – to 'seel' is temporarily to sew together the eyelids of a hawk. While a trace of the 'hawk' metaphor may persist in D'Avenant's elimination of 'pitiful' and his substitution of 'quick-sighted' for 'tender', these changes also eradicate the potential links between 'tender'/'pitiful', and the other references to tenderness and pity in the play, especially the 'Pity, like a naked new-born babe' speech. D'Avenant completely cuts out 'The great bond', with its implications of a relationship that is hugely significant in both ethical and natural terms, and also excises 'Light thickens', with its suggestions of weight and density, of an almost palpable darkness. The replacement of 'rooky wood' by 'thick shady Grove' creates a much more demure, neoclassical impression, and removes the possibility of the contrast between the communal rook and the solitary crow which William Empson will propose, over two centuries later, in *Seven Types of Ambiguity* (1930). The change of 'begin to droop and drowse' to 'grow dark and overcast' means that the sense that this is a time of transition – things are *starting* to droop and drowse – is less prominent; it also eliminates the alliteration of '*d*roop / *d*rowse' and the idea of goodness losing strength, sinking towards sleep and falling into a state of moral inattention.

As well as these linguistic changes which cumulatively alter the whole tone and texture of the play, D'Avenant expands Lady Macduff's role to make her into the virtuous antithesis of Lady Macbeth. In D'Avenant's

Macbeth, the two women are introduced at the same time: when Lady Macbeth first appears in Shakespeare's play, she is alone and reading the letter which Macbeth has sent her; in D'Avenant's version, she is in the company of Lady Macduff – in the next scene, we learn, from Lady Macbeth's words to Duncan, that Lady Macduff has come to stay with her to seek 'a cure for her own solitude'[21] while Macduff has been away at the wars. On their first appearance, the two women engage in a dialogue in which Lady Macduff reveals that she is still suffering from the fears aroused by her husband's absence, even though she now knows he is safe; when Lady Macbeth suggests that her mood should be lifted by the honours that Macduff has gained in battle, Lady Macduff casts doubt upon the value of 'glories gain'd in war'.

As well as introducing Lady Macduff into the first scene with Lady Macbeth, D'Avenant also provides three more scenes in which Lady Macduff appears. In the first of these, she and her husband meet the witches on the heath, and her innocence and virtue are revealed when she refuses to be afraid of them; as Macduff says to her 'if any one wou'd be / Reputed valiant let him learn of you / Virtue both Courage is and safety too'[22]. Her virtuous valour is thus implicitly contrasted with the vicious valour of Lady Macbeth. In the second scene, an exchange takes place between Lady Macduff and her husband in which he confirms that he believes that Macbeth has killed Duncan and argues that he should act against Macbeth to secure justice for the murdered king and defend his country against 'the bloody Tyrant's violence'; his wife is concerned, however, that he may be motivated by ambition for the crown – 'You'd raise your self whilst you would him dethrone' – and that his purpose may only seem 'usurpation at the second hand' which, even if it involved no bloodshed, would be 'unlawful' and 'at best unjustly good'.[23] D'Avenant thus builds in a much more explicit debate than Shakespeare about the ethics and motives of usurpation, which may relate to the uneasiness the issue aroused in the Restoration period.

D'Avenant's third new Lady Macduff scene is especially significant for future *Macbeth* criticism since it provides some explanation of Macduff's apparent desertion of his wife and family – an issue that has been especially troubling for those critics who want to see Macduff as the noble and heroic antithesis of Macbeth. In D'Avenant's scene, Macduff tells his wife that he has resolved to leave her, and when she protests, he argues that it will be safer for her as well as for himself. He gives three reasons for this: Macbeth cannot be 'possessed with such unmanly cruelty' that he will injure her; it will slow them down too much if they all go together; and, as a woman, she will be more exposed to danger by the hardships of the journey than by staying where she is: 'Your sex, which here is your security / Will by the toils of flight your danger be'.[24] The matter is finally settled when a messenger brings news of Banquo's death and Lady Macduff herself urges him to fly and feels herself growing more valiant as she anticipates his departure – 'My heart feels Manhood' – though she is still woman enough to shed tears for his impending absence.[25] This added scene thus mitigates her later denunciation of her husband as lacking 'the natural touch'; in his adaptation, D'Avenant retains this denunciation but eliminates Lady Macduff's son and ends the scene with Lady Macduff saying that she will go 'boldly in', to 'dare' the danger of which she has been warned; in contrast to Shakespeare, and in accordance with neoclassical principles of decorum, the murder takes place offstage.

As well as mitigating Macduff's desertion of his wife and family, D'Avenant's adaptation also removes the questionable responses of Macduff in the scene in which Malcolm tests him by accusing himself of a range of vices which make him unsuitable to be king. In Shakespeare's text, for example, when Malcolm confesses to insatiable lust, Macduff recognizes its dangers to a monarch but does not see it as a disqualification, advising him to gratify it covertly with the 'willing dames' who will be ready to accommodate him because of his regal greatness (4.3.74). D'Avenant cuts down Malcolm's self-accusations considerably and excludes any specific reference to 'lust' (perhaps this ranks among the 'sins too horrible to name' which D'Avenant's Malcolm mentions[26]). Thus Macduff emerges in this scene as a more uncomplicated representative of virtue than in Shakespeare's play.

Whereas Shakespeare's Lady Macbeth disappears after the end of the banquet scene and only reappears once more, in the sleepwalking scene, D'Avenant inserts an extra scene between Lady Macbeth and her husband in which initially, in a reversal of their roles at the banquet, she feels constantly haunted by Duncan's ghost and Macbeth tells her that it is 'the strange error of your eyes'.[27] When the error is temporarily corrected and the ghost disappears for a short while, the scene turns into an ethical debate in which Lady Macbeth urges her husband to give up the crown because it has been won by crime; when he accuses her of provoking him to commit the crime, she affirms that this was due to a collapse in proper gender relationships, in which males should rule over females: 'You were a man / And by the Charter of your sex you should / Have governed me; there was more crime in you / When you obeyed my counsel than I contracted / by my giving it'.[28]

Further notable changes at the end of D'Avenant's *Macbeth* include the return of Fleance and Donalbain, who simply disappear in Shakespeare's play, to join the forces marching against Macbeth; the addition of a speech in which Macduff, as he kills Macbeth, assigns each stroke of his sword to a specific murder for which he is meting out condign punishment – 'This for thy Royal Master Duncan / This for my dearest friend my wife / This for those pledges of our loves: my children'; a dying line from Macbeth himself in which he suggests the cause of his tragedy: 'Farewell vain world, and what's most vain in it Ambition'; and the replacement of Macbeth's severed head by the more decorous metonymy of his sword.[29]

The overall effect of D'Avenant's adaptation is to construct a more evidently moral play than Shakespeare's *Macbeth*. Many of his changes focus on those aspects of Shakespeare's play that will concern later critics – and a significant proportion of those critics, while accepting Shakespeare's text, will aim to interpret it in ways that bring it closer, in terms of its moral import, to D'Avenant's and to eradicate awkward elements that might compromise its ethical stance. D'Avenant's criticism of Shakespeare is only implicit in his adaptation, however; as we enter the seventeenth century, the playwright, poet and editor Nicholas Rowe explicitly addresses the question of the uneasy relationship between Shakespearean drama and neoclassical criteria.

NICHOLAS ROWE

In his preface to his 1709 edition of Shakespeare, 'Some Account of the Life &c. of Mr. William Shakespeare', Rowe states the issue squarely: if neoclassical criteria drawn from Aristotle are applied to Shakespeare's tragedies, 'it would be no very hard task to find a great many faults';[30] Rowe exculpates Shakespeare, however, on the grounds that a general ignorance of the rules of drama prevailed in his time. Shakespeare's 'genius', he contends, is most apparent in those plays 'where he gives his Imagination an entire loose, and raises his fancy to a flight above mankind and the limits of the visible world. Such are his attempts in *The Tempest, Midsummer Night's Dream, Macbeth* and *Hamlet*'. It is Shakespeare's 'magic', which 'has something very solemn and very poetical' in it,[31] that 'raises the fairies in *Midsummer Night's Dream*, the witches in *Macbeth*, and the ghost in *Hamlet*, with thoughts and language so proper to the parts they sustain, and so peculiar to the talent of this writer'.[32] As well as succeeding in this way, *Macbeth*, like *Hamlet*, succeeds in raising not '*Horror*' but '*Terror*' – 'The latter is a proper passion of tragedy, but the former ought always to be carefully avoided'. No dramatist 'ever succeeded better in raising *Terror* in the minds of audience than Shakespeare has done':[33]

■ The whole tragedy of *Macbeth*, but more especially the scene where the King is murdered [2.1.31–72] ... is a noble proof of that manly spirit with which he writ; and both shew how powerful he was, in giving the strongest motions to our souls that they are capable of.[34] □

Rowe finds a way of talking about Shakespearean drama that recognizes its incompatibility with neoclassical criteria, but acknowledges its power in a way that anticipates the Romantic critics such as Hazlitt and Coleridge whom we shall consider in the next chapter of this Guide. Samuel Johnson, however, had more reservations.

SAMUEL JOHNSON

In his 1765 edition of Shakespeare, Samuel Johnson offered the following general observation on *Macbeth*:

■ This play is deservedly celebrated for the propriety of its fictions, and solemnity, grandeur, and variety of its action; but it has no nice discriminations of character, the events are too great to admit the influence of particular dispositions, and the course of the action necessarily determines the conduct of the agents.

The danger of ambition is well described; and I know not whether it may be said in defence of some parts which now seem improbable that in Shakespeare's time it was necessary to warn credulity against vain and illusive predictions.

The passions are directed to their true end. Lady Macbeth is merely detested; and though the courage of Macbeth preserves some esteem yet every reader rejoices at his fall.[35] □

Three aspects of this observation are notable: Johnson's complaint about the way in which character is subordinated to action and event in *Macbeth*; his uneasiness about the improbability of some parts of the play; and his view that the only response that Lady Macbeth arouses is that of detestation. His uneasiness about what he sees as the play's improbable elements is explored further in his first specific note, on the opening stage direction, '*Enter Three Witches*'. Like Nicholas Rowe, Johnson is strongly conscious that Shakespeare's drama could easily be found wanting when judged by prevailing eighteenth-century standards; and Johnson finds *Macbeth* most vulnerable in that very area in which, for Rowe, Shakespeare's 'Genius' is most apparent: the use of 'Magic'. Johnson affirms:

■ A poet who should now make the whole action of his tragedy depend upon enchantment, and produce the chief events by the assistance of supernatural agents, would be censured as transgressing the bounds of probability, be banished from the theatre to the nursery, and condemned to write fairy tales instead of tragedies.[36] □

Here, Johnson's metaphor of the 'nursery' associates the use of the supernatural as a dramatic device with a state of infancy which should be outgrown; it is interesting to compare this pre-Romantic assumption that infancy is an inferior state to its exaltation as a symbol of compassion, creativity and the future in *Macbeth* by twentieth-century critics such as Wilson Knight and Cleanth Brooks.

Like Rowe, Johnson aims to defend Shakespeare by setting him in the context of his times; but whereas Rowe attributes Shakespeare's possible failings to a general ignorance, in the Elizabethan and Jacobean eras, of the precepts of neoclassical drama, Johnson, specifically concerned with what he sees as the transgression of the bounds of probability in *Macbeth*, homes in on the belief in witches that prevailed in those times, especially in the reign of James I, when there was a keen interest in witchcraft – led by the King himself, who had published a book on the topic – and when legislation was enacted to forbid it. 'Upon this general infatuation,' Johnson claims, 'Shakespeare might be easily allowed to found a play', and it cannot be doubted that 'the scenes of enchantment, however they may now be ridiculed, were both by himself and his audience thought awful [in the sense of awe-inspiring] and affecting'.[37] But Johnson does not seem prepared to allow that an educated eighteenth-century audience could be impressed by them or that they might have valid dramatic functions. In his later comment on what he regards as 'the chief scene of enchantment' in *Macbeth*[38] (4:1, the scene which may well include material by Thomas Middleton), he argues defensively that it demonstrates Shakespeare's 'judgement and his knowledge'[39] in selecting appropriate details that conform to 'common opinions and traditions'[40] about witches, and is at pains to show that these details have documentary sources; he makes no explicit case, however, for the dramatic power of the scene or its possible relationships to the broader themes of the play.

Johnson's view that Lady Macbeth is of little interest in her own right is exemplified in his comment on the arguments that she uses, in 1.7, to try to persuade her husband to kill Duncan. The focus of Johnson's observations is not on what these arguments might say about Lady Macbeth as a character but on the way in which they illustrate general aspects of 'human nature':

■ The arguments by which Lady Macbeth persuades her husband to commit the murder afford a proof of Shakespeare's knowledge of human nature. She urges the excellence and dignity of courage, a glittering idea which has dazzled mankind from age to age, and animated sometimes the housebreaker and sometimes the conqueror; but this sophism ['a fallacious argument, especially one used to deceive'] Macbeth has for ever destroyed by distinguishing true from false fortitude in a line and a half, of which it may almost be said that they ought to bestow immortality on the author though all his other productions had been lost.

> I dare do all that may become a man,
> Who dares do more is none.   [1.7.46–7]

This topic, which has been always employed with too much success, is used in this scene with peculiar propriety, to a soldier by a woman. Courage is the distinguishing virtue of a soldier, and the reproach of cowardice cannot be borne by any man from a woman without great impatience.[41] □

With an eighteenth-century confidence, Johnson speaks of 'human nature' as though it were universal and invariable, but it could be argued, from a more relativist twenty-first century perspective, that it is a specific version of 'human nature' that he employs: a 'human nature' which can be aroused to desire and action ('animated') and sometimes disoriented ('dazzled') by certain ideas; which is able to use such ideas to justify dubious behaviour (e.g. burglary); which can, at least in part, be classified in terms of types identified by occupation and moral qualities ('Courage is the distinguishing virtue of a soldier'); and which is strongly gendered – men are particularly vulnerable to accusations of cowardice from women. Here Johnson touches on an aspect of the play with which some later twentieth-century critics will be much concerned: its exploration of what it means to be a man.

Johnson's assumption that 'the course of the action necessarily determines the conduct of the agents' is illustrated in his next remark:

> ■ [Lady Macbeth] then urges the oaths by which he had bound himself to murder Duncan, another art of sophistry by which men have some-times deluded their consciences and persuaded themselves that what would be criminal in others is virtuous in them; this argument Shakespeare, whose plan obliged him to make Macbeth yield, has not confuted, though he might easily have shown that a former obligation could not be vacated by a latter.[42] □

Johnson claims here Shakespeare is working to a 'plan' that compels him to set aside an obvious rational objection that he might have put into Macbeth's mouth (and that indeed might have seemed an appropriate follow-up to the concise demolition of sophistry which Macbeth has just accomplished). Despite his earlier commendation of Shakespeare's 'knowledge of human nature', Johnson does not try to account for Macbeth's failure to make such an objection in terms of 'human nature', or in terms of 'character', but attributes it instead to Shakespeare's compliance with a preconceived design.

In a later comment, Johnson is strongly critical of the line in which Macbeth, describing the dead Duncan, speaks of 'His silver skin laced with his golden blood' (2.3.112). 'No amendment can be made to this line of which every word is equally faulty but by a general blot' – in other words, by cutting it out entirely. He is also uneasy about the description of the daggers used to kill Duncan as 'Unmannerly breech'd with gore' (2.3.115) – if we take 'breech'd' to mean clothed with breeches, or trousers, then the image implicitly likens the blood which stains the daggers to an inappropriate form of dress, as if the daggers were wearing the wrong trousers. Johnson feels that 'breech'd with gore', or, in some editions of his time, 'breach'd with gore', 'are expressions not easily to be understood, nor can it be imagined that Shakespeare would reproach the murderer of his king only with want of manners', and proposes to emend the phrase to 'Unmanly drenched with gore'. He does go on, however, to offer a more general defence of the passage (2.3.112–16) in which the offending images occur:

■ It is not improbable that Shakespeare put these forced and unnatural metaphors into the mouth of Macbeth, as a mark of artifice and dissimulation, to show the difference between the studied language of hypocrisy, and the natural outcries of sudden passion. This whole speech, so considered, is a remarkable instance of judgement, as it consists entirely of antithesis and metaphor.[43] □

Johnson here suggests that the metaphors may be at least partly justified on the grounds that they exemplify a particular linguistic manifestation of a certain sort of human behaviour – 'hypocrisy' – and summon up its opposite – 'the natural outcries of sudden passion'. But he still finds them 'forced and unnatural'. The problems posed by the phrase 'Unmannerly breech'd with gore' have engaged other editors and critics besides Johnson, and figure in one of the most notable twentieth-century critical analyses of *Macbeth*, which we consider in Chapter 4 of this Guide – Cleanth Brooks's 'The Naked Babe and the Cloak of Manliness'.

Johnson clearly has considerable reservations about Shakespeare. In the later eighteenth century, however, a different and deeply influential approach to Shakespeare would emerge, which moved the emphasis from Shakespeare's breaches of decorum to his power of creating and conveying character. A key example of this new approach was provided by William Richardson.

WILLIAM RICHARDSON

In his *Characters of Shakespeare's Plays* (1774), William Richardson, Professor of Humanity at the University of Glasgow, affirms that Shakespeare 'unites the two essential powers of dramatic invention, that of forming characters and that of imitating, in their natural expressions, the passions and affections of which they are composed'.[44] He draws a distinction between the writers – his example is the French neoclassical dramatist Pierre Corneille (1606–84) – who merely *describe* the passions and those who *imitate* them; Shakespeare is the supreme instance of the latter kind of writer because he seems able to imitate *all* the passions. 'Possessing extreme sensibility, and uncommonly susceptible', he is able, like the ancient Greek god Proteus, to change shape, transforming 'himself into every character' and entering 'easily into every condition of human nature'.[45] He is 'most eminently distinguished ... by imitating the passion in all its aspects, by pursuing it through all its windings and labyrinths'.[46]

Richardson focuses on what he sees as 'a very extraordinary', 'violent and total change' in Macbeth's character; from being 'valiant, dutiful to his sovereign, mild, gentle and ambitious ... without guilt', he becomes 'false, perfidious, barbarous, and vindictive'.[47] Applying political metaphors to psychological upheaval, Richardson is concerned to account for how this 'revolution' took place in which 'the usurping principle became so powerful'; he seems to feel, despite his praise of Shakespeare, that *Macbeth* itself does not provide us with a sufficient explanation of its protagonist's transformation. He rejects the idea that the change can be attributed to supernatural agency, even though he acknowledges that the play makes effective use of such a notion; instead, he tries to explain the 'revolution' by relating it to what he sees as more general principles of human nature. Macbeth's transformation comes about, Richardson proposes, as a result of 'the power of fancy, aided by partial gratification, to invigorate and inflame our passions'.[48] His military success at the start of the play brings him honour, praise and reward; his 'ambition, fostered by imagination, and confirmed by success, becomes immoderate' and 'his soul, elevated above nature, aspires to sovereignty'.[49] Richardson sums up the process in this way:

■ Ambition, grown habitual and inveterate in the soul of Macbeth, suggests the idea of assassination. The sense of virtue, compassion, and other kindred principles, are alarmed, and oppose. His ruling passion is repulsed, but not enfeebled. Resigning himself to the hope of profiting by some future emergency, he renounces the idea of violence ['If chance will have me king, why, chance may crown me / Without my stir' (1.3.142)]. A difficulty appears [when Duncan nominates Malcolm as Prince of Cumberland and thus, effectively, his successor]: it renews, rouses and inflames his ambition. The principles of virtue again oppose; but, by exercise and repetition, they are, for a time, enfeebled: they excite no abhorrence: and he reflects, with composure, on his design. But, in reflecting, the apprehension of danger, and the fear of retribution, alarm him. He abandons his purpose; is deemed irresolute: not less innocent for not daring to execute what he dares to design, he is charged with cowardice: impatient of the charge and indignant; harassed by fear, by the consciousness of guilt, and by humanity struggling to resume her influence, he rushes headlong on his bane [poison].[50] □

According to Richardson, the reason that gaining the crown brings Macbeth no rest or happiness is because 'the principles of virtue' are 'inherent in our constitutions' and cannot be wholly eliminated; in the case of Macbeth, 'they return with violence, they accuse and condemn'; Macbeth becomes '[a]mazed at the atrocity of his own proceedings, conscious of perfidy and injustice, and of the resentment they will incite', and 'apprehensive, that both heaven and earth are stirred up against him ... his fancy is haunted with tremendous images, and his soul distracted with remorse and terror'.[51] In these responses, he exemplifies the 'man of uncommon sensibility, adorned with amiable and beneficent dispositions', who 'commits acts of cruelty and oppression' because he has been 'misled by some pernicious appetite' and who is 'more apt, by reflecting on his own conduct, to conceive the resentment and indignation it excites, than men of a different temper'.[52] Richardson sees Lady Macbeth as playing a crucial role; her character is 'invariably savage, perhaps too savage to be a genuine representation of nature' and she 'proceeds easily, and without reluctance, to the contrivance of the blackest crimes'.[53] It is interesting that, despite his emphasis on Shakespeare's supreme capacity to imitate the windings and labyrinths of passion, he does not allow for any deviations in Lady Macbeth's character, omitting to mention her inability to kill Duncan because of his resemblance to her father or her display of obsessive guilt in the sleepwalking scene.

Richardson draws attention to the relationship between '[i]nward contention of mind' and the soliloquy. He discusses the soliloquy not as a dramatic device but as a primal means of self-expression which first manifests itself in early childhood and continues into adulthood in 'men of lively passions'. When the principles contending in the mind are equally strong, our feelings emerge in 'broken and incoherent sentences' and in non-verbal manifestations: 'interrupted gestures, absence of attention, and an agitated demeanour express the disorder of our mind', as when Banquo observes that Macbeth is 'rapt' (1.3.140) after hearing the witches' prophecy, or Lady Macbeth remarks that Macbeth's face 'is as a book where men / May read strange matters' (1.6.60–1) and advises him to conceal his feelings more effectively. When a violent principle has the upper hand, however, a more coherent soliloquy may emerge – Richardson quotes as an example the 'If it were done' soliloquy down to 'And tears shall drown the wind' and the lines from 'We will proceed no further in this business' to 'Not cast aside so soon' (1.7.1–25, 31–5). For Richardson, these passages show Macbeth weighing up the consequences of his plan to murder Duncan and eventually deciding – this time – not to carry it out. Richardson's view of the 'If it were done' soliloquy as relatively coherent can be contrasted with later critics – Cleanth Brooks in the mid-twentieth century, for example – who have pointed to the apparent difficulties and paradoxes of the imagery. But Richardson is concerned, here as elsewhere in this account, with the general meanings that can be abstracted from specific instances.

Richardson concludes by seeing *Macbeth* as exemplifying a more general truth: 'by considering the progress of a ruling passion, and the fatal consequences of its indulgence, we have shown, how a beneficent mind may become inhuman; and how those who are naturally of an amiable temper, if they suffer themselves to be corrupted, will become more ferocious and more unhappy than men of a constitution originally hard and unfeeling'.[54] Although his emphasis throughout his account is on the character of Macbeth, it is not primarily upon the individual idiosyncrasies of that character but on the way in which it exemplifies what Richardson sees as a general law of human nature. There is, nonetheless, an interesting tension in his account between the desire to generalize which he expresses in the introduction to his book – 'to make poetry subservient to philosophy, and to employ it in tracing the principles of human conduct'[55] – and his sense of Shakespeare's capacity to pursue a passion 'through all its windings and labyrinths'; it is that capacity, as it is manifested in the complexities of Shakespeare's language, that will be of interest to a range of prominent twentieth-century critics. Most eighteenth-century critics, however, would pursue Richardson's concern with Shakespeare's characters; and the next significant figure in this respect is Thomas Whately.

THOMAS WHATELY

In his 'Remarks on Some of the Characters of Shakespeare' (1785), Thomas Whately, M. P. and writer on trade, finance and gardening, develops the movement towards character-based Shakespeare criticism by offering a more individualized approach to character than Richardson. Whately clearly departs from Dr Johnson's view that, in *Macbeth*, character is subordinated to plot, at least as far as the main protagonist is concerned, and he also diverges from Richardson's concern with general patterns of behaviour. He focuses on Macbeth and Richard III to demonstrate his general claim for Shakespeare's incomparable excellence in creating distinctive characters – 'the most essential part of drama'.[56] Whately emphasizes the importance, in drama, of 'the distinction and preservation of *character*', which turns a play from a 'tale' into an 'action' in which 'actors' – in the sense of the agents of the action – are 'produced upon the scene'. If the 'proper marks' of character that distinguish real human beings are absent from characters on the stage, 'we immediately perceive that the person before our eyes is but suppositious'. Whately continues to acknowledge the importance of the neoclassical unities of time, place and action, but contends that 'experience' has shown that they can be dispensed with and that any 'absurdity' can be rendered 'invisible' by 'the magic of the scene'. 'Most of Shakespeare's plays abound with instances of such a fascination.'[57]

The majority of tragic dramatists, Whately asserts, have presented general types of behaviour rather than distinctively individualized characters, while comic writers have presented characters that are too idiosyncratic. Shakespeare usually avoids these extremes and his characterization – 'the most essential part of the drama' – is 'excellent beyond compare'. As we saw earlier, Johnson spoke of 'Shakespeare's knowledge of human nature', but Richardson shifted the emphasis from 'knowledge of human nature' to 'the power of imitating the passions' which Shakespeare possesses to a greater degree than any other writer. Whately echoes Johnson in making a claim for Shakespeare's 'knowledge', but this time it is a knowledge not so much of the passions as of the 'heart': 'No other dramatic writer could ever pretend to so deep and so extensive a knowledge of the human heart' (this last phrase will be echoed satirically by L. C. Knights in 1933 in his attack on the character-based approach to Shakespeare which Whately and other eighteenth-century critics helped to create). For Whately, Shakespeare's characters are 'masterly copies from nature'; each differs from the other and they are 'as animated as the originals though correct to a scrupulous precision'. 'Every play of Shakespeare abounds with instances of his excellence in distinguishing characters'.[58]

To demonstrate Shakespeare's capacity to distinguish characters, Whately compares and contrasts Macbeth and Richard III – a coupling that will become a staple of *Macbeth* criticism. Their situations, Whatley suggests, offer many similarities: both are soldiers and usurpers who gain the throne by treason and murder, lose it in battle to the person who claims to be the rightful heir, and have in common 'perfidy, violence and tyranny'.[59] But Shakespeare distinguishes between them by adding, to the sources on which he drew, 'the minute detail by which characters are unravelled'. The character of Macbeth 'is much more complicated than that of Richard' and 'much the more highly finished' because 'it required a greater variety, and a greater delicacy of painting, to express and to blend with consistency all the several properties which are ascribed to him'.[60] Macbeth's 'natural disposition ... is not bad';[61] unlike Richard, he seems to be a man with some human feelings whose reluctance to kill Duncan is largely due 'to reflections which arise from sensibility'. He acts against what Whately variously terms his 'natural temper', 'disposition' and 'nature' because of the 'intervention of a supernatural cause' – the witches – and because of the 'instigations' of Lady Macbeth.

Whately shares with Dr Johnson an interest in the arguments that Lady Macbeth uses to persuade her husband to undertake the murder; but whereas Johnson focuses on Lady Macbeth's use of the idea of courage to try to motivate Macbeth, Whately focuses on the 'I have given suck' speech (1.7.54–9) and claims that this provides 'no incentive either to [Macbeth's] courage or his ambition'. In contrast to Johnson, Whately does not interpret Lady Macbeth's deployment of the idea of courage in explicitly gendered terms; instead, he draws out what he sees as the general argument that Lady Macbeth is making: 'that the strongest and most natural affections are to be stifled upon so great an occasion [as the opportunity of gaining the throne]'. This is not a general argument with universal appeal, however; it is specifically tailored to Macbeth's character, which is 'liable to be swayed' by such affections.

Whately then makes a claim which, as we shall see, would be strongly contested by J. P. Kemble: that while both Macbeth and Richard III possess courage, 'in Richard, it is intrepidity, and in Macbeth no more than resolution; in him it proceeds from exertion, not from nature'.[62]

■ [Even when Macbeth] proceeds to the bloody business of killing Duncan without further recoils ... a certain degree of restlessness and anxiety still continues, such as is constantly felt by a man, not naturally very bold, worked up to a momentous achievement. His imagination dwells entirely on the circumstances of horror which surround him ... But a resolution, thus forced, cannot hold longer than the immediate occasion for it: the moment after that is accomplished for which it was necessary, his thoughts take the contrary turn, and he cries out in agony and despair, 'Wake Duncan with thy knocking. I would thou couldst'. □   [2.2.72][63]

Whately acknowledges that Macbeth is less agitated when he commits further murders – though it is worth noting, as Whately does not, that he employs hirelings to do these later killings; for Whately, however, his reduced anxiety is not inconsistent: 'on the contrary, it confirms the principles upon which [his character] is formed'. His later murders are attempts to ensure his safety, 'and he gets rid of fear by guilt, which, to a mind so constituted, may be the less uneasy sensation of the two'.[64] Whereas Richard III is able to hide his true feelings and reactions and act a part whenever necessary, Macbeth cannot do so; and Whately sees the 'weakness of mind' which prevents him from doing this as also evident in 'that hesitation and dullness to dare which [Macbeth] feels in himself'.

In Whately's perspective, it is the qualities of Macbeth's character that his essay has identified – his sensibility, his imagination, his restlessness, his anxiety, his lack of natural boldness, his capacity for fear, his inability to dissimulate – that make his final despair inevitable:

> ■ A mind so framed and tortured as that of Macbeth, when the hour of extremity presses upon him, can find no refuge but in despair; and the expression of that despair by Shakespeare is perhaps one of the finest pictures that ever was exhibited. It is wildness, inconsistency, and disorder ... It is presumption without hope, and confidence without courage; that confidence rests upon his superstition; he buoys himself up with it against all the dangers that threaten him, and yet sinks upon every fresh alarm.[65] □

Whately, then, provides one of the most sustained demonstrations so far of a character-based interpretation of *Macbeth*. He assumes that the course of events in *Macbeth* is driven by the character of its main protagonist, rather than by the plot of the play, and that the language of the play gives access to Macbeth's character; and, while he acknowledges that the *character* of Macbeth is inconsistent, he argues that the *characterization* is consistent – that Macbeth is consistently characterized as an inconsistent character because of those persistent characteristics that make him prone to fear and regret. It was the imputation that Macbeth, compared to Richard, was a coward that stung J. P. Kemble into a response.

J. P. KEMBLE

J. P. Kemble was an actor, theatre manager and producer, whose *Macbeth Re-considered: An Essay* (1786) aimed to defend Macbeth, as a character, against Whately's imputations of cowardice. Kemble is not simply concerned to defend Macbeth as a free-standing character, however; it is crucial to the moral effectiveness of the play that Macbeth should not be a coward. Kemble starts from the general premise that plays should promote 'the cause of morality' but can only do so when they teach their audiences 'to love virtue and abhor vice' by 'a catastrophe resulting from principles natural to the agents who produce it'.[66] But *Macbeth* cannot teach the love of virtue if the guilt and remorse of its protagonist are due only to cowardice and imbecility – and this, in Kemble's view, is what Whately's argument implies. We 'shall never be amended by a wretch who is uniformly the object of our contempt'.[67] Kemble sets out to show that Macbeth is truly courageous prior to his meeting with the witches, as the testimonies to his valour in putting down the king's enemies demonstrate; for Kemble, it is ambition, and not, as Whately suggests, personal fear, that drives Macbeth to want to destroy Banquo and Macduff; and Macbeth, Kemble asserts, is as intrepid as Richard in meeting similar or perhaps greater challenges. Kemble then aims to identify 'the essential difference' between these two 'great bad men'[68] (a phrase that William Hazlitt will take up and, with an appropriate alteration of gender, apply to Lady Macbeth):

■ Ambition is the impulse that governs every action of Richard's life. He attains the crown by dissimulation, that owns no respect for virtue; and by cruelty, which entails no remorse on the valour that would maintain his ill-acquired dignity. Ambition is the prominent vice of Macbeth's nature; but he gratifies it by hypocrisy, that reveres virtue too highly to be perfectly itself; and by murders, the recollection whereof at times renders his valour useless, by depriving him of all sense but that of his enormous wickedness. Richard's character is simple, Macbeth's mixed. Richard is only intrepid, Macbeth intrepid and feeling.[69] □

As we can see, Kemble echoes Whately's contention that Macbeth is a more complex character than Richard III, but affirms, against Whately, that both Macbeth and Richard are intrepid. Richard Cumberland would also take up the comparison between Macbeth and Richard III, but would pay more attention to Lady Macbeth than Johnson, Whately or Kemble had done.

RICHARD CUMBERLAND

In his essay collection *The Observer* (5 vols., 1785–91), Richard Cumberland identifies an 'essential difference in the development' of Macbeth and Richard III which is to the advantage of Macbeth as a character and elevates the whole play, and Shakespeare himself, to the highest level of dramatic achievement:

■ The struggles of a soul naturally virtuous whilst it holds the guilty impulse of ambition at bay, affords the noblest theme for the drama, and puts the creative fancy of our poet upon a resource in which he has been rivalled only by the great father of tragedy Aeschylus [ancient Greek dramatist, 525/524–456 BC, author of the *Oresteia* trilogy][70] □

Indeed, in his creation of character, of 'imaginary beings', Shakespeare outstrips his classical rival: 'in the variety of character, in all the nicer touches of nature, in all the extravagances of caprice and humour, from the boldest feature down to the minutest foible, Shakespeare stands alone'.[71] Cumberland's argument here is an example of the way in which, as the eighteenth century advanced, Shakespeare, far from being criticized for his failure to adhere to neoclassical principles derived from ancient Greek drama and criticism, was promoted to the equal, or even the superior, of the ancient Greek playwrights.

Cumberland's discussion of Lady Macbeth, like Johnson's, sees her primarily in relation to her husband, but also in terms of her function in the overall ethical significance of the play. 'The part which Lady Macbeth fills in the drama has a relative as well as positive importance, and serves to place the repugnance of Macbeth in the strongest point of view'.[72] The 'natural influence which so high and predominant a spirit asserts over the tamer qualities of her husband' turns the witches into 'secondary agents for bringing about the main action of the drama', and this is crucial to the moral effect of *Macbeth*:

■ if [the witches], which are only artificial and fantastic instruments, had been made the sole or even principal movers of the great incident of [Duncan's] murder, nature would have been excluded from her share in the drama, and Macbeth would have become the mere machine of an uncontrollable necessity, and his character, being robbed of its free agency, would have left no moral behind.[73] □

Cumberland stresses that the witches and their prophecies are not invoked in the debates between Lady Macbeth and her husband about whether to kill Duncan, and he sees this omission as deliberate on Shakespeare's part: it is Lady Macbeth's forcefulness and her manipulation of her husband that carry the day. The quality of 'intrepidity', which Whately found in Richard but not in Macbeth, and which Kemble saw in both Macbeth and Richard, is transferred by Cumberland to Lady Macbeth, whose 'vaunting display of hardened intrepidity', in the 'I have given suck' speech (1.7.54–9), 'presents one of the most terrific pictures that was ever imagined'[74] – 'terrific' here is used in its now archaic sense of 'causing terror'. Later on, Cumberland explains the sleepwalking scene in terms of 'the intrepidity of [Lady Macbeth's] character' which 'is so marked that we may well suppose no waking terror could shake it'. We might see Cumberland here as anticipating a psychological explanation of Lady Macbeth's behaviour, but he goes on to place the scene within the history of drama rather than of psychology: 'Dreams have been a dramatic expedient ever since there has been a drama'. Cumberland points out that Aeschylus, whom he has earlier called 'the father of tragedy', uses this expedient in the *Oresteia*, with Clytemnestra's dream just before Orestes kills her, and that many playwrights have imitated him since; but Shakespeare goes one better:

■ To introduce upon the scene the very person walking in sleep, and giving vent to the horrid fancies that haunt her dream, in broken speeches expressive of her guilt, uttered before witnesses, and accompanied with that natural and expressive action of washing the blood from her defiled hands, was reserved for the original and bold genius of Shakespeare only. It is an incident so full of tragic horror, so daring and at the same time so truly characteristic that it stands out as a prominent feature in the most sublime drama in the world, and fully compensates for any sacrifices the poet might have made in the previous arrangement of his incidents.[75] □

In this appreciation of the sleepwalking scene, Cumberland affirms Shakespeare's superiority in some of the terms that will feature most prominently in the Romantic apotheosis of Shakespeare. He has no doubt of Shakespeare's originality and boldness; and while his discussions of Lady Macbeth still subordinate consideration of her 'character' to her functions in the play – as an essential element of its moral effect, as a foil that makes the virtuous facets of Macbeth shine – he does suggest that Lady Macbeth is more than the merely detestable figure dismissed by Johnson and begins to open up the possibility that she, as well as her husband, could be analysed in terms of 'character'. As the next chapter will show, the high valuation of Shakespeare, and the concern with the characters of both Macbeth and Lady Macbeth, will be taken up and developed by Romantic and Victorian criticism.

CHAPTER TWO

The Nineteenth Century: Romantic and Victorian *Macbeth*

The late eighteenth and early nineteenth centuries saw, in Romanticism, an explosion of cultural energy across Europe which linked up with the tumultuous political events of that period – the American War of Independence, the French Revolution and the Napoleonic wars – to give a sense of a world in turmoil. In the drama, fiction and poetry which emerged at this time, the constraints of the eighteenth century were challenged, stretched and sometimes snapped and thrown off, and this had its impact on the way that the dramatic and literary texts of the past were understood – and certainly on the way in which people responded to Shakespeare. Those elements of his work which seemed faults in the perspective of neoclassical criticism appealed much more to the Romantic imagination. This did not mean a wholesale rejection of eighteenth-century approaches, however: the emphasis on character which had emerged in the later eighteenth century was continued and developed as Shakespeare, and some of his protagonists, were reconstructed as proto-Romantic figures. A key text in this process was *Characters of Shakespeare's Plays* (1817), a work of great vivacity and perception by the essayist, journalist and critic William Hazlitt.

WILLIAM HAZLITT

In his combative preface to *Characters of Shakespeare's Plays*, Hazlitt stakes out his general position and implicitly defines himself in relation to his eighteenth-century predecessors; he approvingly cites the 1725 'Preface' to Shakespeare's works by the poet Alexander Pope (1688–1744), in which Pope praises Shakespeare's capacity to create original and individual characters;[1] he commends Whately's comparison between Macbeth and Richard III as 'an exceedingly ingenious piece of analytical criticism' (though mistakenly identifying Whately as 'Mason'); and he quotes approvingly, and at some length, from the influential *Lectures on*

Shakespeare by the German critic August von Wilhem Schlegel (1767–1845). While Hazlitt commends Schlegel's lectures as 'by far the best account of the plays of Shakespeare that has hitherto appeared',[2] he identifies two ways in which Schlegel's approach might be improved: by eschewing the quasi-mystical style he sometimes adopts and by supporting particular points with specific passages from Shakespeare's texts. The implication is that Hazlitt's own book will effect these improvements.

Hazlitt then launches a sustained and devastating attack on what he sees as Dr Johnson's inadequacies when it comes to appreciating Shakespeare. Johnson, he charges, was too rigid, generalizing, mechanical, rational and matter-of-fact; he was constricted by common sense and by a style that always demanded balance and equilibrium; he lacked genius, a quick, natural organic sensibility and a capacity to respond properly to poetry once it exceeded the bounds of prose. This is more than an assault upon the supposed failings of an individual critic; it challenges a powerful eighteenth-century set of critical assumptions and criteria – though, as Hazlitt himself has already acknowledged, other ways of looking at Shakespeare, especially in terms of a concern with character, had also developed in the eighteenth century. With regard to their approach to Shakespeare's characters, Hazlitt compares Johnson unfavourably with Pope; whereas Pope recognized Shakespeare's capacity to create individual characters, Johnson saw in Shakespeare only examples of general types – species rather than individuals: 'he did not find the individual traits, or the dramatic distinctions which Shakespeare has engrafted on this general nature, because he felt no interest in them'. It is these 'dramatic distinctions'[3] that Hazlitt will pursue in his essays on individual plays.

Hazlitt's discussion of *Macbeth* incorporates an account of Macbeth's character; a comparison, echoing and developing that of Whately, between Macbeth and Richard III; a more extended consideration of the character of Lady Macbeth than previous critics had offered; an evocation of the peculiar nature of the witches; and some observations on the structure, themes and language of the play. Hazlitt identifies two distinctive features of *Macbeth*, as compared with Shakespeare's three other principal tragedies, *Lear, Othello* and *Hamlet*: its wild and lofty imaginative quality and its speed and intensity of action – and, he argues, 'the one is made the moving principle of the other'[4] and the imaginative quality drives the action.

■ The overwhelming pressure of preternatural agency urges on the tide of human passion with redoubled force. Macbeth himself appears driven along by the violence of his fate like a vessel drifting before a storm: he reels to and fro like a drunken man; he staggers under the weight of his own purposes and the suggestions of others; he stands at bay with his situation; and from the superstitious awe and breathless suspense into which the communications of the Weird Sisters throw him, is hurried on with daring impatience to verify their predictions, and with impious and bloody hand to tear aside the veil which hides the uncertainty of the future.[5] □

Like Richard Cumberland, discussed in the previous chapter of this Guide, Hazlitt sees Lady Macbeth as a foil to Macbeth who brings out his virtuous aspect; her 'obdurate strength of will and masculine firmness give her the ascendancy over her husband's faltering virtue'.[6] But Hazlitt is more concerned than Cumberland with the way in which her resolution highlights, not her husband's virtue, but his instability; and he develops his discussion of her as a character in her own right, even applying to her the adjectives that J. P. Kemble applied to Macbeth and Richard III when he called them 'great bad men':

■ The magnitude of her resolution almost covers the magnitude of her guilt. She is a great bad woman, whom we hate, but whom we fear more than we hate. She does not excite our loathing like Regan and Goneril [Lear's 'wicked' daughters in *King Lear*]. She is only wicked to gain a great end; and is perhaps more distinguished by her commanding presence of mind and inexorable self-will, which do not suffer her to be diverted from a bad purpose, when once formed, by weak and womanly regrets, than by the hardness of her heart or want of natural affections.[7] □

This is a more complicated figure than the 'merely detestable' Lady Macbeth of Dr Johnson's account, or, in Cumberland's interpretation, the foil to Macbeth which reinforces the moral lesson of the play. The Lady Macbeth who emerges from Hazlitt's description is a woman with qualities which could, in other contexts, seem admirable: 'she is herself wound up to the execution of her baneful project with the same unshrinking forti-tude in crime, that in other circumstances she probably would have shown patience in suffering'.[8] Hazlitt's implication that Lady Macbeth is a character who could be taken out of the play and placed 'in other circumstances' marks a development away from considering 'character' as a function of a specific text and towards the sense that the 'characters' of Shakespeare have a quasi-independent existence which makes it possible to imagine them in different circumstances or at different times of their lives: it leads towards a situation in which it is possible to ask the kind of ques-tion that L.C. Knights, in 1933, would mock as epitomizing the character-based approach to Shakespeare: 'How many children had Lady Macbeth?'

Hazlitt contrasts the 'solid, substantial, flesh-and-blood display of passion' that Lady Macbeth shows as she urges her husband to murder

Duncan with the 'cold, abstracted, gratuitous, servile malignity of the witches, who are equally instrumental in urging Macbeth to his fate for the mere love of mischief, and from a disinterested delight in deformity and cruelty':[9]

■ They are hags of mischief, obscene panders to iniquity, malicious from their impotence of enjoyment, enamoured of destruction, because they are themselves unreal, abortive, half-existences, and who become sublime from their exemption from all human sympathies and their contempt for all human affairs, as Lady Macbeth does by the force of passion![10] □

Although Hazlitt, later in the essay, says that the witches are 'ridiculous on the modern stage',[11] the virulence of this description suggests that they still have the power to disturb, at least when the play is read rather than performed; and it seems that, in a sense, the witches are disturbing for Hazlitt because they are not 'human' characters in the way that Lady Macbeth is, even at her most 'sublime'. It is interesting to compare and contrast Hazlitt's negative account of the witches with that of Terry Eagleton, who, as we shall see in Chapter 6 of this Guide, claims in his 1986 study of Shakespeare that 'positive value in Macbeth lies with the witches' and that indeed they are 'the heroines' of the play.[12]

Despite his focus on the characters of Macbeth and Lady Macbeth, Hazlitt does give attention to other key aspects of the play: structure, theme and language. He observes that 'Macbeth (generally speaking) is done upon a stronger and more systematic principle of contrast than any other of Shakespeare's plays. It moves upon the verge of an abyss, and is a constant struggle between life and death'.[13] The idea of the play as 'a constant struggle between life and death' would be echoed and developed in the twentieth century by G. Wilson Knight, whose influential interpretation in *The Imperial Theme* opens: 'The opposition of life and death forces is strong in *Macbeth*'.[14] Hazlitt also suggests that the 'principle of contrast' he has identified accounts for the distinctive features of the language of Macbeth: 'the abruptness and violent antitheses of the style, the throes and labour which run through the expression' and turn 'defects' into 'beauties'.[15] Hazlitt gives examples (his apparent misquotes have been corrected here): 'So fair and foul a day I have not seen' (1.3.36); 'Such welcome and unwelcome things at once' (4.3.139); 'good men's lives / Expire before the flowers in their caps, / Dying or ere they sicken' (4.3.172–4); 'Look like the innocent flower, but be the serpent under it' (1.5.63–4). The 'same contradictory principle' can be found in the description of the witches: they are neither of the air nor the earth but both (1.3.39–40); they 'should be women ... yet their beards forbid [it]' (1.3.43–4). Thus, while Hazlitt is certainly concerned with character, his observations on structure, theme and language engage with aspects of *Macbeth* which, as the later chapters of this Guide will show, take on a more central importance for later critics. In the early nineteenth century, however, another major Romantic critic of Shakespeare, the poet and thinker Samuel Taylor Coleridge, would try, as Hazlitt had done, to convey the general nature of *Macbeth* and would then consider the characters of Macbeth and Lady Macbeth, and the nature of the witches.

SAMUEL TAYLOR COLERIDGE

Coleridge begins his 'Notes on Some Other Plays of Shakespeare' by comparing *Macbeth* with *Hamlet*, especially in terms of their openings. *Hamlet* begins by moving from 'simple conversation' to 'the language of impassioned intellect', but the intellect still remains 'the seat of passion';[16] *Macbeth* at once invokes the imagination and its associated emotions. The opening of *Macbeth* sets a pace which is sustained until the end. Coleridge, like Hazlitt, remarks on the speed of the action: 'the movement throughout is the most rapid of all Shakespeare's plays'.[17] The initial appeal to the imagination and emotions is also sustained throughout the play and one sign of this, in Coleridge's view, is 'the absence of any puns' or plays on words, which Coleridge presumably sees as the products of the intellect. There is also 'an entire absence of comedy'. The only place where wordplay and comedy are evident is the Porter section (2.3.1–39), which Coleridge calls 'disgusting' and dismisses as 'an interpolation of the actors'[18] or as largely 'written for the mob by some other hand';[19] the 'ever-present being of Shakespeare' is only evident, he asserts, in the lines 'I'll devil-porter it no further: I had thought to have let in some of all professions, that go the primrose way to the everlasting bonfire' (2.3.16–18).[20] Not only comedy, but also 'irony and philosophic contemplation' are absent from Macbeth: the play is 'wholly and purely tragic'.

Moreover, the language of the play is also devoid, according to Coleridge, of 'equivocal morality', of 'sophistry and self-delusion'. The only exceptions – which might be rather larger ones than Coleridge is ready to acknowledge – are interpreted by Coleridge as cognitive errors – mistranslations – caused by ambition or fear:

■ Previously to the dreadful act, Macbeth mistranslates the recoilings and ominous whispers of conscience into prudential and selfish reasonings, and, after the deed done, the terrors of remorse into fear from [of] external dangers – like delirious men who run away from the phantoms of their own brains, or, raised by terror to rage, stab the real object that is within their reach.[21] □

Coleridge makes the interesting critical move here of supplying what he sees as the correct translation, or interpretation, of Macbeth's words at key moments in the play, an interpretation which involves identifying an ethical and psychological 'reality' that those words partly mask, but which is accessible to the perceptive critic. It could be argued, however, that Macbeth's 'prudential and selfish reasonings' before the deed and his post-regicide fears of 'external dangers' relate, at least partly, to threats which have, within the dramatic conventions of which he is part, a sharp reality of their own and are more than mistranslations of conscience and remorse; we might adapt a point that Oscar James Campbell makes against Cleanth Brooks, in an essay which we consider in Chapter 4 of this Guide: 'Macbeth, like all murderers in Elizabethan plays, is afraid ... of the knife in the hands of a human avenger'.[22]

Apart from these 'exceptions', Coleridge asserts, 'Macbeth's language is the grave utterance of the very heart, conscience-sick, even to the last faintings of moral death'. This aspect of the language of the play is not peculiar to the words of Macbeth, however, but 'is the same in all the other characters'. The variety of the language 'arises from rage, caused ever and anon by disruption of anxious thought, and the quick transition of fear into it'.[23]

Coleridge's view that Macbeth proceeds to 'moral death' is developed later in his essay, which offers a psychological, ethical and quasi-religious explanation of the 'Tomorrow, and tomorrow, and tomorrow' speech (5.5.18–27). After his wife's demise, Macbeth 'puts on despondency, the final heart-armour of the wretched, and would fain think everything shadowy and unsubstantial, as indeed all things are to those who cannot regard them as symbols of goodness'. Coleridge therefore sees this speech as a psychologically rather than philosophically motivated judgement; it is not a general comment on human existence, but proceeds from a state of despondency that provides a defence ('heart-armour') against remorse.

Coleridge's psychological analysis of Macbeth is complemented and surpassed by his compelling account of the psychology of Lady Macbeth. Hazlitt, focusing largely on her words and behaviour prior to Duncan's murder, had remarked on her resolution and firmness; Coleridge sees her as a fantasist:

■ Lady Macbeth, like all in Shakespeare, is a class individualized: of high rank, left much alone, and feeding herself with day-dreams of ambition, she mistakes the courage of fantasy for the power of bearing the consequences of the realities of guilt. Hers is the mock fortitude of a mind deluded by ambition; she shames her husband with a superhuman audacity of fancy which she cannot support, but sinks in the season of remorse, and dies in suicidal agony. Her speech:

> Come, you spirits
> That tend on mortal thoughts, unsex me here, etc. [1.5.38–52]

is that of one who had habitually familiarized her imagination to dreadful conceptions, and was trying to do so still more. Her invocations and requisitions are all the false efforts of a mind accustomed only hitherto to the shadows of the imagination, vivid enough to throw the every-day substance of life into shadow, but never as yet brought into direct contact with their own correspondent realities.[24] □

Here, Coleridge constructs a psychologically consistent Lady Macbeth, supplying an answer, in advance, to a question which Sigmund Freud will later address: if she were indeed the resolute, obdurate character whom Hazlitt describes, it might be difficult to account for her collapse, after Duncan's murder, into guilt – why should she not continue to be resolute, especially as she has now obtained what she wants? But if she is, as Coleridge argues, a fantasist – a kind of combination of a bored housewife and romantic dreamer – whose visions of remorse-free killing do not engage with the reality of Duncan's murder and its aftermath, then her character after the murder is a consistent development of her character before it. Of course, this view rests on the assumption that Lady Macbeth is to be understood as a coherent character, but within those terms, it is a penetrating and plausible interpretation, and the most fully developed psychological account of Lady Macbeth so far.

While Coleridge is able to analyse Lady Macbeth's character in psychological terms, he finds, like Hazlitt, that the witches are more puzzling:

■ The Weird Sisters are as true a creation of Shakespeare's, as his Ariel and Caliban [in *The Tempest*] – fates, furies, and materializing witches being the elements. They are wholly different from any representation of witches in the contemporary writers, and yet presented with a sufficient external resemblance to the creatures of vulgar prejudice to act immediately on the audience. Their character consists in the imaginative disconnected from the good; they are the shadowy obscure, and fearfully anomalous, of physical nature, the lawless of human nature – elemental avengers without sex or kin.[25] □

Although Coleridge, in contrast to Hazlitt, applies the term 'character' to the witches, and tries to relate them to both physical and human nature, he cannot accommodate them to the natural and human order.

As with Hazlitt's view of the witches, it is interesting to compare Coleridge's view with that of Terry Eagleton.

Coleridge's generalizations about the language of Macbeth and his almost complete dismissal of the Porter scene are open to question; but his focus on the psychology of Lady Macbeth is significant, posing a question about her apparent change of character after Duncan's murder that will be taken up by later literary critics and by Freud. A third notable Romantic critic of Macbeth, Thomas De Quincey, moves the focus away from character and on to audience response – initially, his own – to an aspect of the play that earlier critics seemed to have overlooked.

THOMAS DE QUINCEY

The writer Thomas De Quincey, best known as the author of *Confessions of an English Opium Eater* (1821–22), produced a celebrated essay in 1823 called 'On the Knocking at the Gate in *Macbeth*'. De Quincey starts by telling us how he had been perplexed since boyhood by the effect that the knocking on the gate which follows the murder of Duncan had on his feelings: 'it reflected back upon the murder a peculiar awfulness and a depth of solemnity'. His essay explores the question of '*why* it should produce such an effect'.[26]

De Quincey, who would later write a notable piece of black humour called *On Murder Considered as One of the Fine Arts* (1827), sees Shakespeare as aiming to express the 'murderous mind' which Macbeth and Lady Macbeth, although clearly differentiated as characters, both exhibit when they kill Duncan. In view of 'the unoffending nature of their victim', this 'murderous mind' had to be 'expressed with peculiar energy'. It should make us feel that what De Quincey calls 'the human nature'[27] – which he defines as 'the divine nature of love and mercy, spread through the hearts of all creatures, and seldom utterly withdrawn from man'[28] – was 'gone, vanished, extinct, and that the fiendish nature had taken its place'. The dialogues and soliloquies achieve this effect 'marvellously'; but it is 'finally consummated' by the knocking on the gate.[29] As De Quincey memorably puts it:

■ [In *Macbeth*,] the retiring of the human heart, and the entrance of the fiendish heart was to be expressed and made sensible ['sensible' here means 'readily perceived', present to the senses]. Another world has stepped in; and the murderers are taken out of the region of human things, human purposes, human desires. They are transfigured: Lady Macbeth is 'unsex[ed', 1.5.41]; Macbeth has forgot that he was born of woman; both are conformed to the image of devils; and the world of devils is suddenly revealed. But how shall this be conveyed and made palpable? In order that a new world may step in, this world must for a time disappear. The murderers, and the murder must be insulated – cut off by an immeasurable gulf from the ordinary tide and succession of human affairs – locked up and sequestered in some deep recess; we must be made sensible that the world of ordinary life is suddenly arrested – laid asleep – tranced – racked into a dread armistice; time must be annihilated; relation to things without abolished; and all must pass self-withdrawn into a deep syncope ['temporary loss of consciousness'] and suspension of passion. Hence it is, that when the deed is done, when the work of darkness is perfect, then the world of darkness passes away like a pageantry in the clouds: the knocking at the gate is heard; and it makes known audibly that the reaction has commenced; the human has made its reflux upon the fiendish; the pulses of life are beginning to beat again; and the re-establishment of the goings-on of the world in which we live, first makes us profoundly sensible of the awful parenthesis that had suspended them.[30] □

De Quincey is concerned with the way in which *Macbeth* evokes an extreme state of mind and enables the audience to feel sympathy for that state of mind – sympathy not in the sense of 'pity' but in what De Quincey insists is 'its proper sense': 'the act of reproducing in our minds the feelings of another'.[31] While this state of mind is undoubtedly that of two clearly differentiated characters – Macbeth and Lady Macbeth – it also exemplifies a state of mental extremity that could manifest itself in others: 'the murderous mind', the psychological state of mind in which murder is perpetrated. This state of mind is in a parenthesis – that is, it is as if it were enclosed in brackets, and the knocking of the gate functions as the closing bracket. In De Quincey's perspective, therefore, this action is much more than a dramatic bit of stage business: it is a key part of the overall effect of *Macbeth*. It contributes not only to the evo-cation of a state of mind but also to the play's opposition of contraries: the human, informed by divine love and mercy, is opposed to the fiendish and inhuman. As we see in Chapter 3 of this Guide, the view that the whole play could be understood in terms of such oppositions was to become important in the strands of twentieth-century criticism of *Macbeth* represented by G. Wilson Knight and L. C. Knights.

De Quincey concludes his essay with a general affirmation: in Shakespeare's work, as in nature, 'there can be much or too little, nothing useless or inert'; if we study his plays 'with entire submission of our own faculties', we shall 'see proofs of design and self-supporting arrangement where the careless eye had seen nothing but accident'! This is a long way from the defensiveness of Johnson, uneasy about what he sees as Shakespeare's defects, or indeed Coleridge, ruthlessly excising most of the Porter's words as non-Shakespearean.

De Quincey's affirmation anticipates an approach to Shakespeare which will become of central importance in twentieth-century criticism: *Macbeth*, like each of Shakespeare's other plays and indeed his total *oeuvre*, is to be approached as a whole in which the smallest detail plays an active and significant part. But later nineteenth-century criticism continued to focus on character; and it was a woman writer, Anna Jameson, who would give further attention to Lady Macbeth.

ANNA JAMESON

In her *Characteristics of Women, Moral, Poetical, and Historical* (1833), Anna Jameson points to a relative dearth of discussion of Lady Macbeth in existing criticism of Shakespeare. Whereas Macbeth's character 'is considered as one of the most complex in the whole range of Shakespeare's dramatic creations',[32] Lady Macbeth has, so far, been underestimated. Her sublimity has been acknowledged, but she has been seen as a simpler figure than her husband, secondary to him and existing to advance the action of the play rather than as 'an individual conception of amazing power, poetry, and beauty' in her own right.[33] Jameson instances Dr Johnson's dismissal of her as 'merely detested' and finds Hazlitt's account slightly 'superficial'[34] although she admires it. She does not mention Coleridge's account and was perhaps not familiar with it.

While Jameson feels that Lady Macbeth's 'amazing power of intellect', 'inexorable determination of purpose' and 'superhuman strength of nerve' make her 'as fearful in herself as her deeds are hateful', this does not mean that she is 'a mere monster of depravity'. 'She is a terrible impersonation of evil passions and mighty powers', but she is 'not so far removed from our own nature, as to be cast beyond the pale of our sympathies';[35] the reason for this is that she 'remains a woman to the last – still linked with her sex and with humanity'. In order to explain how Lady Macbeth retains our sympathy, Jameson aims 'to trace minutely the action of the play, as far as she is concerned in it, from its very commencement to its close'.[36]

Jameson identifies 'ambition' as the 'ruling motive' of Lady Macbeth,[37] but sees her as retaining 'a touch of womanhood' in that the ambition is more for her husband than for herself.[38] It is important, in Jameson's view, to recognize that the evil did not originate with her; it was already in the mind of Macbeth – she cites the 'supernatural soliciting' speech – and extends itself to her 'through the medium of her husband'. If Lady Macbeth then seems to take the initiative and to become more actively evil than her husband, it is because of her superior, commanding intellect rather than her greater wickedness. She employs eloquence, sophistry, sarcasm (when she taunts Macbeth with being a 'coward') and boldness of address to goad her husband on to Duncan's murder. In the murder scene itself, she drives on Macbeth with 'obdurate inflexibility of purpose', but she has already shown, in the 'I have given suck' speech, that she is capable of maternal tenderness, and she now reveals a filial tenderness when she explains why she could not kill Duncan: 'Had he not resembled / My father as he slept, / I had don't' (2.2.12–13). Jameson sees this as an 'unexpected touch of feeling, so startling, yet so wonderfully true to nature', which brings 'home at once to our very heart' the sense that Lady Macbeth is not absolutely depraved and ferocious.

After Duncan's murder, Lady Macbeth shows herself to be, in her way, a good wife: she supports, sustains and soothes her husband, but she does not goad him to further crimes – she has no hand in the murder of Banquo or of Macduff's wife and children. Moreover, according to Jameson, the 'bond of entire affection and confidence' which unites the Macbeths claims from us 'an involuntary respect and sympathy' and sheds 'a softening influence over the whole tragedy'. Her tenderness towards him, for example, when she tries to soothe him as the banquet approaches – 'Come on, gentle my lord, / Sleek o'er your rugged looks, be bright and jovial / Among your guests tonight' (3.1.28–30) – makes us feel that Lady Macbeth's 'influence over the affections of her husband, as a wife and woman, is at least equal to her power over him as a superior mind'.[39] It is true that, in the banquet scene, she is harsh with her erratic spouse when the guests are present, but once they have gone, she is submissive and caring, and her relative silence at this point contains, for Jameson, 'a touch of pathos and tenderness' which is 'one of the most masterly and most beautiful traits of character in the whole play'.[40]

Jameson commends the way in which conscience is finally shown to awaken in Lady Macbeth. Her courage means that she will not, in contrast to her husband, see spectres or start at shadows when she is conscious; nor will she give voice to remorse. The sleepwalking scene, however, provides 'a glimpse into the depths of [her] inward hell' which touches 'our human sympathies', making us 'sigh over the ruin [rather] than exult in it'.[41] It is possible, Jameson acknowledges, that her view of Lady Macbeth might seem to engage 'our sympathies on behalf of a perverted being' and that this would be morally wrong; in her defence, she cites the observation of the American theologian William Ellery Channing (1780–1842) on the interest aroused by the figure of Satan in *Paradise Lost* (1667) by John Milton (1608–74): 'our interest fastens, in this and like cases, on what is *not* evil in the character'.[42]

Jameson moves on to compare and contrast Lady Macbeth with other evil women in ancient Greek tragedy; in her view, Clytemnestra in the *Agamemnon* of Aeschylus is a 'shameless adulteress, cruel murderess, and unnatural mother' who cannot justly be likened to Lady Macbeth;[43] the Electra of Sophocles (about 496–406 BC) is closer to Lady Macbeth but evokes less sympathy, and the murder scene is 'too shocking, too *physical*' compared with 'the exhibition of various passions' in the murder scene in *Macbeth* which does not detract from but nonetheless relieves the horror of Duncan's slaughter.[44] For Jameson, the only female character who comes close to Lady Macbeth is the Medea of Euripides (about 480–406 BC), who abandons all for Jason and then, when he leaves her, takes a terrible revenge by killing their children; but, Jameson asserts, 'although Medea's passions are more feminine [than those of Lady Macbeth], her character is less so'.[45] Taking up 'Schlegel's distinction between the ancient or Greek drama, which he compares to sculpture, and the modern or romantic drama, which he compares to painting',[46] Jameson suggests that Medea can be seen as a sculpture and Lady Macbeth as a painting, and she focuses this distinction more precisely by comparing Medea to the Medusa of Greek gems and bas-reliefs and Lady Macbeth to the Medusa of the Renaissance artist Leonardo da Vinci (1452–1519). This comparison, which concludes her account of Lady Macbeth, is an interesting one to consider in the light of the psychoanalytic interpretation of the Medusa as an image of the castrating female.

Jameson's discussion of Lady Macbeth is very much in a Romantic idiom but, along with Coleridge's account, it does help to demonstrate that Lady Macbeth is a figure of considerable interest in her own right. Although Jameson considers her as a character, she does not endow her with an existence outside the play – she does not ask, for example, 'How many children had Lady Macbeth?' – but concentrates on what can be inferred about her from her words and actions within the drama. Her inferences are linked, however, with broader ideas of femininity and of woman's 'nature', and with representations of women in drama, particularly ancient Greek drama, and in these respects she opens up important areas for exploration, even though the relationship of *Macbeth* to constructions of femininity – and masculinity – would not be more extensively examined until the later twentieth century. But the elevation of Lady Macbeth as a significant character in her own right who is in some respects superior to her husband would find an echo and amplification in Edward Dowden's account of the play in the later Victorian era.

EDWARD DOWDEN

A key example of the Victorian response to *Macbeth*, and to Shakespeare more generally, is Edward Dowden's *Shakspere: A Critical Study of His*

Mind and Art (1877) – 'Shakspere' was Dowden's preferred spelling. In this book, Dowden sees Shakespearean tragedy as 'concerned with the ruin or restoration of the soul, and of the life of man'; 'its subject is the struggle of good and evil in the world' and this 'strikes down upon the roots of things'.[47] Shakespearean tragedy declares, emphatically, that here, 'upon the earth, evil *is*' but that there is 'also in the earth a sacred passion of deliverance, a pure redeeming ardour'.[48] It provides no answers or happy endings, however; in these respects, it is severe and stern, but it does 'discover the supreme fact, – that the moral world stands in sovereign independence of the world of the senses'.[49]

When Dowden comes to consider *Macbeth*, the witches rouse him to extreme language, as they aroused Hazlitt and Coleridge: like Hazlitt, he finds them 'sublime' but he also sees them as 'grotesque'[50] and 'terrible':

■ They tingle in every fibre with evil energy, as the tempest does with the electric current; their malignity is inexhaustible; they are wells of sin springing up into everlasting death; they have their raptures and ecstasies in crime; they snatch with delight at the relics of impiety and foul disease; they are the awful inspirers of murder, insanity and suicide.[51] □

There is an important difference between the attitude of Dowden and those of Hazlitt and Coleridge, however. Both earlier writers seemed troubled by the difficulty of categorizing the witches: Hazlitt called them 'unreal, abortive, half-existences'[52] and Coleridge saw them as the 'fearfully anomalous, of physical nature'.[53] Dowden also suggests that they are difficult to categorize – he finds them '[n]ameless' and 'sexless' (sex is presumably being used here in the sense of 'gender') – and counsels us not to try to identify them further: 'It is enough to know that such powers auxiliary to vice do exist outside ourselves'. But in calling them 'powers auxiliary to vice' – and in seeing them as wholly evil, as he does in the passage we have just quoted – he is, in fact, placing them in a definite category and also affirming the existence of forces beyond those recognized by the materialist and scientific worldviews of the later nineteenth century. He is concerned to rebut the idea that the witches merely embody inner temptation and declares that they have an objective, external existence: to recognize this is a mark of realism rather than a sign of fantasy: 'no great realist in art has hesitated to admit the existence of what theologians name divine grace [and] Satanic temptation'.[54] Dowden does not himself endorse these theological terms, however, but employs a late nineteenth-century mixture of historical, sociological and quasi-scientific language: 'The history of the race, and the social medium in which we breathe, have created forces of good and evil which are independent of the will of each individual man and woman ... There is in the atmosphere a zymotic poison of sin ["zymotic" is a historical medical term and means "relating to or denoting contagious disease regarded as developing after infection, like the fermenting of yeast"]; and the constitution which is morally enfeebled supplies appropriate nutriment for the germs of disease; while the hardy moral nature repels the same germs.' Macbeth, it seems, has a weak moral constitution.

Dowden challenges the idea that we see in Macbeth a 'sudden transformation of a noble and loyal soul into that of a traitor and murderer' – an idea which was held, for example, by William Richardson in the eighteenth century. Instead, Dowden finds him, at the start of the play, an unformed, inchoate figure, in 'a careless attitude of suspense or indifference between virtue and vice [which] cannot continue long'; he is one of those who 'lack energy of goodness, and drop into a languid neutrality between the antagonist spiritual forces of the world'.[55] Dowden makes no mention of the martial valour, or brutality, Macbeth displays in the fight against the rebels and invaders at the start of the play; indeed, his lack of energy and his languor make him sound more like an anticipation of a *fin-de-siècle* poet of the last decade of the nineteenth century than a soldier. His resemblance to such a poet is further suggested by another quality which Dowden finds in him: he is 'excitably imaginative, and his imagination alternately stimulates, and enfeebles him'.[56]

By contrast, Lady Macbeth 'sees things in the clearest and most definite outlines. Her delicate frame is filled with high-strung nervous energy. With her to perceive is forthwith to decide, to decide is to act'. If the reference to 'high-strung nervous energy' can make Dowden's Lady Macbeth sound like a late nineteenth-century female neurotic, a candidate for the psychoanalyst's couch that would soon emerge as the primary site for the investigation of neurosis, her capacity to commit herself to a course of action and drive herself along with her conscious will turn her into an existentialist heroine who enacts the precepts of the philosopher Friedrich Nietzsche. But the power of the will has its limits: '[a]s long as her will remains her own, she can throw herself upon external facts and maintain herself in relation with the definite, actual surroundings; it is in her sleep, when the will is incapable of action, that she is persecuted by the past which perpetually renews itself, not in ghostly shapes, but by the imagined recurrence of real and terrible incidents'.[57] Even in sleep, she remains in contact with reality, even if it is of the past rather than the present. And, Dowden suggests, it is finally she, rather than her husband, who is 'slain by conscience'. Macbeth himself, in contrast, indulges in 'vague, imaginative remorse' and, while his 'soul ... never quite disappears into the blackness of darkness',[58] he falls 'deeper and deeper into solitude and gloom'[59] and finally meets a 'savage, and almost brutal' end.[60]

Like Dowden, A. C. Bradley, at the start of the twentieth century, will seek to place his discussion of Macbeth and Lady Macbeth within a more general account of Shakespearean tragedy, and he will explicitly identify Macbeth as having the imagination of a poet. He will do this within a book, published in 1904, that would prove both influential and controversial. It is a moot point whether Bradley is best seen as the last major nineteenth-century critic of Shakespeare or the first major twentieth-century one; his synthesis certainly owed much to the nineteenth and indeed to the eighteenth century; but it provided a vital stimulus and source-book for twentieth-century critics – even if they usually reacted against it. We therefore consider Bradley in Chapter 3.

CHAPTER THREE

The Early Twentieth Century: Tragedy, Psychoanalysis and Imagery

In between 1900 and 1940, literary criticism, including criticism of Shakespeare, was transformed. There were a range of reasons for this, but two main ones stand out. One was the emergence of those literary texts which have come to be called modernist – texts such as *Ulysses* (1922) by James Joyce (1882–1941) and *The Waste Land* (1922) by T. S. Eliot (1888–1965); these texts were difficult to read in terms of nineteenth-century poetry and fiction – difficult, it could be said, in the way in which Shakespeare was difficult – and if they were to be properly understood, new and more rigorous techniques of interpretation were required. The other main reason was the development of the study of literature as an academic discipline: literary criticism could no longer simply be the occupation of the man of letters: it was a professional activity which required specialist expertise – in particular, the ability to read and interpret demanding texts; and, here again, Shakespeare's texts, not least *Macbeth*, were notably demanding. In this transformation of literary criticism, especially as it applied to Shakespeare, A. C. Bradley's *Shakespearean Tragedy* played a complex role. Bradley certainly gave close attention to the text and he tried to weave his local observations into broader interpretations and into a general theory; but many of his assumptions seemed open to question and came under strong attack. His book has not gone away, however: still in print, it remains valuable, both for its suggestive insights and for the ways in which it helps us to understand the subsequent development of *Macbeth* criticism in the twentieth century.

A. C. BRADLEY

In *Shakespearean Tragedy*, A. C. Bradley offered a general definition of Shakespearean tragedy which stresses the part that the character and

43

actions of the hero play in the tragic effect, and the way in which tragedy reveals a moral order despite the suffering and waste that it evokes. For all his concern with character, his view of tragedy is ultimately a philosophical one, derived from the German thinker G. W. F. Hegel (1770–1831), in which individuals are incarnations of larger dynamic processes. For Bradley, Shakespearean tragedy can be defined initially as a story of 'exceptional suffering and calamity'[1] which affects a hero who is a man of high social standing (king, prince, noble, general), and ultimately leads to his death. The suffering and calamity which, partly because of the hero's high social standing, 'generally extend far and wide beyond him, so as to make the whole scene a scene of woe, are an essential ingredient in tragedy, and a chief source of the tragic emotions, and especially of pity' – although Bradley also makes the interesting, and debatable, remark that, in *Macbeth*, pity 'is directed ... chiefly to minor characters',[2] an observation which, if it were accepted, could have significant implications for the interpretation of the 'Pity, like a naked new-born babe' passage. In Shakespearean tragedy, however, the woes which affect the hero are not due primarily to chance or fate: 'the calamities of tragedy do not simply happen, nor are they sent; they proceed mainly from ... the actions of men'. The suffering which accompanies a 'series of inter-connected deeds', and the ensuing catastrophe, are represented 'not only or chiefly as something which happens to the [principal] persons concerned, but equally as something which is caused by them'. The hero 'always contributes in some measure to the disaster in which he perishes'.[3] Bradley sums up the matter in this way:

■ The 'story' or 'action' of a Shakespearean tragedy does not consist, of course, solely of human actions or deeds; but the deeds are the predominant factor. And these deeds are, for the most part, actions in the full sense of the word ... acts or omissions thoroughly expressive of the doer ... characteristic deeds. The centre of the tragedy, therefore, may be said with equal truth to lie in action issuing from character, or in character issuing in action. ... Shakespeare's main interest lay here ... the calamities and catastrophe follow inevitably from the deeds of men, and ... the main source of these deeds is character.[4] □

Bradley acknowledges that Shakespeare's tragedies sometimes portray extreme states of minds and that the actions which proceed from these cannot be called 'actions in the full sense of the word'. He argues, however, that these extreme states produce no actions of dramatic importance; the vision of the dagger does not make Macbeth kill Duncan but appears to him because he is thinking of killing Duncan; Lady Macbeth's sleepwalking has no effect on subsequent events. The intervention of supernatural beings – the witches in *Macbeth* are a notable example – does contribute to the action, but it is always related closely to character, confirming and crystallizing thoughts and desires that are already present and pressing for expression: for example, 'the half-formed thought [of murder] or the memory of guilt in Macbeth'.[5] Chance and accident also play their part in the tragic action but Shakespeare employs them only sparingly, and he is justified in using them because they constitute a fact of human life which does, in actuality, sometimes take on tragic dimensions when it affects the outcomes of actions that men have initiated.

Bradley also argues that Shakespearean tragedy is always uplifting; the contrast between the greatness of the hero, and the suffering and catastrophe which, to a large extent, he brings upon himself, highlights the positive potential of human nature and produces what Bradley calls 'the centre of the tragic impression': a sense of waste. In this respect, tragedy becomes an image of 'the mystery of the whole world'.[6] Shakespearean tragedy does not present a Christian vision of existence – if it did, Bradley suggests, it would not finally be tragic – but neither does it offer a morally indifferent one: 'the ultimate power in the tragic world is a moral order' which 'shows itself akin to good and alien from evil'.[7] Thus, the main source of suffering and death is always evil – for instance, '[g]uilty ambition, seconded by diabolic malice and issuing in murder, opens the action in *Macbeth*';[8] and evil 'exhibits itself everywhere as something negative, barren, weakening, destructive, a principle of death' which 'isolates, disunites, and tends to annihilate not only its opposite but itself'. This view of evil as 'a principle of death' will be echoed and developed in the work of later critics such as G. Wilson Knight. Nonetheless, for Bradley, evil is also an aspect of this ultimately moral order:

■ the evil against which [the order] asserts itself, and the persons whom this evil inhabits, are not really something outside this order, so that they can attack it or fail to conform to it; they are within it and a part of it. It itself produces them … . We do not think of Hamlet merely as failing to meet its demand, of Antony as merely sinning against it, or even of Macbeth as simply attacking it … we feel … that they are *its* parts, expressions, products; that in their defect or evil *it* is untrue to its soul of goodness, and falls into conflict and collision with itself; that, in making them suffer and waste themselves, *it* suffers and wastes itself; and that when, to save its life and regain peace from this intestinal struggle, it casts them out, it has lost a part of its own substance – a part far more dangerous and unquiet, but far more valuable and nearer to its heart, than that which remains – a Fortinbras, a Malcolm, an Octavius. There is no tragedy in its expulsion of evil: the tragedy is that this involves the waste of good.[9] ☐

Shakespearean tragedy is finally, for Bradley, representative of a tragedy which is that of life itself: the 'inexplicable fact' or 'appearance' of a world struggling for perfection but generating both 'glorious good' and 'an evil which it is able to overcome only by self-torture and self-waste'.[10]

Bradley's approach to Shakespearean tragedy, then, is certainly concerned with character and the way it is expressed in action; it also, however, places character and action in a broader, Hegelian perspective in which they are elements of the whole dynamic process of existence as it struggles towards perfection but, in the course of doing this, produces evil. Within this general perspective, Bradley finds that a distinctive 'tone or atmosphere' usually characterizes each Shakespearean tragedy, and in *Macbeth* its effect 'is marked with unusual strength'.[11] Like Hazlitt, Bradley provides a vivid impressionistic account of this atmosphere, but he does not stop there; he goes on to analyse, in some detail, the elements which contribute to it. His analysis focuses partly on the settings and events of the play, and partly on its language; and it is his discussions of language which are especially significant for twentieth-century criticism and which anticipate some aspects of the work of Caroline Spurgeon, G. Wilson Knight and L. C. Knights. Bradley draws attention to the references to darkness, to blackness, and to blood; to the 'vividness, magnitude, and violence'[12] of such imagery as dashing out the smiling baby's brains (1.7.54–9) or pouring the sweet milk of concord into hell (4.3.99); and to the repeated mentions of sleep and lack of sleep. He also points to the use in *Macbeth*, more extensively than in any other Shakespeare play, of dramatic irony, where the character's words and actions take on meanings for the audience that are unknown to the character himself or, often, to the other characters. When Macbeth says in his very first words in the play, 'So fair and foul a day I have not seen' (1.3.36), he does not know that this echoes the witches' 'Fair is foul, and foul is fair' (1.1.10), but an attentive audience does.

In turning to the character of Macbeth, Bradley reiterates the view of earlier critics such as Whately and Hazlitt – that Macbeth is a man of courage, conscience and ambition – but focuses on one further 'marked peculiarity' – that he 'has, within certain limits, the imagination of a poet – an imagination on the one hand extremely sensitive to impressions of a certain kind, and, on the other, productive of violent disturbance both of mind and body'. It is through his imagination that his conscience, honour and best and deepest self communicate to him, with images that 'alarm and horrify',[13] but he does not 'accept as the principle of his conduct the morality which takes shape in his imaginative fears'.[14] And his imagination, though 'excitable and intense', is also 'narrow':[15]

> ■ What appals him is always the image of his own guilty heart or bloody deed, or some image which derives from them its terror or gloom. These, when they arise, hold him spellbound and possess him wholly, like a hypnotic trance which is at the same time the ecstasy of a poet.[16] □

If Dowden's languid, careless, excitably imaginative Macbeth resembles a *fin-de-siecle* poet of the 1890s, Bradley's Macbeth seems more like a late Victorian or early Edwardian version of the poets of the Romantic era: he is a spellbound, rapt, ecstatic figure tortured by guilt, a kind of combination of Percy Bysshe Shelley (1792–1827) and Lord Byron (1788–1824).

Bradley's approach to Shakespearean tragedy would prove widely influential. But in the 1930s it would be displaced – and sometimes directly attacked – by critics who felt that he placed too much emphasis on character and that it was more productive, and more in accord with the ways in which Shakespeare's plays actually worked, to look closely at the images they contained, at the patterns those images seemed to form and at the way in which those patterns of imagery related to overall themes. Between 1904 and 1930, however, another writer – not primarily a literary critic – produced an interpretation of *Macbeth* which is of considerable interest both in its own right and as a harbinger of a major strand of *Macbeth* criticism in the later twentieth century. The writer in question is the founder of psychoanalysis, Sigmund Freud.

SIGMUND FREUD

In his celebrated discussion of *Hamlet* in *The Interpretation of Dreams* (1900), Sigmund Freud makes a passing but intriguing reference to *Macbeth*: 'Just as *Hamlet* deals with the relation of a son to his parents, so *Macbeth* (written at approximately the same period) is concerned with the subject of childlessness'.[17] Freud explores this idea further in 'Some Character-Types Met With in Psycho-Analytical Work' (1916), where he suggests that the action of *Macbeth* is based on the contrast between 'the curse of unfruitfulness and the blessings of continuous generation' – a contrast, he proposes, that was demonstrated in contemporary reality by the accession to the throne of James I, after the death of the childless Elizabeth I (1533–1603); like Macbeth and Lady Macbeth, Elizabeth had no direct descendant to carry on the line, so that she was succeeded by a son of her arch-rival, Mary Queen of Scots (1542–87), whose execution Elizabeth had ordered, as Macbeth had ordered the killing of Banquo.

According to Freud, it is not enough for Macbeth to have satisfied his own ambition by gaining the crown, because he 'wants to found a dynasty',[18] to become, not only a king, but also the father of kings. Freud cites Macduff's words soon after hearing about the killing of his wife – 'He has no children' (5.1.217) – and takes them to apply to Macbeth – rather than, as has sometimes been argued, to Malcolm – and to mean: 'Only because he is himself childless could he murder my children'. Macduff's words provide a vantage-point from which to survey the whole play and to see a range of crucial references to the father–children relationship:

■ The murder of the kindly Duncan is little else than parricide [the murder of a father]; in Banquo's case, Macbeth kills the father while the son escapes him; and in Macduff's, he kills the children because the father has fled from him. A bloody child, and then a crowned one, are shown him by the witches in the apparition scene [4.1]; the armed head which is seen earlier [in this scene] is no doubt Macbeth himself. But in the background rises the sinister form of the avenger, Macduff, who is himself an exception to the laws of generation, since he was not born of his mother but ripp'd from her womb.[19] □

Although Freud's approach to *Macbeth* is largely character centred, it is interesting to note that here, he does draw attention to a recurrent motif in the play – the father–children references – and in this respect he anticipates both G. Wilson Knight and Cleanth Brooks.

Freud's sense of the importance of the father–children relationship in the play, and of the contrast between 'unfruitfulness' and 'continuous generation', provides him with a possible explanation of Lady Macbeth's psychological collapse after she has succeeded in helping to make her husband king and herself queen: 'what was it that broke this character which had seemed forged from the toughest metal?'[20] We saw in Chapter 2 that Coleridge considered this issue and concluded that it was because Lady Macbeth was a fantasist who falsely imagined that Duncan's murder would bring no remorse and who collapsed when confronted with the bloody reality of the killing; Freud does not mention Coleridge, but he does acknowledge the possibility that the change in Lady Macbeth could be explained by seeing the resolution she exhibits before the murder as a state of 'concentration and high tension which could not endure for long' – an explanation which would not be incompatible with that of Coleridge. Freud feels, however, that it could be better explained in terms of 'a deeper motivation' that would 'make this collapse more humanly intelligible to us'[21] – and the deeper motivation, he suggests, could be her childlessness, which convinces her that she is powerless against the forces of nature and prevents her from providing *Macbeth* with the children who would help to ensure that his line, rather than Banquo's, succeeded to the throne.

Freud feels that there is a flaw in this explanation: the change happens too quickly. In a way, he wants to rewrite the play to incorporate the time-lapse that we find in Shakespeare's source, Holinshed; there, Macbeth, partly on his wife's instigation, murders Duncan and becomes king, but for ten years he is an effective ruler: it is only after a decade that he starts to turn into a tyrant – that he arranges for Banquo's murder, for example. As Freud acknowledges, Holinshed does not suggest that Macbeth's childlessness drives him towards tyranny; but the ten years of relatively beneficent rule would, he speculates, give time for the Macbeths to experience 'a long-drawn-out disappointment of their hopes of offspring' which would 'break the woman down and drive the man to defiant rage'.[22] The implication is that, if this ten-year period had been, in some way, represented in Shakespeare's play, then Freud's explanation would fit the bill:

> ■ [*Macbeth* would then] be a perfect example of poetic justice in the manner of the talion [punishment in kind] if the childlessness of Macbeth and the barrenness of his Lady were the punishment for their crimes against the sanctity of generation – if Macbeth could not become a father because he had robbed children of their father and a father of his children, and if Lady Macbeth suffered the unsexing she had demanded of the spirits of murder.[23] □

Freud recognizes, however, that the pace of events in Shakespeare's tragedy prevents the development of character which would support his proposed explanation and concedes that it is 'impossible to guess'[24] the 'motives ... which in so short a space of time could turn the hesitating, ambitious man into an unbridled tyrant, and his steely-hearted instigator into a sick woman gnawed by remorse'.[25] He feels, however, that the powerful effect of the tragedy on the spectator justifies the attempt to study 'its psychological mechanism',[26] even if no conclusion can be reached.

Freud's approach largely assumes that the effect of *Macbeth* on the spectator, and the 'psychological mechanism' of the play, are best understood by looking at the psychology of the *characters*, and approaching them as though they had conscious and unconscious motives, as people in real life do, even if it is impossible to determine those motives or to match them adequately to the play as we have it. At the end of his discussion of *Macbeth*, however, he draws on a paper by his colleague Ludwig Jekels (1867–1954), which seems never to have been published, but which takes a different and potentially fruitful approach to the issue of the 'psychological mechanism' of Shakespeare's plays by suggesting that they often split a character into two figures which cannot be wholly understood if they are considered separately. If this were the case with Macbeth and Lady Macbeth, 'it would of course be pointless to regard her as an independent character and seek to discover the motives for her change, without considering the Macbeth who completes her'.[27] While Freud does not pursue this idea in detail, he does offer some suggestive examples of the transmission of qualities between the two 'characters' which reinforces the possibility that they could be seen as dual aspects of a psychological whole:

■ the germs of fear which break out in Macbeth on the night of the murder do not develop further in *him* but in *her*. It is he who has the hallucination of the dagger before the crime; but it is she who afterwards falls ill of a mental disorder. It is he who after the murder hears the cry in the house: ' "Sleep no more!" ... "Glamis [Macbeth] hath murdered sleep ..." and so "Macbeth shall sleep no more" ' [2.2.40–1]; but we never hear that *he* slept no more, while the Queen, as we see, rises from her bed and, talking in her sleep, betrays her guilt. It is he who stands helpless with bloody hands, lamenting that 'all great Neptune's ocean' will not wash them clean, while she comforts him 'A little water clears us of this deed' [2.2.58, 65]; but later it is she who washes her hands for a quarter of an hour and cannot get rid of the bloodstains: 'all the perfumes of Arabia will not sweeten this little hand' [5.1.42–3]. Thus what he feared in his pangs of conscience is fulfilled in her; she becomes all remorse and he all defiance. Together they exhaust the possibilities of reaction to the crime, like two disunited parts of a single psychical individuality.[28] □

This opens up an alternative way of discussing *Macbeth* in psychoanalytical, psychological terms that regards the characters as aspects of psychic processes rather than as individuals with conscious and unconscious motives.

It would be some decades, however, before psychoanalytical perspectives became prominent in the interpretation of *Macbeth*, and when they did so, they would be closely allied with questions of feminism and gender, as we shall see in Chapter 7. In the earlier twentieth century, the crucial change in *Macbeth* criticism – and in Shakespearean criticism more generally – came about in the 1930s and the three key figures in this change were Caroline Spurgeon, G. Wilson Knight and L. C. Knights.

CAROLINE SPURGEON

Caroline Spurgeon's *Shakespeare's Imagery and What It Tells Us* was first published in 1935, but parts of it had been given as lectures in 1930 and

1931, and indeed Wilson Knight refers to it in his discussion of *Macbeth* in *The Imperial Theme*.[29] We therefore discuss it first, before considering Wilson Knight and L. C. Knights. Spurgeon aims to look at Shakespeare's imagery in a systematic way, to identify those images which recur within and across his plays, to articulate the ideas which those images suggest and to relate them to the themes of the plays; she is important for the way in which she helped to bring about a shift in Shakespeare criticism from a concern with character to a concern with language and, in particular, to a concern with how specific images in Shakespeare's plays could be seen as part of larger patterns of imagery and theme. It was an approach that encouraged critics to pay close attention to the details of the language of any given Shakespeare play and to try to relate those details to a sense of that play's overall significance – a significance that would not primarily lie in the representation of 'character'. As we shall see, Spurgeon still sometimes uses the imagery of Shakespeare's plays to make inferences about 'character', but the 'character' is seen more as emerging through the imagery than as its source, and the imagery is related not only to 'character' but also to ideas and themes.

Spurgeon finds the imagery in *Macbeth* richer, more varied and more imaginative than in any other of Shakespeare's plays, and she identifies four main recurrent images. One is that of a man wearing clothes that do not belong to him, suit him, or fit him; she suggests that this image conveys the idea of Macbeth's inadequate moral and spiritual stature. Macbeth himself employs such an image early in the play, when Ross greets him as Thane of Cawdor: 'The Thane of Cawdor lives: why do you dress me / In borrowed robes?' (1.3.106–7). A little later, Banquo observes of Macbeth: 'New honours come upon him, / Like our strange garments, cleave not to their mould / But with the aid of use' (1.3.143–4). When Macbeth urgently debates the murder of Duncan with Lady Macbeth, one reason he gives for his reluctance to do the deed is that he has 'bought / Golden opinions from all sorts of people, / Which would be worn now in their newest gloss, / Not cast aside so soon' (1.7.32–5) – to which Lady Macbeth responds 'Was the hope drunk / Wherein you dressed yourself?' (1.7.35–6). After the murder, Macduff says of Macbeth's impending coronation: 'Well, may you see things well done there. Adieu, / Lest our old robes sit easier than our new!' (2.4.38–9). Near the end of the play, with Macbeth's defeat imminent, Caithness employs the metaphor of a man trying unsuccessfully to fasten a big garment with a small belt – 'He cannot buckle his distempered cause / Within the belt of rule' (5.2.15–16) – while Angus observes: 'Now does he feel his title / Hang loose about him, like a giant's robe / Upon a dwarfish thief' (5.2.20–2) – images which evoke, according to Spurgeon, an 'imaginative picture of a small, ignoble man encumbered and degraded by garments unsuited to him'[30] (as we shall see in Chapter 4, Cleanth Brooks does not feel that Spurgeon grasps the crucial implication of these images). While Spurgeon still sees Macbeth as a great figure, she feels that these images prevent him from achieving the sublime grandeur that Coleridge and Bradley attribute to him. Her mention of Coleridge and Bradley in this context helps to signal the way in which she does maintain a concern with 'character' in discussing the 'clothes' imagery in *Macbeth*; but the pattern of images she picks out clearly has implications, not only or even primarily for Macbeth's character, but also for the moral and political themes and intimations of the play. Her identification of the 'clothes' imagery has been perhaps her most enduring contribution to *Macbeth* criticism and many subsequent critics have drawn on it.

The second recurrent image to which Spurgeon points is that of sound resounding over the earth and the heavens, and this helps to convey the idea of the enormity of evil. There is, for example, the famous soliloquy in 1.8, with its images of the angels pleading trumpet-tongued against the damnable act of Duncan's murder and of the 'blast' which the 'naked new-born babe' strides; this finds an echo later in Macduff's account of the state of Scotland under Macbeth's rule: '[e]ach new morn / New widows howl, new orphans cry; new sorrows / Strike heaven on the face, that it resounds / As if it felt with Scotland, and yelled out / Like syllable of dolour' (4.3.4–8). Sound also reverberates in Ross's words to Macduff as he prepares to tell him that his wife and children have been murdered on Macbeth's orders: 'I have words / That would be howled out in the desert air, / Where hearing should not latch them' (4.3.194–6).

The third recurrent image is that of light, which is associated with the good, and dark and night, which are associated with evil; one particularly significant idea which emerges from this pattern of imagery is that of an evil which can only operate in darkness and which threatens the eyesight. When Duncan effectively designates his eldest son, Malcolm, as his successor by conferring upon him the title of Prince of Cumberland, he declares that others who merit it will also receive rewards: 'signs of nobleness, like stars, shall shine / On all deservers' (1.4.41–2); in contrast, Macbeth, balked by Malcolm's preferment, says: 'Stars, hide your fires, / Let not light see my black and deep desires' (1.4.50–1). Darkness becomes the element in which evil deeds are contemplated and committed. As Duncan approaches Dunsinane Castle, Lady Macbeth says: 'Come, thick night, / And pall thee in the dunnest smoke of hell' (1.5.48–9) – an invocation that contrasts with her later need, of which we learn during the sleepwalking scene, to have 'light by her continually' after darkness falls (5.1.19–20). As the moment of Duncan's murder draws near, Banquo observes to Fleance: 'There's husbandry in heaven, / Their candles are all out' (2.1.4–5), and, after the slaying, Ross observes that night seems to persist into the next day, when light ought to prevail: 'By th'clock 'tis day, / And yet dark night strangles the travelling lamp [i.e. the sun]' (2.4.6–7), and 'darkness does the face of earth entomb / When living light should kiss it' (2.4.9–10). In his soliloquy after he hears of his wife's death, Macbeth famously sums up the frailty and transience of life by seeing it as a candle whose flame burns only briefly before it is extinguished. The idea of an evil that threatens eyesight is vividly conveyed in Macduff's words about the murdered Duncan: 'Approach the chamber, and destroy your sight / With a new Gorgon' (2.3.68–9; in ancient Greek mythology, the Gorgon was a monstrous woman, one of three sisters, who turned men to stone when they looked at her face); and when the witches conjure up the procession of Kings, Macbeth sees one who is 'too like the spirit of Banquo' and cries: 'Thy crown does sear mine eye-balls' (4.1.128–9).

The fourth chief image in *Macbeth* – an image which, as Spurgeon observes, recurs throughout Shakespeare's drama – is that of sickness, which signifies sin; this pattern of imagery will also be discussed by L. C. Knights. There are, for example, Malcolm's words to Macduff, after the latter has heard of the murder of his wife and children: 'Let's make us medicines of our great revenge, / To cure this deadly grief' (4.3.215–16). Caithness describes Malcolm as 'the medicine of the sickly weal [state]' (5.2.27) and says that the blood they will shed in their battle against Macbeth will be 'our country's purge' (5.2.27–8). Macbeth himself recognizes Scotland is sick when he wishes that the doctor who attends Lady Macbeth could 'cast the water of my land' – that is, analyze its urine, an image that Spurgeon discreetly refrains from explicating fully – and 'purge it to a sound and pristine health' (5.3.52–4) – though Macbeth identifies the English invaders, not himself, as the disease. Spurgeon also draws attention to the 'remedial or soothing ... character' of all Macbeth's images of sickness – balm for a sore, sleep after fever, a purge, physic for pain, a 'sweet oblivious antidote' (5.3.45) – and suggests that this 'intensifies to the reader or audience his passionate and constant longing for well-being, rest, and, above all, peace of mind'.[31]

In these last observations, Spurgeon is, as with the 'clothes' images, using imagery to make inferences about Macbeth's character; but, once again, the imagery that she discusses clearly has implications, not only or even primarily for Macbeth's character, but also for the moral and political themes of the play.

Spurgeon's approach is open to question in several respects. It tends to play down the development of *Macbeth* in terms of its unfolding in time, and thus to give insufficient consideration to the cumulative effect of the imagery; it does not give enough attention to the contexts in which specific examples of imagery occur; and it does not fully pursue the ways in which different strands of imagery might be

t is an approach which, at its most reductive, could lead
:al scanning of a Shakespeare text for repeated words and
l with sensitivity and with an awareness of its limitations,
ﬂvﬁ e search for recurrent images is valuable; and, in the
early 1930s, it was an enormously fruitful development that, as we
shall now see, would be pursued, in different ways, by Wilson Knight
and L. C. Knights.

G. WILSON KNIGHT

In *The Wheel of Fire*, first published in 1930, Wilson Knight outlines the
idea of a 'spatial' rather than 'temporal' approach to Shakespeare – an
idea which was to prove fertile and influential. He begins by making a
distinction between 'criticism' and 'interpretation'. 'Criticism' entails
turning the work that is being examined into an object; comparing it
with other works, especially in terms of quality; assessing its strengths
and weaknesses; and making a judgement as to its enduring worth.
'Interpretation' involves merging with the work that is being considered, trying to grasp it in its own terms and eschewing evaluation.
'Criticism is a judgement of vision; interpretation a reconstruction of
vision.'[32] In practice, most commentary on literary texts involves a mixture of 'criticism' and 'interpretation'; but, in Wilson Knight's view, any
fruitful and enduring response to work as great as Shakespeare's will
inevitably consist much more of 'interpretation' than of 'criticism'.
    The 'interpretation' of a Shakespeare play means, first, receiving it as
a total vision, in an uncritical and, in a sense, passive and child-like way;
and, second, reconstructing and reexpressing this vision in intellectual
terms. But what is the best way to reexpress this vision? Here Wilson
Knight makes a bold and innovative suggestion: in order 'to receive the
whole Shakespearean vision into the intellectual consciousness', it is
necessary 'to see the whole play in space as well as time', because 'there
are throughout the play a set of correspondences which relate to each
other independently of the time-sequence which is the story'. If we can
'see the whole play laid out, so to speak, as an area', we will be 'simul-
taneously aware of these thickly-scattered correspondences in a single
view of the whole' and 'possess the unique quality of the play in a new
sense'. Wilson Knight acknowledges that, in Shakespeare, the temporal
dimension – the succession of events – and the spatial dimension – the
sets of correspondences – are closely fused, but he feels that the spatial
perspective has been neglected and that it helps to illuminate and
explain the plays, sometimes in striking ways. Wilson Knight does not
see the spatial approach, however, as merely an additional method
which highlights one hitherto overlooked aspect of the plays; it is,

rather, crucial to grasping their metaphysical significance, to 'cutting below the surface to reveal that burning core of mental or spiritual reality from which each play derives its nature and meaning'.[33] This heightened language is characteristic of Wilson Knight's interpretations of Shakespeare, in which a spatial approach is wedded to a kind of metaphysical melodrama. We now see how this works in relation to *Macbeth*.

Wilson Knight finds that '*Macbeth* is Shakespeare's most profound and mature vision of evil'[34] – and this evil is absolute, not relative, supernatural rather than natural, and objective rather than subjective. It is not simply located in Macbeth, or Lady Macbeth, as 'characters'; it can also be found in Banquo, Macduff and Malcolm; it pervades the whole play. Lady Macbeth is not to be understood in terms of 'ambition' or 'will'; she is 'a woman possessed ... of an evil passion' and once that passion has done its work she reverts to an ordinary state of feminine frailty, collapsing into remorse; the change in her is not to be explained in the psychological terms of either Coleridge or Freud.

A range of elements combine to create the sense of evil which pervades *Macbeth*. There is a constant sense of uncertainty – 'questions, rumours, startling news' and surprise are everywhere. Wilson Knight suggests that more questions may be asked in *Macbeth* than in any other Shakespeare play. It starts with questions: 'When shall we three meet again?' and 'Where the place?' (1.1.1, 6), and these continue as the action proceeds: 'What bloody man is that?' (1.2.1); 'Where has thou been, sister? ... Sister, where thou?' (1.3.1, 3); Banquo marks his first entrance with two successive questions: 'How far is't called to Forres? What are these' (1.3.37); as the time to kill Duncan approaches, Macbeth and Lady Macbeth trade questions: 'What news?', 'Why have you left the chamber?', 'Hath he asked for me', 'Know you not he has' (1.7.28–30)'; questions punctuate the moment and immediate aftermath of the murder: 'Didst thou not hear a noise? – Did not you speak? – When? – Now. – As I descended?' (2.2.14–16); 'But wherefore could I not pronounce Amen?' (2.2.29); 'Will all great Neptune's ocean wash this blood / Clean from my hand?' (2.2.58–9). There are numerous other examples.

There is also a 'heavy proportion of second-hand or vague knowledge' in *Macbeth*. We know little about the rebellion (Wilson Knight does not draw any political implications from this, as some later historically or politically oriented critics might). Many rumours and fears circulate during the action of the play. These uncertainties extend to the reader or audience, and Wilson Knight gives examples of them:

■ Why does Macbeth not know of Cawdor's treachery? Why does Lady Macbeth faint? Why do the King's sons flee to different countries when a whole nation is ready in their support? Why does Macduff move so darkly mysterious in the background and leave his family to certain death? Who is the Third Murderer? And, finally, why does Macbeth murder Duncan?[35] ☐

In other perspectives, these questions might look like faults in *Macbeth* or puzzles requiring interpretation; for Wilson Knight they indicate the way in which the play creates a sense of uncertainty in which its readers or spectators participate; they too are in the dark, prey to doubt and ambiguity. Of course, such uncertainty would not be sufficient in itself to create a vision of evil (it could, in other contexts, be the stuff of comedy). In *Macbeth*, however, it serves to reinforce the sense of evil which emerges from the language and events of the play.

Macbeth is not wholly a vision of evil, however. Other elements in the play are opposed to evil, and in the further interpretation of *Macbeth* which appeared a year after *The Wheel of Fire*, in *The Imperial Theme* (1931), Wilson Knight expands his account of these. In this later reading, the idea of *Macbeth* as a play which conveys a vision of metaphysical evil is still strong; but now there is a more powerful counterweight. *Macbeth* is a play of metaphysical oppositions, in which life and death themes, especially creation and destruction, are opposed – an opposition that is evident in both the action and the language of the play. Wilson Knight identifies four typically Shakespearean life-themes which *Macbeth* expresses:

1. Warrior-honour
2. Imperial magnificence
3. Sleep and feasting
4. Ideas of creation and nature's innocence.

These are contrasted with 'forces of death and ill-omen, darkness and disorder'.[36]

In Wilson Knight's view, 'warrior-honour' is the honour of a loyal fighter in a noble cause – which is what Macbeth is at the start of the play. Wilson Knight does not register the excessive aspect of the violence which Macbeth visits on Macdonald – 'unseamed him from the nave to th' chops' (1.2.22) – or raise the issue of whether the bloody way in which the rebellion and invasion is repulsed might reflect adversely on the 'nobility' of the cause; in this respect, he appears to endorse the distinction between violence that is good because it preserves the existing power structure and violence that is evil because it opposes it – a distinction which, as we see in Chapter 5, some critics in the 1980s, such as Alan Sinfield, started to question. For Wilson Knight, courage detached from honour – for example, the courage one may show in ruthlessly pursuing one's individual ambitions – is of no value, as Macbeth discovers once he has murdered Duncan. Honour is bound up with fidelity to one's king, country, clan and family, which are all 'units of peace, concord, life'. The 'Sons, kinsmen, thanes' whom Duncan evokes (1.4.35) are all 'bound close together' by a 'natural law ... in proper place and allegiance'.[37] The 'evil' in Macbeth rejects and opposes this order.

The second positive theme Wilson Knight identifies, closely entwined with the first, is 'imperial magnificence': Macbeth cannot achieve this because he has no real rights to it; he never really possesses the crown. The third life-theme is 'sleep and feasting', which are both 'creative, restorative forces of nature', 'twin life-givers'. By murdering Duncan in his sleep after feasting him, Macbeth has struck against these forces, he has 'murdered sleep' (2.2.40), and as a result, a spectre haunts his banquet and sleep eludes him. 'Nature' is the fourth life-theme, and '[n]ature-references blend with human themes, especially in point of procreation and childhood'.[38] Among positive references to nature in the play, the most notable is Banquo's description of Macbeth's castle to Duncan on their arrival:

■ King Duncan: This castle hath a pleasant seat. The air
Nimbly and sweetly recommends itself
Unto our gentle senses.
Banquo: This guest of summer,
The temple-haunting martlet, does approve
By his loved mansionry, that the heavens' breath
Smells wooingly here. No jutty, frieze,
Buttress, nor coign of vantage but this bird
Hath made his pendant bed, and procreant cradle;
Where they most breed and haunt, I have observed
The air is delicate. □   (1.6.1–10)

Knight draws attention to terms suggestive of sensuousness, eroticism and the creation of life – 'senses', 'wooing', 'delicate', 'breed', 'procreant cradle' – and suggests that the dialogue provides 'a perfect contrast in microcosm to the Macbeth-evil. Macbeth's crime is a blow against nature's unity and peace, a hideous desecration of all creative, family, and social duties, all union and concord'.[39] Towards the end of the play, nature strikes back when Birnam wood seems to march against Macbeth: 'This is creative nature accusing, asserting her strength after her long torment of destruction'.[40]

Knight also finds the life-theme of 'nature' in the references to 'milk', to which Lady Macbeth opposes herself; for example, she says that Macbeth is 'too full of the milk of human kindness' (1.5.15), asks the spirits that tend on mortal thoughts to 'take my milk for gall' (1.5.46) and imagines that she could dash out the brains of 'the babe that milks me' (1.7.55). This last example is also one of the many references to babies and children that reinforce the 'nature' theme and contribute to the play's ultimate affirmation of life. Wilson Knight concludes that the whole play can be seen 'as a wrestling of destruction with creation':

■ with sickening shock the phantasmagoria of death and evil are violently loosed on earth, and for a while the agony endures, destructive; there is a wrenching of new birth, itself disorderly and unnatural in this disordered world, and then creation's more firm-set sequent concord replaces chaos. The baby-peace is crowned.[41] □

Wilson Knight's conclusion could itself be seen to demonstrate a certain 'wrenching' of *Macbeth* into a metaphysical pattern that would be questioned by some later critics; but his interpretation provides a vivid and provocative vision of the play, shifts the emphasis away from 'character' and provides copious examples from the text to support its case. An interpretation of *Macbeth* that had some similarities to that of Wilson Knight would be provided by his near-namesake, L. C. Knights, but in a cooler tone, and with significant differences of emphasis.

L. C. KNIGHTS

In 1933, L. C. Knights posed, in the title of a landmark essay, a famous question that he had no intention of pursuing: 'How Many Children Had Lady Macbeth?' His title functioned, not to announce the topic of his essay, but to parody an approach to Shakespeare that treated the characters of his plays as if they were akin to real people who could be detached from the dramas in which they appeared and whose life outside the play one could speculate about; an approach which, as we have seen, developed in the later eighteenth century, persisted through the nineteenth century and reached its climax in the early twentieth century with A. C. Bradley, but which had already begun to be implicitly challenged by Caroline Spurgeon. For L. C. Knights, as for Wilson Knight, Bradley is the key target, and Knights signals this in his essay title: one of the appendices to Bradley's *Shakespearean Tragedy* considers whether Macbeth (not, as it happens, Lady Macbeth) had children, although Bradley does say that the question cannot be answered, and 'does not concern the play'.[42] But for Knights, the matter is not even worth considering; it is the wrong kind of question to ask of a Shakespeare play because it assumes that the characters in the play have an existence prior to and beyond the drama that produced them. In opening his attack, Knights satirically echoes the claim of the eighteenth-century writer Thomas Whately, which was quoted in Chapter 1 of this Guide, that no playwright except Shakespeare had 'so deep and so extensive a knowledge of the human heart'.[43]

■ The most fruitful of [critical] irrelevancies is the assumption that Shakespeare was pre-eminently a great 'creator of characters'. So extensive was his knowledge of the human heart (so runs the popular opinion) that he was able to project himself into the minds of an infinite variety of men and women and present them 'real as life' before us.[44] □

For Knights, this assumption distracts critics from grasping the true nature of a Shakespeare play.

Knights affirms that '[a] Shakespeare play is a dramatic poem',[45] an 'indivisible unity'[46] constituted by a 'unique arrangement of words', a 'precise particular experience'[47] which requires 'a full complex response'[48] that 'can only be obtained by an exact and sensitive study of the quality of the verse, of the rhythm and imagery, of the controlled associations of the words and their emotional and intellectual force'. A Shakespeare play, that is, requires 'close reading' which focuses on specific textual details while constantly relating them to an overall poetic whole. To exemplify this kind of reading, Knights offers an interpretation of *Macbeth* which partly overlaps with Wilson Knight's but has distinctive insights of its own.

Like Wilson Knight, Knights identifies several themes in the play, though they are not the same as his fellow-critic's:

1. the reversal of values
2. unnatural disorder
3. the deceitful appearance and consequent doubt, uncertainty and confusion

To demonstrate his claim that these themes are stated in the first act of *Macbeth*, Knights gives close attention to specific words and phrases. For example, the reversal of values and deceitful appearance leading to confusion are announced in the words of the first scene: 'Fair is foul, and foul is fair' (1.1.10); 'hurly-burly' and 'When the battle's lost and won' (1.1.3, 4) 'suggest the kind of metaphysical pitch-and-toss that is about to be played with good and evil'.[49] The lines which, in the second scene, evoke the battle with the rebels – 'Doubtful it stood, / As two spent swimmers that do cling together / And choke their art' (1.2.7–9) – relate not only to the battle with the rebels but also to Macbeth's doubtful future. Moreover, the account of the battle conveys what Knights calls 'unnatural violence' – for example, in the phrase 'to bathe in reeking wounds' (1.2.39) – and 'a kind of nightmare gigantism', for instance in the lines 'Where the Norwegian banners flout the sky / And fan our people cold' (1.2.49–50). Uncertainty is prevalent in the encounter with the witches, who 'look not like th'inhabitants o'th'earth / And yet are on it', who 'should be women' but have 'beards' that 'forbid' Banquo 'to interpret / That [they] are so' (1.3.39–44), and who may be 'fantastical' or 'that indeed / Which outwardly [they] show' (1.3.53–4). This uncertainty is epitomized in Macbeth's soliloquy, 'This supernatural soliciting / Cannot be ill; cannot be good' (1.3.130–1), which has what Knights memorably calls a 'sickening see-saw rhythm'.[50]

By contrast with the three earlier scenes, Knights, in a very similar way to Wilson Knight, sees 4:1 as invoking the 'natural order' through its deployment of terms that apply to 'natural relationships': 'children', 'servants', 'Sons', 'kinsmen' – and 'honourable bonds and the political order' – 'liege', 'thanes', 'service', 'loyalty', 'duties', 'throne', 'state', 'honour' (1.4.25, 35, 3, 35, 22, 24, 25, 27). Human 'love' (1.4.27) is associated with images of husbandry, as in Duncan's words to Macbeth – 'I have begun to plant thee, and will labour / To make thee full of growing' (1.4.28–9). For Knights, 'the natural order' includes 'birds, beasts and reptiles' and the human order marked by 'propriety and degree'; 'it represents society in harmony with nature, bound by love and friendship, and ordered by law and duty. It is one of the main axes of reference by which we take our emotional bearings in the play'.[51]

This is one aspect of Knights's approach that will be strongly challenged by a later, more politicized or historical criticism which will argue that this notion of the 'natural order' is in fact deeply ideological and aims to mystify questionable, historically specific relationships by treating them as if they were akin to organic growths. Knights's classification of 'servants' as a 'natural relationship' could seem especially vulnerable from such perspectives; the word does not have the biological connotations of 'children', 'Sons' and 'kinsmen'; and it could be argued that it seems 'natural' only in a certain kind of hierarchical society; while 'throne', which Knights regards as part of 'the political order', might appear – indeed, Shakespeare's plays often suggest this – to indicate a political apparatus that is likely to generate uncertainty and, not infrequently, usurpation; the 'political order' that Duncan represents has, after all, to be defended by violence. Like Wilson Knight, Knights constructs and deploys binary oppositions without questioning his categories or asking whether they are as separate and contrary as he supposes. Is it appropriate to accept a political 'order' that includes a monarchy and nobles as 'natural' or as a temporary and dubious historical construction?

The supposed positive value of 'natural order' is reinforced by what Knights calls the 'holy supernatural', setting it against the 'supernatural soliciting' of the witches.[52] He instances the reference to the 'temple-haunting martlet' (1.6.4) when Duncan and Banquo first arrive at Macbeth's castle, and the exchange in 3.6 between Lennox and 'another Lord', both of whom are not 'characters', but 'completely impersonal', and whose dialogue contains references to 'the most pious Edward', 'the holy King' who has received Malcolm 'with such grace', 'some Holy angel', 'a swift blessing' and 'prayers'. In this scene, Knights especially singles out the following lines which link up with key images in the rest of the play:

> ■ ... by the help of these – with Him above
> To ratify the work – we may again
> Give to our tables meat, sleep to our nights,
> Free from our feasts and banquets bloody knives,
> Do faithful homage, and receive free honours,
> All which we pine for now. □   (3.6.32–7)

For Knights, this suggests that food, sleep, society and the political order have a supernatural sanction, and the idea of such a sanction is strengthened later in the play, for example in 4.3, where the discussion of King Edward's healing power includes phrases and words such as 'A most miraculous work', 'Heaven', 'holy prayers', the 'healing benediction', 'virtue', 'blessings' and 'grace'. The opposition of these qualities to the 'evil' that Macbeth is taken to represent is echoed by the contrasting images of health and disease in the sleepwalking scene (5.1), and the disease imagery links up with the theme of disorder and the unnatural.

When Knights turns to the scene between Macduff and Malcolm in 4.3, which, he says, has often puzzled editors and critics, he argues that its function is not to develop Macduff and Malcolm as characters but to provide the kind of commentary that a tragic chorus gives. Alternating speeches state, explicitly, impersonally and unsparingly, the evil for which Macbeth is responsible. Malcolm, in making his self-accusing speech, ceases to be a person in a play. 'His lines repeat and magnify the evils that have already been attributed to Macbeth, acting as a mirror wherein the ills of Scotland are reflected'.[53] Although Malcolm says that he would 'Pour the sweet milk of concord into hell' (4.3.99), he is neither cannily testing Macduff nor projecting, in fantasy, his own potential for evil: he is, in effect, describing Macbeth's actions. Knights's interpretation certainly provides one way of explaining some of the oddities of this scene, but it does not engage with Malcolm's status as the future king of Scotland, which makes it difficult to confine his function to a choric one. He may not be a 'character' but he is more than a mere bystander.

In Knights's reading, as in that of Wilson Knight, virtue and order are restored at the end of Macbeth, but Knights offers a different interpretation of the Birnam wood scene. For Wilson Knight, as we saw in the previous section, the apparent movement of the trees shows 'creative nature ... [re-] asserting her strength' against Macbeth;[54] for Knights, it presents rather more of a problem, since it could seem to portray the representatives of good making use of the deceit that has previously been associated with evil in the play. Knights's solution to this is to acknowledge that this is indeed 'a peculiar "reversal" ' in which deceit is now associated with the good rather than the bad, but to argue that it functions both to emphasize the disorder which Macbeth has produced – presumably by showing that such disorder forces even the good to adopt dubious measures – and to free our minds from the weight of horror that has been aroused by previous deceitful appearances – for the moving wood, like the birth of Macduff, can be explained in simple terms and is thus only temporarily deceitful and ambiguous.

Knights also considers the 'Tomorrow and tomorrow and tomorrow' speech (5.3.18–27) and links this with one of the key themes that he has earlier identified in *Macbeth* – the theme of the deceitful appearance; Macbeth is saying that life itself deceives us, and that he has seen through the imposture. As Knights recognizes, the poetic power of this claim poses a threat to an affirmative interpretation of *Macbeth*: 'we are almost bullied into accepting an essential ambiguity in the final statement of the play, as though Shakespeare were expressing his own "philosophy" in the lines'. Knights suggests, however, that the speech plays a new variation on the theme of the deceitful appearance: whereas earlier examples of deceitful appearances in the play – most obviously, the witches – were strongly marked as untrustworthy, the 'Tomorrow and tomorrow and tomorrow' speech can seem to be on the side of truth, an apparent revelation of the reality that lies behind illusion which can almost convince us that the view of life it offers could be valid. But that view of life is itself a deceitful appearance, and the deception becomes visible when it is placed within the context of the affirmative movement of the last act. The 'Tomorrow and tomorrow and tomorrow' speech is neither a final judgement on human existence nor a demonstration of Macbeth's grandeur in despair; it is a crucial part of the play's system of values; its extreme negativeness strengthens, by contrast, the positive affirmations of the play.

Knights's clear-cut distinctions between good and evil, nature and the unnatural, deceitful appearance and honest reality are, like those of Wilson Knight, open to question; but his interpretation remains a rich and subtle one which combines close attention to textual detail with a sense of the play as a whole. As we shall see in Chapter 4, Knights himself would take up *Macbeth* again and develop and extend his interpretation nearly twenty-five years later, in *Some Shakespearean*

Themes (1959). Another critic of the 1930s who also gave close and rewarding attention to textual detail, though he did not produce a book or essay on Shakespeare as influential as those of Caroline Spurgeon, Wilson Knight or L. C. Knights, was William Empson, and we turn to him next.

WILLIAM EMPSON

William Empson's remarks on passages in *Macbeth* in his seminal *Seven Types of Ambiguity* (1930) are fascinating in themselves, and more generally important because they exemplify an approach to Shakespeare which looks closely at the ways in which his language – and not only through its imagery – generates complex meanings. Empson first cites *Macbeth* when he is trying to grasp the way in which poetry creates 'atmosphere' – which he seeks to define more precisely as 'the consciousness of what is implied by the meaning'.[55] He attempts to show how this consciousness of implication is produced in the passage in which Macbeth invokes the approach of darkness on the evening on which he has arranged for the murder of Banquo and Fleance:

■ Light thickens, and the crow
Makes wing to th'rooky wood.
Good things of day begin to droop and drowse,
Whiles night's black agents to their preys do rouse □   (3.2.51–4)

Empson suggests the lines are an example of what the Victorian art and cultural critic John Ruskin (1819–1900) called the Pathetic Fallacy – the poetic convention in which natural phenomena are described as if they were reflecting human moods. The image of the crow flying towards the wood as light fades might, in other contexts, seem soothing; but this context implies an analogy between the crow moving towards the wood and the murderer – Macbeth himself, and the killers he has hired – moving towards his victims. This analogy is partly suggested by Macbeth's situation at this point in the play; but it is reinforced by the language and ambiguous syntax – for example, it is unclear whether the crow is one of the 'good things of day' or one of 'night's black agents' – and, above all, by the associations of the words 'rook' and 'crow':

■ *Rooks* live in a crowd and are mainly vegetarian; *crow* may be either another name for a *rook*, especially when seen alone, or it may mean the solitary Carrion crow. This subdued pun is made to imply here that Macbeth, looking out of the window, is trying to see himself as a murderer, and can only see himself as in position of the *crow*; that his *day*

of power, now, is closing; that he has to distinguish himself from the
other *rooks* by a difference of name, *rook-crow*, like the kingly title, only;
that he is anxious, at bottom, to be at one with the other rooks, not to
murder them; that he can no longer, or that he may yet, be united with
the rookery; and that he is murdering Banquo in a forlorn attempt to
obtain peace of mind.[56] □

In a footnote to the second edition of *Seven Types of Ambiguity*, published
in 1947, Empson questioned his own analysis, pointing out that 'the
passage is still impressive if you have no opinions at all about the difference between crows and rooks'.[57] But it remains an interesting attempt
to investigate the question of *why* a certain passage in *Macbeth* produces
the effect it does.

An example from *Macbeth* also features in *Seven Types of Ambiguity* in
Empson's discussion of dramatic irony. Empson sees dramatic irony as a
way in which a single part of a play can remind the reader of the whole
drama – since the reader has to be aware of the whole drama, or at least
significant aspects of it, in order to grasp the irony. Empson quotes the
lines in which Ross tells Macbeth that Duncan 'finds thee in the stout
Norwegian ranks, / Nothing afeard of what thyself didst make, Strange
images of death' (1.3.93–5) and observes that Ross's remark seems out
of place: why should a soldier be afraid of seeing the dead enemies
whom he has killed; as they are no longer alive, they are surely no
longer a threat to him? The assertion that Macbeth was *not* frightened of
the images of those whom he has killed could imply the possibility that
he *might have been* frightened of them – that he is susceptible to this kind
of fear; and this will, of course, later prove to be the case. The lines provide an example of dramatic irony because those familiar with the rest
of the play will know, as Macbeth and Ross do not, that Macbeth, while
he has not been frightened by these dead enemies, will be frightened by
the images of the dead enemies he will soon kill – Duncan and Banquo.
If we take it that Ross is relaying one of Duncan's remarks, it could also
suggest that Duncan, naïve though he may be about those whom he
trusts, nonetheless has some insight into the way Macbeth's mind
works. Moreover, the remark could also be seen to imply a similarity
between killing in battle and murder, despite the convention by which
the former is approved and the latter condemned: in thus referring both
kinds of killing, it adds a further component of dramatic irony for the
reader who knows that Macbeth will soon move from one kind to the
other.

It is interesting to observe here that the line 'Nothing afeard of what
thyself didst make, Strange images of death' (1.3.93–5) contains a possible ambiguity which Empson does not discuss. On one level, the line
means that Macbeth, fighting against the Norwegian soldiers, showed

no fear of seeing the dead men whom he had killed. If we take 'Nothing' to apply, not to 'afeard', but to Macbeth himself, the line could mean: Macbeth himself, who is Nothing, *is* afraid of the images of death he has produced. This would link with his words, after meeting the witches – 'nothing is / But what is not' (1.3.140–1) – and, of course, with the idea of 'Signifying nothing' near the end of the play (5.5.27). It may hint that Macbeth already 'signifies nothing' even when he is fighting for Duncan.

Macbeth provides Empson with examples of both his second and seventh type of ambiguity. In the second type of ambiguity, in which 'two or more meanings are resolved into one',[58] several different metaphors may be used at once, and a 'resounding example of such multiple metaphor is Macbeth's 'If it were done, when 'tis done, then 'twere well / It were done quickly. If th'assassination / Could trammel up the consequence, and catch / With his surcease success: that but' (1.7.1–4). This is how Empson draws out the different metaphors and their implications:

> ■ 'Consequence' means causal result, and the things to follow, though not causally connected, and, as in 'a person of consequence', the divinity that doth hedge a king. 'Trammel' was a technical term used about netting birds, hobbling horses in some particular way, hooking up pots, levering and running trolleys on rails. 'Surcease' means completion, stopping proceedings in the middle of a lawsuit, or the overruling of a judgement; the word reminds you of 'surfeit' and 'decease', as does 'assassination' of hissing and, as in 'supersession', through 'sedere' [Latin for 'to sit'], of knocking down the mighty from their seat. 'His' may apply to Duncan, 'assassination' or 'consequence'. 'Success' means fortunate result, result whether fortunate or not, and succession to the throne. And 'catch', the single little flat word among these monsters, names an action; it is a mark of human inadequacy to deal with these matters of statecraft. ... The meanings cannot all be remembered at once, however often you read it; it remains the incantation of a murderer, dishevelled and fumbling among the powers of darkness.[59] □

We can see that Empson finally resolves these multiple metaphors into one meaning, and that meaning is 'murderer'.

If Empson's second type of ambiguity offers the possibility of this kind of resolution, his seventh type is more recalcitrant. This is the most ambiguous type, in which, in a given context, two opposite meanings are implied. Such an ambiguity can occur even in what may seem like momentary rejections of the anxiety that ambiguity can bring. Empson considers the words which terminate the scene in which Macbeth, aroused and alarmed by the witches' prophecy and its almost instant partial fulfilment (he is now, as they forecast, Thane of Cawdor), has been, to use L. C. Knights's term, see-sawing between the idea of killing

Duncan to secure the crown and the idea of leaving it to chance: 'Come what come may, / Time and the hour runs through the roughest day' (1.3.145–6).

Empson explicates the opposite meanings implied in these lines in this way:

> ■ Either, if he wants it to happen: 'Opportunity for crime, or the accomplished fact of crime, the crisis of action or of decision, will arrive whatever happens; however much, swamped in the horrors of the imagination, one feels as if one could never make up one's mind. I need not, therefore, worry about this at the moment'; or, if he does not want it to happen: 'This condition of horror has lasted only a few minutes; the clock has gone on ticking all this time; I have not yet killed him; there is nothing, therefore, for me to worry about yet.' These opposites may be paired with predestination and freewill: 'The hour will come, whatever I do, when I am fated to kill him, so I may as well keep quiet; and yet if I keep quiet and feel detached and philosophical all these horrors will have passed over me and nothing can have happened.' And in any case (remembering the martial suggestions of 'roughest day'), 'Whatever I do, even if and when I kill him, the sensible world will go on, it will not really be as fearful as I am now thinking it, it is just an ordinary killing like the ones in the battle'.[60] □

Empson also suggests that the opposite meanings he has teased out of the lines can be divided between the two terms 'Time' and 'the hour', even though the fact that, grammatically, they take the singular might suggest that they should be treated as having one meaning. He proposes that the two terms can be read as opposites: 'the hour' implies 'the hour of action' and thus the impulse to take control either over the situation, by committing the murder, or over 'suggestion' by firmly deciding not to commit it; 'time' suggests the rest of time, detachment from action, and thus the impulse to yield, either to fear, which would lead to inaction, or to suggestion, which would lead to action. (It is interesting to note here, although Empson does not make the point explicitly, that either taking control or yielding to suggestion could have the same consequences in terms of action). These two impulses are echoed in the transitive and intransitive meaning of 'runs through': as Empson puts it: ' "time and the hour" force the day to its foregone conclusion, as one runs a man through with a dagger, or "time and the hour" are, throughout the day, after all, always quietly running on'.[61] In a footnote to the second edition of *Seven Types of Ambiguity*, Empson acknowledges that his analysis of this *Macbeth* passage looks too elaborate, but he does not renounce it, feeling that the lines do have the meanings he has suggested (and they are not, in contrast to his earlier comments about the

'Light thickens' lines, dependent on one's knowledge or opinions about rooks and crows).

Although Empson's interpretations of specific passages in *Macbeth* are deeply informed by his knowledge and awareness of the play as a whole and its broader themes, he does not provide a developed overall reading in the way that Wilson Knight and Knights do. But even where his readings are open to question, he does convey a strong sense of the complexity of Shakespeare's language in *Macbeth*, both in its most obviously impressive passages – the 'Light thickens' lines – and in passages that do not, at first glance, seem especially significant – Ross's remark about Macbeth not being afraid of the corpses of those he had killed in battle, or the 'Time and the hour' lines. Empson helps to demonstrate that Shakespeare's words are always worthy of close and fully alert attention and thus offers a corrective to a quest for patterns of imagery that may result in the neglect of other important elements of Shakespeare's language.

The work of Spurgeon, Wilson Knight, Knights and Empson in the 1930s brought the interpretation of *Macbeth* to a new level of depth and precision. In their respective ways, they had helped to establish the importance of 'close reading': of scrutinizing the language of the play carefully and responsively, trying to describe its effects with precision and sensitivity, and relating specific details to overall themes. Later critics would take issue with their interpretations in a range of ways: but, in order for their challenges to be effective, they too would have to engage in close reading, to try to support their case by paying careful attention to the text. This would produce a rich range of interpretations of *Macbeth*, as the subsequent chapters of this Guide will show. But, while the practice of close reading had been established, there were still vital questions about the topics on which critics should choose to focus when they interpreted a text, and on the relations between a literary text and its historical context. We start the next chapter by looking at critics in the 1940s and early 1950s who raised questions which would not be more thoroughly pursued until the 1980s – questions about historical context, and questions of what would later be called gender.

CHAPTER FOUR

The Mid-Twentieth Century: History, Nature and Evil

W hatever their differences, the interpretations of *Macbeth* which we considered in Chapter 3 had one thing in common: they paid little attention to the historical and political aspects and contexts of the play. Only Freud makes a historical comparison, linking the theme of child-lessness in *Macbeth* with the theme of Elizabeth I's childlessness, but this is not central to his argument. In 1944 and 1950, however, there would be two significant pieces of writing – one a short chapter, the other a whole book – that did raise historical and political questions. Another question – of what would later come to be called gender – would be raised in an essay of 1950 by Eugene M. Waith. These historical, political and gender aspects of the play would not be pursued in the 1950s; but they are worth considering both in their own right and for the way in which they feed into later twentieth-century criticism. The first of them – the short chapter – occurs in E. M. W. Tillyard's *Shakespeare's History Plays* (1944).

E. M. W. TILLYARD

In *Shakespeare's History Plays* (1944), E. M. W. Tillyard argued that *Macbeth* was not only 'the last of the great tragedies', but also 'the epilogue of the Histories'.[1] For Tillyard, *Macbeth* is related to the history plays in two key respects: it shows Macbeth violating and eventually being defeated by the 'body politic' – in this case, 'Scotland', which is 'a more organic part' of the play 'than Denmark is of *Hamlet*, Venice of *Othello*, or even Rome of *Coriolanus*'; and it offers, in Malcolm, Shakespeare's 'culminating version' of the ideal ruler, which he had failed to produce in *Henry V*, and which he had attempted again, though more marginally, with the figures of Guiderius in *Cymbeline* and Fortinbras in *Hamlet*. By seeing *Macbeth* as a play which exemplifies the defeat of a bad ruler by the body politic, Tillyard provides a new angle on the well-worn comparison between Macbeth and Richard III, which, as we have seen, goes back to the eighteenth century; his focus is not so much on the characters of the protagonists as on the analogies between the situations and events depicted in the two plays – which, according to Tillyard, would have been evident to an audience who had 'the Elizabethan proclivity to finding examples of history repeating itself'.[2] Both Macbeth and Richard III are tyrants who bring terror to their people; Malcolm's exile at the English court, covertly watched by Macbeth's spies, mirrors the exile of the Earl of Richmond at the court in Brittany, where Richard III keeps him under surveillance; the slaughter of Macduff's children grimly echoes the murder of the princes in the tower; Macbeth's followers desert him at Dunsinane as Richard's do at Bosworth. As well as these specific similarities, there is a broader analogy: a crime works itself out, the villain is punished, and orderly rule is established.

Against its portrayal of the bad king, *Macbeth* sets its portrait of the good king, who is, Tillyard argues, of little interest as a character, but very interesting in what he represents:

■ [Malcolm] is entirely devoted to the good of his country, he has his personal passions in tight control, he is Machiavellian in his distrust of other men till he is absolutely assured of their integrity [hence his self-denunciation in 4.3, which can be seen as a way of testing Macduff's integrity], and he is ready to act. ... He is in fact the ideal ruler who has subordinated all personal pleasures, and with them all personal charm, to his political obligations. He is an entirely admirable and necessary type and he is what Shakespeare found that the truly virtuous king, on whom he had meditated so long, in the end turned into. As a subordinate character he fits perfectly into the play and does not risk letting his creator down, as Henry V had done.[3] □

Tillyard does not consider a question that could be raised in the light of Michael Hawkins' account of *Macbeth*, which we shall discuss in Chapter 5 of this Guide: if Malcolm is the good ruler, what implications does this have for a judgement of Duncan's qualities as king? Duncan is the reverse of 'Machiavellian in his distrust of other men'; he trusts them too easily – first MacDonald, the Thane of Cawdor, a man in whom he 'built / An absolute trust' (1.3.13–14), then Macbeth, who inherits the title of Thane of Cawdor. Given Duncan's position, his propensity to unquestioning trust could be seen as a weakness.

Macbeth is, Tillyard concludes, both a major tragedy and representative of its age in demonstrating how the cosmic, political, and individual spheres should be combined. Like Wilson Knight and Knights, Tillyard affirms the importance, in *Macbeth*, of the theme of order disrupted then restored, and he acknowledges that this has a metaphysical dimension;

the cosmic order is mirrored, on a smaller scale, by the political order, and the political order is mirrored, more minutely, in the order of the individual; but Tillyard links these ideas of order much more explicitly with the thought of the Elizabethan and Jacobean world and gives greater prominence to the political aspect of *Macbeth* than Wilson Knight or Knights had done. Fertile though Tillyard's suggestions are, however, there is no space to develop them in the short chapter he devotes to *Macbeth*: it would be Henry N. Paul who would undertake a much more extensive investigation into the historical context of the Scottish play.

HENRY N. PAUL

Where Tillyard aimed to relate *Macbeth* to Elizabethan and Jacobean political thought, Henry N. Paul's fascinating book *The Royal Play of Macbeth: When, Why and How it was Written by Shakespeare* (1950) aims to link it much more concretely to the Jacobean era – to the ideas and ideology of King James I and to the fall-out from the Gunpowder Plot. Of course, other critics had done this before, but not on the same scale as Paul. While Paul provides plenty of information and documentary material, many of his inferences are unwarranted; there is no hard evidence for his central claim that *Macbeth* was a kind of royal command performance which was first played before King James I and a visiting head of state, the King of Denmark, at Hampton Court on 7 August 1605,[4] although this idea has achieved widespread currency. But Paul's overall assumption that *Macbeth* is intimately related to the early years of James's reign, to James's ideas about kingship and witches, and to the Gunpowder Plot has been taken up, in the later part of the twentieth century, by cultural materialist critics such as Alan Sinfield and New Historicist critics such as Stephen Greenblatt.

Two aspects of Paul's book are particularly significant for future developments in *Macbeth* criticism. One is his discussion of James's book *Basilicon Doron* [ancient Greek for 'kingly gift'] in which he sets out 'the true difference between a lawful, good king and usurping tyrant' in a passage that would be, according to Paul, notorious when the book was printed and for a long time afterwards:

■ A good king thinking his highest honour to consist in the due discharge of his calling ... and as their natural father and kindly master thinks his greatest contentment stands in their prosperity, and his greatest surety in having their hearts ... where by the contrary an usurping Tyrant thinking his greatest honour and felicity to consist in attaining *per fas, vel nefas* [justly or unjustly], to his ambitious pretenses ... building his surety upon the people's misery ... [Some good kings] may be cut off by the treason of some unnatural subjects, yet live their fame after them; and some notable plague fails never to overtake the committers in this life, besides their infamy to all posterities hereafter. Where, by the contrary, a Tyrant's miserable and infamous life, arms in the end his own subjects to become his bureaux [i.e., *bourreaux*, torturers, hangmen].[5] □

Paul's confident assertion that Shakespeare *decided* to use *Macbeth* to illustrate a difference which he had read about in the King's book is unwarranted; but he has a stronger claim when he affirms that those with an awareness of James I's 'antithetical teachings about "lawful good kings" and "usurping tyrants" can better appreciate the sharp contrast which the play creates between Duncan and Macbeth'.[6] In the light of some of the influential interpretations we considered in the previous chapter of this Guide – most notably, those of Wilson Knight and Knights – it might be said that we can appreciate that contrast anyway, through the play's imagery, and that it is a contrast which is better grasped in metaphysical and ethical terms rather than historical and political ones; but Paul opens up a historical and political perspective which implicitly challenges the assumption that the antitheses the play establishes are primarily metaphysical; rather than being absolute, they emerge from a specific moment of absolutist political theory and, insofar as *Macbeth* does reinforce those antitheses, it could be seen as powerful propaganda for a particular ideology rather than a profound insight into the eternal truth of the human condition. Paul also suggests how James I's distinction between 'a lawful good king' and 'an usurping tyrant' recurs at moments of political crisis – in the conflict between Charles I and Parliament, in the controversies between Whigs and Tory in the final years of King Charles II's reign. Its recurrence in the rather more marginal field of later twentieth-century Shakespeare criticism may also be related to a sense of political crisis in the modern world.

James I's distinction between a lawful true king and an usurping tyrant raised the question of whether it was ever justifiable to kill a tyrant, and he himself had come out strongly against this, both in *Basilikon Doron*, where he states that it is 'ever unlawful' for subjects to rebel even against an usurping tyrant, and in his earlier book *The True Law of Free Monarchies* (1598) where he argued that subjects should not rebel against a bad king 'in respect they had once received and acknowledged him for their king'.[7] Paul points out that James 'strongly condemned the justification of tyrannicide' offered by his old tutor, George Buchanan (1506–82) in his work of political theory, *De Jure Regni apud Scotos* [*The Powers of the Crown in Scotland*] (1579), and his history of Scotland, *Rerum Scoticarum historia* [*History of Scotland*] (published in Latin in 1582). But James's rejection of killing a king in any circumstances posed a problem in relation to *Macbeth*, a play in which a tyrannical King of Scotland is killed by the Scotsman Macduff. Paul personalizes and reduces the scale of this problem by seeing it as a question of exculpating Macduff; because, in Paul's view, Shakespeare is writing the play to be performed before a king who condemned king-killing in any circumstances, 'Macduff must be kept free from the charge of regicide or from violation of his allegiance in his killing of Macbeth'. Paul's argues that Shakespeare achieves this by showing a Macduff who instantly condemns Duncan's murder as 'sacrilegious' and never swears an oath of allegiance to Macbeth; it is questionable whether this disposes of the problem, however. The value of this aspect of Paul's book lies not in his account of how the play supposedly reconciles itself with James's views on kingship and tyrannicide, but in his highlighting of the contest between the views of James and Buchanan and of the way *Macbeth* may relate to these. The contest between these two views is central to Alan Sinfield's account of the play in the essay which we shall consider in Chapter 5 of this Guide.

The other aspect of Paul's book which is particularly significant for future critical developments is his discussion of the possible relationship between *Macbeth* and the Gunpowder Plot – and especially the new notion of 'equivocation' which the Plot had highlighted. Paul was not the first to notice this link; for example, S. L. Bethell, as quoted by Kenneth Muir in his introduction to the Arden edition, says in *Shakespeare and the Popular Dramatic Tradition* (1944) that the 'whole atmosphere of treason and distrust which informs *Macbeth* found a parallel in the England of the Gunpowder Plot';[8] but by considering it within a book-length study of *Macbeth*, Paul does insert the issue definitively into the field of mid-twentieth-century discourse on the play, although it will be some time before its explosive potential is realized. When one of the alleged Gunpowder Plot conspirators, Father Henry Garnett, Superior of the Order of Jesus for England, was tried for treason, he defended the practice of equivocation – of making a statement on oath which appeared to have one clear meaning while making a private mental reservation which contradicted that apparent meaning. Thus, if one were asked upon oath whether a priest were in such a place and one knew that a priest was indeed in such a place, one could nonetheless reply 'No', without perjury and without troubling one's conscience, if one made the private mental reservation that the priest was not in that place in order that any person should have to reveal that he was there. Thus a statement might have two meanings, one of them entirely opposite to its apparent meaning. The most direct reference to this idea of equivocation – and, perhaps, to Father Garnett's arrival in Hell – seems to occur in *Macbeth* 2.3, where the Porter says, as he goes to answer the knocking: 'Faith, here's an equivocator that could swear in both the scales against either scale, who committed treason enough for God's sake, yet could not equivocate to heaven' (2.3.7–10). A further reference occurs in the Porter's sentence which starts sixteen lines later, where he says 'Therefore much drink may be said to be an equivocator with lechery: it makes him and it mars him; it sets him on and it takes him off; it persuades him and disheartens him, makes him stand to and not stand to; in conclusion, equivocates him into a sleep, and, giving him the lie, leaves him' (2.3.28–33). The term recurs later in the play, when Macbeth says that he is starting 'To doubt th' equivocation of the fiend, / That lies like truth' (5.5.40–2). But as well as the uses of the term 'equivocation', 'equivocator' and 'equivocate(s)' which Paul points out, it is also the case that the *idea* of equivocation – of 'palter[ing] in a double sense', as the witches do – runs throughout the play and can be related both to its major themes (for example, the 'reversal of values' identified by L. C. Knights, which we considered in Chapter 3) and to the destabilizing activity of its language (as discussed by Malcolm Evans in Chapter 5).

For over two decades, critics did not pursue the implications of Paul's suggestion that *Macbeth* was profoundly shaped by the political and ideological pressures and current events of its time, or of Tillyard's suggestion that *Macbeth*, even if it remained primarily a tragedy, could also be seen as a history play; metaphysical, philosophical and theological interpretations would remain dominant, and there would still be a strong focus on the imagery: but, as we shall see, the historical, political and ideological aspects of the play would start to receive more attention in the 1980s. Another aspect of *Macbeth* which would start to receive more attention in the 1980s was that of gender, particularly with regard to the play's representations of masculinity – a topic that was broached by Eugene M. Waith in 1950.

EUGENE M. WAITH

Eugene M. Waith's essay 'Manhood and Valor in Two Shakespearean Tragedies' (1950) considered the 'complex and confusing relationship of valor to manhood in *Macbeth* and *Antony and Cleopatra*'[9] (in this Guide we shall concern ourselves only with his comments on *Macbeth*). Waith points to a widespread cultural assumption, which goes back to the ancient world, that 'valor is an all-inclusive virtue', 'the very emblem of manhood', and that the man who most fully embodies this is the brave soldier: but he also highlights the ambivalence and confusion in the symbol of the soldier which arises because 'bravery in battle is often closely allied to the most unfeeling cruelty'. He cites a comment by Thomas Beard, in *The French Academy* (1602), who condemns the soldier who pursues war as 'pernicious', behaving in a way 'which savoureth more of brutishness than of humanity', but who also sees a long peace as making men, among other things, 'effeminate'.[10] Macbeth's mistake, Waith suggests, is to counter the threat of effeminacy by embracing brutishness.

There are two key antitheses in *Macbeth*: one is between manly valour and effeminacy and the other is between 'man and beast'. This latter antithesis emerges explicitly when Macbeth says 'I dare do all that may become a man / Who dares do more is none' and Lady Macbeth retorts: 'What beast was't then / That made you break this enterprise to me?' (1.7.46–8). Waith contends that 'Macbeth's mental torment grows out of the conflict between the narrow concept of man as the courageous male and the more inclusive concept of man as a being whose moral nature distinguishes him from the beasts',[11] and that these two concepts are active throughout the play. While Macbeth, partly as a result of his wife's urgings, tries to act in accordance with the narrow concept, he is also agonizingly aware of the larger concept – a concept which Waith sees as embodied in Macduff, especially in the lines where, hearing of the murder of his wife and children and urged by Malcolm to 'Dispute it like a man', he says: 'I shall do so; But I must also feel it as a man' (4.3.221–3). Waith sees Macduff as 'a complete man: he is a valiant soldier, ready to perform "manly deeds", but is neither ashamed of "humane" feeling nor unaware of his moral responsibilities'. Macbeth, by contrast, embracing the narrow concept of manhood urged on him by Lady Macbeth, becomes more and more narrowed in character, leading to a 'supreme irony': when Lady Macbeth dies, 'tortured by the conscience she despised, Macbeth is so perfectly hardened, so completely the soldier that she wanted him to be' that he is almost desensitized to fear and feeling, so that her death arouses hardly any emotion in him. Although Macbeth dies, in accordance with the narrow definition of manhood, 'like a man', it is Macduff who is more of a man, who shows valour in combat but 'fights only in a good cause, and in whose nature valor is not the sole virtue'.[12]

Waith's essay, which would become a classical point of reference, thus suggests the importance of concepts of manhood in the play and this issue would be further explored, particularly by feminist-psychoanalytic critics, in the later twentieth century. But the accounts of *Macbeth* offered by Tillyard, Paul and Waith would take time to bear fruit; the most influential and controversial interpretation of *Macbeth* in the immediate post-war era would come from the American 'New Critic' Cleanth Brooks and would concentrate on the imagery of the play and its philosophical significance.

CLEANTH BROOKS

Cleanth Brooks was one of the leading 'New Critics' in the United States in the mid-twentieth century. American New Criticism took as its model literary text the lyric poem whose major practitioner was the seventeenth-century 'Metaphysical' poet John Donne (about 1572–1631); such a poem employed paradox, irony, ambiguity and an elaborate, tightly condensed pattern of imagery to weave complex and conflicting attitudes into a tense, vibrant, concentrated unity. In his essay 'The Naked Babe and The Cloak of Manliness', first published in 1946 and collected in *The Well Wrought Urn* (1947), Brooks seeks to extend the reach of New Criticism to incorporate Shakespeare; he acknowledges that Shakespeare is a much greater poet than Donne, but claims that the characteristics of Donne's lyric poetry can also be found, on a larger scale, in Shakespearean drama – and his example is *Macbeth*.

Brooks explores the significance of two key symbols in *Macbeth*: the unclothed, exposed baby, and the clothed, concealed man. He admits that the symbols on which he focuses are not the only or most obvious ones – darkness and blood are more frequent – but he claimed that they encompass 'an astonishingly large area of the total situation'[13] in the play and that 'the naked babe' is 'perhaps the most powerful symbol in the tragedy'.[14] Brooks cites Caroline Spurgeon's analysis of the 'clothes' imagery in *Macbeth* which we considered in the previous chapter and adds one further example that, as he points out, she does not include: the daggers 'unmannerly breech'd with gore' (2.3.114) which, as we saw in Chapter 2, Dr Johnson, like other editors, wanted to emend; Brooks does not, however, mention Wilson Knight's discussion of the 'babe' imagery, although this ties in quite closely with his own.

In considering the 'babe' imagery, Brooks starts by pointing out the oddness of the comparison in the 'Pity, like a naked new-born babe' passage (1.6.21–5):

■ Is the babe natural or supernatural – an ordinary, helpless baby, who, as newborn, could not, of course, even toddle, much less stride the blast? Or is it some infant Hercules, quite capable of striding the blast, but, since it is powerful and not helpless, hardly the typical pitiable object?[15] □

The passage, Brooks suggests, goes on to offer two options: 'pity is like the babe or "heaven's cherubim" who quite appropriately, of course, do ride the blast'. As we see later in this chapter, Helen Gardner will take issue with Brooks's idea that riding the blast is appropriate for the cherubim, arguing that 'cherubim', if one sets it in the context of its meaning elsewhere in Shakespeare, has peaceful connotations that make it complement rather than contradict the image of the 'babe'. Brooks, however, sees the image as presenting a paradox: the powerful helplessness of pity.

Brooks points to other occurrences of the babe image, which sometimes appears as a metaphor, as in the 'Pity, like a naked new-born babe' passage; sometimes as a character, like Macduff's child (although as Oscar James Campbell suggests, Brooks stretches the idea of a babe to include Macduff's highly articulate little boy);[16] and sometimes as a symbol, like the crowned and bloody babes in the visions conjured up by the witches. For Brooks, the image of the babe symbolizes 'the future which Macbeth would control and cannot control' and also 'all those enlarging purposes which make life meaningful'[17] and 'all those emotional, and – to Lady Macbeth – irrational ties which make man more than a machine – which render him human'.[18] Brooks sees Lady Macbeth as sharing the characteristic which, according to Robert Penn Warren (1905–89), is common to all Shakespeare's villains: she is a rationalist. She seems to offer Macbeth a way to control the future if he can stop being a baby and clothe himself in the cloak of manliness. But her view of manhood is constricted and her rationality, in rejecting one aspect of what the babe symbolism represents – pity – also rejects another aspect of what it represents, the very future that she wants her husband and herself to grasp.; her proclaimed readiness to dash out her baby's brains if necessary is, ironically, to dash out the future of which the child is the symbol.[19]

As Macbeth is more aware of the force of pity than Lady Macbeth, so he is more aware of the unpredictability of the future. In his anxiety about the future, he is typical, a kind of Everyman figure; what makes him tragic is his desperate attempt to control the future despite that anxiety – an anxiety which Lady Macbeth's rationalism initially scorns.

■ it is not merely his great imagination and his warrior courage in defeat which redeem [Macbeth] for tragedy and place him beside the other great tragic protagonists; rather it is his attempt to conquer the future, an attempt involving him, like Oedipus, in a desperate struggle with fate itself. It is this which holds our imaginative sympathy, even after he has degenerated into a bloody tyrant and has become the slayer of Macduff's wife and children.[20] □

But if Macbeth's 'war on the future'[21] is his redeeming feature, it is also the source of his degeneration, driving him to 'make war on children'[22] to try to avert the fulfilment of the weird sisters' prophecy that the children of others will rule after him. Brooks does not mention Freud in this essay, but, like Freud in the analysis which we considered in Chapter 3, he sees in Macbeth a 'desire to found a dynasty' which is thwarted by his lack of children.[23] It should be noted here, however, that Brooks, in considering this aspect of Macbeth, seems to work with a questionable interpretation of the half-line 'we'd jump the life to come' (1.7.7), when he says that 'it is idle to speak of jumping the life to come if one yearns to found a line of kings'.[24] As Oscar James Campbell points out, Brooks appears to take 'jump' to mean 'leap over' or 'skip, and to take 'the life to come' to mean the future life in this world, whereas 'jump' probably means 'risk' and 'the life to come' probably means the future life after death, beyond this world. Thus Macbeth is saying that if it were possible that a decisive act, such as the murder of Duncan, could at once bring success and have no further harmful consequences, it would be worth risking damnation after death.

Discussing the pattern of clothes imagery that Spurgeon picks out, Brooks provides a different slant on her interpretation of the lines of Caithness and Angus as they march against Macbeth: 'He cannot buckle his distemper'd cause / Within the belt of rule' and 'now does he feel his title / Hang loose about him, like a giant's robe / Upon a dwarfish thief' (5.2.15–16, 20–2). As we saw in Chapter 3, these images evoke, for Spurgeon, an 'imaginative picture of a small, ignoble man encumbered and degraded by garments unsuited to him'.[25] Brooks argues, however, that the 'crucial point of the comparison ... lies not in the smallness of the man and the largeness of the robes, but rather in the fact that – whether the man be large or small – they are not *his* garments: in Macbeth's case they are actually stolen garments. Macbeth is uncomfortable in them because he is continually conscious of the fact that they do not belong to him'. This links up with 'the oldest symbol for the hypocrite' – 'the man who cloaks his true nature under a disguise'.[26]

Brooks argues that a 'series of masking or cloaking images' runs parallel to the pattern of clothes imagery traced by Spurgeon, and that both sets of imagery convey the idea that Macbeth is hiding a 'disgraceful' self.[27] This provides a context in which to interpret the imagery that so offended Dr Johnson, of Duncan's 'silver skin lac'd with his golden blood' and the image of the daggers used to kill him being 'Unmannerly breech'd with gore'. The 'golden blood', royal blood, clothes both the king and the blades of the daggers; the daggers 'are like men in "unmannerly" dress ... , naked except for their red breeches [trousers]'. Brooks concedes that this image of the daggers is 'fantastic' but claims that:

■ The metaphor fits the real situation on the deepest levels. As Macbeth and Lennox burst into the room, they find the daggers wearing, as Macbeth knows all too well, a horrible masquerade. They have been carefully 'clothed' to play a part. They are not honest daggers, honourably naked in readiness to guard the king, or, 'mannerly' clothed in their own sheaths. Yet the disguise which they wear will enable Macbeth to assume the robes of Duncan – robes to which he is no more entitled than are the daggers to the royal garments which they now wear, grotesquely.[28] □

Thus Brooks justifies the images which Dr Johnson and others found highly questionable by integrating them into the specific situation in which they occur, into the broader pattern of clothes imagery in *Macbeth*, and into some of the key themes of the play.

As well as the images of the babe and the clothes, Brooks also draws attention to 'other symbols of growth and development, notably that of the plant'.[29] He cites, for example, Banquo's words to the witches: 'If you can look into the seeds of time, / And say which grain will grow and which will not' (1.3.58–9). Like Wilson Knight and L. C. Knights, he quotes Duncan's welcome to Macbeth: 'I have begun to plant thee, and will labour / To make thee full of growing' (1.4.28–9).[30] He also instances Macbeth's reflection that the witches had hailed Banquo as 'father to a line of kings', whereas 'Upon my head they placed a fruitless crown, / And put a barren sceptre in my grip' (3.1.59–61). He points to Macbeth's image of himself 'as the winter-stricken tree':[31] 'I have liv'd long enough: my life / Is fall'n into the sear, the yellow leaf' (5.3.22). The plant imagery supplements the child imagery and sometimes merges with it, for instance when Macbeth says that he has given his soul to the devil 'To make them kings, the seed of Banquo kings' (3.1.69), and at least once the plant and clothing symbolism are fused, when the army advancing on Macbeth's castle 'clothes' itself in trees, thus turning Macbeth's own device of dissimulation against him: 'the garment which cloaks the avengers is the living green of nature itself, and nature seems, to the startled eyes of his sentinels, to be rising up against him'.[32] It is worth comparing this view of the moving wood with those of Wilson Knight and L. C. Knights which we considered in Chapter 3.

Brooks's remarkable essay provoked notable counter-attacks from Oscar James Campbell and Helen Gardner; we have already mentioned three of their objections, and we now look at their assaults on Brooks in more detail.

OSCAR JAMES CAMPBELL

In 'Shakespeare and the "New" Critics', Oscar James Campbell commended Brooks as 'a critic of unusual sensitivity and insight',[33] but charged him with distorting the meaning of specific passages in *Macbeth* by trying to force all the references to clothes, and all the references to babes, into chains of imagery that provided structural principles for the play. For example, he takes issue with Brooks's interpretation of Macbeth's description of the daggers used to kill Duncan as 'Unmannerly breech'd with gore'. As the previous section showed, Brooks tries to fit this into the image-pattern of unsuitable, stolen and concealing clothes by arguing that these improperly trousered daggers are not correctly clothed in their sheaths, or honourably naked as they might be if they were performing their proper function of protecting the king; they have been 'clothed' with blood in order to hide Macbeth's guilt so that he can win the throne and wear the king's robes – robes which, however, will not fit him properly, as the blood is not fit clothing for the daggers. Campbell, however, accounts for the image, not as one link in a chain of symbolism that runs throughout the play, but as contributing to the vivid representation of Macbeth's psychological condition at this intensely dramatic moment in the play – when he has been challenged by Macduff to explain why he killed the grooms:

■ Shakespeare has designed the series of extravagant images [from 'Here lay Duncan / His silver skin lac'd with his golden blood ... ' to 'Unmannerly breech'd with gore' (2.3.108–13)] as a means of revealing Macbeth's neurotic embarrassment, which is here on the verge of betraying his guilt to Macduff, Malcolm, and Donalbain. In other words, the figure [in the sense of metaphor] epitomizes the murderer's state of mind and nerves at one of the play's high emotional moments.[34] □

Campbell thus seeks to recall us from imagery and overall themes to the ways in which specific images, at particular moments in the play, provide a concentrated expression of character and action. It could be argued, however, that Campbell, despite his objection that Brooks distorts the meaning of specific passages, is *less* specific than Brooks in discussing the images in this passage; what seems to count for Campbell is the general quality of 'extravagance' which all those images share, a quality which could, in principle, be conveyed by other over-the-top images. Campbell does not offer any alternative explication of the *specific* meaning of the 'unmannerly breech'd with gore' line, but lumps it with the other images in the passage and accounts for all of them in terms of what they signify about Macbeth's psychological state at this moment.

Campbell also challenges Brooks's interpretation of the 'babes' imagery as symbolizing the future which Macbeth cannot control, finding that it 'reduces the rich complexity of Macbeth's human nature to a bare general proposition'. Macbeth's anxieties are, in any given instance, much more specific: for example, in the soliloquy which leads up to the 'naked new-born babe' image, the powerful metaphor of 'Bloody instructions' which 'return to plague the inventor' (1.7.9–10) shows that 'Macbeth, like all murderers in Elizabethan plays, is afraid, not of his inability to control the future, but of the knife in the hands of a human avenger'.[35] We observed in Chapter 2 how this point, suitably adapted, could also constitute an objection to Coleridge's view that Macbeth 'mistranslates' conscience and remorse into prudence and fear of external dangers. Campbell's perspective would not exclude conscience and remorse but would see them as specific manifestations, at particular moments of the play, of 'the rich complexity of Macbeth's human nature'. This sense of complexity and multiplicity also informs Campbell's affirmation that Macbeth's tragedy does not lie, as Brooks argues, in his failed attempt to control the future but 'in the multitudinous fears and superstitions that form the psychological punishment for his crime'.[36]

Campbell charges that Brooks's desire to wrest specific images from their contexts and forge them into a chain of imagery is also evident in his observation, which we considered in the previous section, that Lady Macbeth's vaunted willingness to dash out her baby's brains if necessary in order to attain the future is ironical because the babe symbolizes the future and thus, in rejecting the claims of the babe, she is also rejecting the future. In Campbell's view, this account weakens 'the stark simplicity of Lady Macbeth's utterance', which he sums up in this way: 'Rather than be such an irresolute coward as you now are, I had rather be guilty of the most fiendishly unnatural deed of which a mother is capable'.[37] As we shall see later in this chapter, L. C. Knights suggests the limitations of Campbell's paraphrase of this passage in the course of a more general defence of an approach to Shakespeare's plays which seeks out recurrent imagery. Campbell contends, however, that Shakespeare's plays do not work like metaphysical poems; while images do indeed recur in those plays, they are employed, not as parts of a chain of imagery, but 'for an immediate imaginative purpose relevant only to a specific situation'.[38]

Campbell's uneasiness about the New Critical approach was shared by Helen Gardner, who also launched an attack on Brooks's interpretation of *Macbeth* from a different angle.

HELEN GARDNER

In *The Business of Criticism* (1959), Helen Gardner focuses, in particular, on Cleanth Brooks's observations on the 'Pity, like a naked new-born babe' passage, accusing him of using Shakespeare's words as the basis for pursuing his own associations and bending the sense of the passage in order to demonstrate that it conforms to the favoured New Critical qualities of ambiguity, irony and paradox. She contends that the 'interpretation he gives is shallower and less in keeping with the play as a whole than the interpretation we can arrive at by using Shakespeare to comment on Shakespeare'.[39] First of all, Gardner attacks Brooks's remark that 'heaven's cherubim' do 'quite appropriately ... ride the blast'[40] and his implication that they are powerful and threatening. In accordance with her declared approach of 'using Shakespeare to comment on Shakespeare', she instances Othello's cry 'Patience, thou young and rose-lipped cherubin' (4.2.65) and Prospero's reference in *The Tempest* to 'O, a cherubin / Thou wast that did preserve me!' (1.2.152–3) as demonstrating that, elsewhere in Shakespeare's plays, the term 'cherubin' has positive associations of youth, beauty, innocence, and heavenly, smiling and serene patience. She acknowledges that these examples do not necessarily mean that the 'cherubim' in *Macbeth* may not carry a menacing and vengeful significance, but argues that the context of the 'Pity, like a naked new-born babe' passage demonstrates otherwise:

■ The final image of the wind dropping as the rain begins is the termination of the whole sequence of ideas and images. It is to this close that they hurry. The passage ends with tears stilling the blast. The final condemnation of the deed is not that it will meet with punishment, not even that the doer of it will stand condemned; but that even indignation at the murder will be swallowed up in universal pity for the victim. The whole world will know, and knowing it will not curse but weep. The babe, naked and new-born, the most helpless of all things, the cherubim, innocent and beautiful, call out the pity and the love by which Macbeth is judged. It is not terror of heaven's vengeance which makes him pause; but the terror of moral isolation. He ends by seeing himself alone, in a sudden silence, where nothing can be heard but weeping, as, when a storm has blown itself out, the wind drops and we hear the steady falling of the rain, which sounds as if it would go on for ever. The naked babe 'strides the blast' because pity is to Shakespeare the strongest and profoundest of human emotions, the distinctively human emotion. It rises above and masters indignation. The cherubim are borne with incredible swiftness about the world because the virtues of Duncan are of such heavenly beauty that they command universal love and reverence.[41] □

This is certainly an interesting interpretation, which traces a progress in the passage from storm to calm in which contradictions are resolved and the moral and spiritual affirmations of the play supposedly emerge; but it is open to question in several key respects. For example, is it the case, as Gardner contends, that the passage ends with 'tears stilling the blast' and the end of the storm? The storm may no longer be present to the senses of sight and hearing (if we assume that 'drown' implies 'drown the noise of'); but it could still be continuing. Moreover, the 'tears' are not necessarily as benign as Gardner implies; the physical experience to which the metaphor can be related – the wind blowing into the eyes and bringing tears to them – is a painful one, and could be seen as an image of the pain and anger (surely something more than 'indignation'?) that Duncan's death is likely to bring; these emotions might be exacerbated rather than dissolved by 'pity'. Gardner's assertion that 'the naked babe "strides the blast" because pity is to Shakespeare the strongest and profoundest of human emotions' is not only a dubious generalization which presumes to be able to infer the mind of Shakespeare from his plays, but it also avoids the strangeness of the image – for, as we saw Brooks pointing out, a newborn baby cannot walk, or even toddle: it would be perfectly possible to deploy a newborn baby in a cradle as a symbol of the power of pity without endowing it with such ambulatory precocity. It is also questionable whether Duncan's virtues command 'universal love and reverence'; his kingdom is experiencing rebellion and invasion when the play opens, and his continued rule relies partly on fear and violence – the fear and violence that Macbeth, while he is still loyal to Duncan, visits upon Duncan's enemies, and can expect to be visited on him if he takes over Duncan's throne (recall Campbell's 'knife in the hand of a human avenger'). Pity, in the world of *Macbeth*, does not quell violence, and may arouse and legitimate it.

Gardner goes on to charge that the 'reappearance of "the babe symbol" in the apparition scene and in Macduff's revelation of his birth has distracted the critic's attention from what deeply moves the imagination and the conscience in this vision of a whole world weeping at the inhumanity of helplessness betrayed and innocence and beauty destroyed'.[42] But the references to babies – and, more widely, to children – do, after all, occur in *Macbeth* and it could be suggested that here, Brooks – like Wilson Knight before him – is only doing what Gardner herself recommends: using Shakespeare to comment upon Shakespeare. If it is possible, as Gardner does, to draw examples of the positive associations of 'cherubim' from other plays to challenge the view that the 'cherubim' in *Macbeth* are menacing, why is it not legitimate to use examples of the references to babies and children in other parts of *Macbeth* to interpret the 'naked new-born babe' passage? And those examples could well be seen to reinforce the powerful, avenging, threatening aspects of the 'naked new-born babe', since, especially in the shadow of the witches' prophecy, the babes, or children, of Banquo and his descendants are a powerful threat – as Macbeth himself is well aware – to Macbeth's peace of mind and do constitute a kind of revenge for the murders of Duncan and Banquo. The babe strides the blast not only because pity is powerful but because the babe – incapable of walking at present, as Brooks points out – will, if it survives, learn to walk, and will become a man capable of threatening Macbeth. Might one indeed see the babe, with its preternatural qualities, as a symbol of the man not of woman born – born, rather, in the 'naked new-born babe' passage, of Macbeth's vivid but also worldly imagination – who is already stalking the earth in the shape of Macduff?

While both Campbell and Gardner present salutary challenges to Brooks – and, more generally, to an image-based interpretation of Shakespeare – their alternative readings of specific passages are themselves open to question and can seem to perpetrate the error of which they both, in their respective ways, accuse Brooks: distorting particular aspects of the play in order to make it accord with a general perspective. Partly in response to Campbell, L. C. Knights would offer, in 1959, a defence of image-based interpretation and a reading of *Macbeth* which complements and richly develops the one he had produced in 1933.

L. C. KNIGHTS AGAIN

In the opening chapter of *Some Shakespearean Themes* (1959), L. C. Knights points to the major reorientation in early twentieth-century Shakespeare studies which we traced in Chapter 3 of this Guide. The most important aspect of this reorientation was the change from a primary concern with 'character' and 'plot' in Shakespearean drama to a view of his plays as poetic wholes in which patterns of imagery played a vital structural and thematic role; a change to which, as we have seen, Knights himself made a vital contribution in 1933 with his essay, 'How Many Children Had Lady Macbeth?' Now Knights is concerned to consolidate rather than create change and to defend the importance of grasping patterns of imagery against Oscar Campbell's view, which we have just considered, that Shakespeare's images are relevant only to specific dramatic situations and particular characters; Wilson Knight affirms that, in Shakespeare's greatest dramas, the recurrent images *'reverberate'* and 'exercise [a] mutually attractive power', that 'there is a process of what I. A. Richards calls interanimation between the image on which we are focusing and some scores of others throughout the play'.[43] Taking one of Campbell's own examples, the 'I have given suck ... Have done to this' (1.7.54–9) passage from *Macbeth*, Knights acknowledges that Campbell's paraphrase – 'Rather than be such a coward, I had rather be guilty of the most fiendishly unnatural deed of which a mother is capable' – is valid as far as it goes, but questions its adequacy; it does not register the unnatural violence of the image or the way in which it reverberates, not only with other violent images and actions in *Macbeth* – for example, 'to bathe in reeking wounds' (1.2.39), 'Even till destruction sicken' (4.1.76) – but also 'with the insistence on "unnatural deeds" so pervasive throughout the play'. Moreover, the violence in the passage is aimed not only at others but at Lady Macbeth herself, at her own 'nature', and this relates to the 'unnatural tension of the will' which is a key element of the play.

Knights concedes that Shakespeare's images can sometimes be mere embellishments; he gives an example from *The Life and Death of King John* (Probably 1595 or 1596) and contrasts it with three key lines from *Macbeth*:

■ But even this night, whose black contagious breath
Already smokes about the burning cresset
Of the old, feeble, and day-wearied sun. □   (*King John*, 5.4.33–5)

■   Light thickens, and the crow
Makes wing to th'rooky wood.
Good things of Day begin to droop and drowse ... □   (3.2.51–3)

Knights affirms that the lines from *Macbeth*, even taken in isolation, are more compressed, striking and surprising than those from *King John* – 'there is more *going on*'.[44] But their significance is enhanced when they are seen in relation to the other 'images of darkness and of torpor' in the play. This enhancement of significance in *Macbeth* is not the result of a mere accumulation of images; it is due to the intense poetic quality of each image and the way in which the imagery is an essential element of the total poetic vision of the play. 'You cannot discuss imagery apart from the living tissue of which it forms a part'.[45] The 'living tissue' of *Macbeth* is much richer and more vital than that of *King John*: the verse of the later play is 'more fluid, more vivid and compressed' and it activates the reader or spectator's mind in different ways:

■ The compression, the thick clusters of imagery (with rapidly changing metaphors completely superseding the similes and drawn-out figures to be found in the earlier plays), the surprising juxtapositions, the overriding of grammar, and the shifts and overlapping of meaning – all these, demanding an unusual liveliness of attention, force the reader to respond with the whole of his active imagination.[46] □

It is only when the reader responds in this way that 'meanings from below the level of "plot" and "character" take form as a living structure':

■ If that structure of meaning seems especially closely connected with recurring and inter-related imagery, that is not because possible associations and recurrences are puzzled out by the intellect, but because the mind at a certain pitch of activity and responsiveness combines the power of focusing lucidly on what is before it with an awareness of before and after, sensing the whole in the part, and with a triumphant energy relating part to part in a living whole. But it is only in relation to that larger all-embracing meaning – determined by the 'plain sense' of what is said, and by its overtones, by the dramatic situation and the progress of the action, by symbols and by the interplay of different attitudes embodied in the different persons of the drama – it is only in relation to this total meaning that the imagery, or any other component that may be momentarily isolated, takes on its full significance. We only hear Shakespeare's deeper meanings when we listen with the whole of ourselves.[47] □

What deeper meanings emerge from *Macbeth* in Knights's 1959 interpretation, and how does it relate to his 1933 reading? Echoing and elaborating his earlier claim that '*Macbeth* is a statement of evil',[48] he starts by asserting: '*Macbeth* defines a particular kind of evil – the evil that results from a lust for power'.[49] The themes of the play which Knights identifies in 1959 are identical or similar to those which he found in 1933: the reversal of values, unnatural evil, deceitful appearances. But he relates his later interpretation of *Macbeth* to a more developed account of Shakespeare's idea of nature, based especially on his reading of *King Lear*, to a notion of 'automatism', and to Shakespeare's preoccupation with finding positive values that could withstand the power of time.

According to Knights, Shakespeare sees non-human nature as something very different from human nature, and does not regard it as, in itself, moral or benign; but there are correspondences between non-human nature and the creative and destructive aspects of the human mind. These aspects of the human mind, if they are not to cause chaos, must be assimilated and transmuted by our distinctively human nature; and the human being who acknowledges that distinctively human nature can recognize the difference between humanity and the natural world but can also be open to that world and see it as symbolic of that which is distinctively human, despite the difference between the two modes of nature. Knights claims that this rather complex notion 'lies behind and validates the elaborate and imaginatively powerful analogy between the human order and the order of nature in *Macbeth*'.[50]

In Knights's interpretation, it is human nature which defines and judges the 'evil' in *Macbeth*. One indispensable element of that human nature is its ability and need to form relationships; it is this need which produces the human order and which makes killing wrong: 'if you accept your humanity then you can't murder with impunity'.[51] In killing Duncan, Macbeth also violates his own human nature and thwarts his need to form relationships, breaking the 'great bond' that unites him with his fellow human beings; this is why the killing is 'unnatural'. The play counters this unnatural evil by evoking situations in which human nature and human order are uppermost and in which the creative and orderly aspects of non-human nature can therefore be perceived, appreciated, and used to symbolize human nature and order;

one notable example, already discussed by Knights in his 1933 essay and also, as Knights acknowledges, employed by Wilson Knight in his *Wheel of Fire* interpretation, is the exchange between Duncan and Banquo which marks Duncan's arrival at Macbeth's castle, with its references to the nimble, sweet, wooing, 'delicate' air and to the nest-building and breeding bird, the 'temple-haunting martlet' (1.6.1–10). This passage evokes 'a natural and wholesome *order*' which has its human equivalent 'in those mutualities of loyalty, trust and liking that Macbeth proposes to violate'.[52]

As well as setting *Macbeth* within this more complex idea of nature, Knights's 1959 interpretation also introduces another, related notion: that of the 'automatism of evil', to which the play opposes 'the creative energy of good', which employs and controls the powers of nature. It is the idea of 'automatism' which provides Knights with a way of approaching the issue of the relationship between free will and compulsion in *Macbeth*. In Knights's perspective, the play suggests that human beings inhabit the worlds of both human nature and non-human nature, and are free to choose between them; but only human nature has an ethical and intellectual dimension; non-human nature has no inherent morality or reflective capacity. To reject the ethical promptings of human nature is to grant undue power to the forces of non-human nature, to fail to inhabit the human world of creative activity, and to betray 'life' to 'automatism':

■ Automatism is perhaps most obvious in Lady Macbeth's sleep-walking, with its obsessed reliving of the past, but Macbeth also is shown as forfeiting his human freedom and spontaneity ... Most readers have felt that after the initial crime there is something compulsive in Macbeth's murders; and at the end, for all his 'valiant fury', he is certainly not a free agent. He is like a bear tied to a stake, he says [5.7.1–2]; but it is not only the besieging army that hems him in; he is imprisoned in the world he has made.[53] □

It is this self-made imprisonment, which stems from Macbeth's rejection of the ethical promptings of human nature and his 'betrayal of life to automatism',[54] that also helps to account for the loss of significance evoked in the 'Tomorrow and tomorrow and tomorrow' speech (5.5.19–28): 'time appears to him as meaningless repetition because he has turned his back on, has indeed attempted violence on, those values that alone give significance to duration, that in a certain sense make time'.[55] In 1933, as we saw in the previous chapter of this Guide, Knights acknowledged that the poetic quality of this speech might almost make us feel that it was presenting a valid view of human existence which could undermine the positive values of the play; by 1959, Knights sees the speech as reinforcing those positive values by saying, in effect: this is how life looks when you reject them.

Knights's 1959 interpretation is complex, rich and fascinating, but also prompts a range of questions. Like Wilson Knight, his assumption that the 'order' represented by Duncan, Macduff and Malcolm is in accordance with 'human nature' could be seen as an ideological one. His notion of 'automatism' is an interesting contribution to the debate about the relationship between freedom and determination in the play, but it leads to problems: for example, what exactly is this 'automatism'? Is it a psychological phenomenon, and, if so, why is it necessarily excluded from 'human nature'? If it is an aspect of non-human nature, why does it manifest itself in actions that, however brutal they may be, have a rational element – Banquo's son really could be a threat to Macbeth's life and power – or are expressive of the ethical dimension of human nature (as Lady Macbeth's handwashing is)? Then there is the question of the point at which Macbeth's actions are determined more by 'automatism' than by free choice; if, as Knights contends, 'there is something compulsive in Macbeth's murders' after the killing of Duncan, if by the end 'he is certainly not a free agent', how positive is the view of 'human nature' that this implies? Does it not grant a power to 'automatism' that undermines the positive affirmations Knights wants to find in the play? And is it not this quest for positive affirmations – this desire that *Macbeth*, despite its violence, despite its representation of 'automatism', despite the power of the 'Tomorrow and tomorrow and tomorrow' speech, should be ultimately affirmative – that drives Knights to neglect the possible ambiguities and negative aspects of the play? It is these ambiguities and negative aspects which, as we shall see, some later twentieth-century critics will confront more directly.

Published in 1959, Knights's book is important both for its intrinsic merits and as the apotheosis of a critical approach to *Macbeth* which emphasized its patterns of imagery and its exploration of an evil which was balanced and eventually defeated by good. This kind of approach would continue, but influential interpretations with a different emphasis emerged in the 1960s; these shifted the focus back to Macbeth's character, but spoke of it in existentialist or Nietzschean terms, and they found the forces of nihilism and evil in the play more powerful, and more complex, than Knights, or Wilson Knight, had allowed. The next two sections provide examples of such interpretations, the first by Jan Kott, the second by Wilbur Sanders.

JAN KOTT

Shakespeare Our Contemporary (1964) by the Polish poet and critic Jan Kott, made a great impact when it first appeared, especially on innovative theatre directors such as Peter Brook. It remains an exciting, provocative and suggestive book, even if the historical context which helped to give it such force has changed. As Kott's title suggests, his aim is to show the relevance of Shakespeare to a twentieth century that had seen two world wars and the concentration camps; if one response to these catastrophes was to affirm the continued power of human creativity, another was to emphasize the capacity for destruction which recent history seemed to demonstrate and the sense of absurdity which came with it – and it could be argued that Shakespeare's darkest plays, like *Macbeth* or *Lear*, anticipated this post-holocaust vision. In his intense account of *Macbeth*, Kott starts by pointing out the similarity of its plot to those of the History plays, particularly *Richard III*: here he revives a comparison which, as we have seen, goes back to the eighteenth century, and was also taken up by E. M. W. Tillyard in 1942. But for Kott, whereas the History plays show history as a mechanism, *Macbeth* shows history as a nightmare, as harrowing personal experience, as blood, as murder: 'There is only one theme in Macbeth: murder. History has been reduced to its simplest form, to one image and one division: those who kill and those who are killed ... In Macbeth's world – the most obsessive of all worlds created by Shakespeare – murder, thoughts of murder and fear of murder pervade everything'.[56]

In this perspective, Macbeth murders not only, or even primarily, out of ambition or a lust for power but to show that he is a man capable of murder, to free himself from the fear of murder, to try to put an end to murder, and to escape the nightmare that is history. There is no escape, however; his act only plunges him deeper into nightmare.

■ Macbeth has killed the King, because he could not accept a Macbeth who would be afraid to kill a king. But Macbeth, who has killed, cannot accept the Macbeth who has killed. Macbeth has killed in order to get rid of a nightmare. But it is the necessity of murder that makes the nightmare ... Macbeth has murdered for fear, and goes on murdering for fear.[57] □

Like the concentration camp Nazis, he undergoes what Kott calls 'the Auschwitz experience', passing a threshold beyond which any atrocity is possible. But this might make him merely brutal and callous; it is not the whole picture. It is not, finally, the nightmare of history from which Macbeth is trying to escape:

■ Macbeth, the multiple murderer, steeped in blood, could not accept the world in which murder existed. In this, perhaps, consists the gloomy greatness of this character, and the true tragedy of Macbeth's history. For a long time Macbeth did not want to escape the reality and irrevocability of nightmare, and could not reconcile himself to his part, as if it were somebody else's. Now he knows everything. He knows there is no escape from nightmare, which is the human fate and condition, or – in more modern language – the human situation. There is no other.[58] □

Kott's Macbeth has come to see the truth of the human situation. In this perspective, the 'Tomorrow and tomorrow and tomorrow' speech is not, as Bradley would have it, 'the despair of a man who had knowingly made war on his own soul',[59] or, as L. C. Knights proposes, the loss of meaning that results from rejecting and indeed assaulting 'those values that alone give significance to duration'.[60] It is a speech that tells it like it is.

Kott also considers Lady Macbeth and raises an issue that previous critics had not addressed explicitly: her sexual relationship with her husband:

■ In this particular union, in which there are no children, or they have died, Lady Macbeth plays a man's part. She demands murder from Macbeth as a confirmation of his manhood, almost as an act of love ... . The two are sexually obsessed with each other, and yet have suffered a great erotic defeat.[61] □

This implication of sexual failure – impotence on Macbeth's part, perhaps, for which his excessive penetrative violence in battle ('unseamed him from the nave to th' chops', 1.2.22) might be a desperate attempt at compensation – is fascinating, though it could easily lead into speculation unsubstantiated by evidence from the text of the play itself.

Kott offers a different, darker *Macbeth* to those of Wilson Knight and Knights; he stresses the nightmarish, bloody horror of the play, the power of its protagonist's nihilism, and the erotic enigma of its primary couple; the affirmations which Wilson Knight and Knights found there are absent. Wilbur Sanders, to whom we now turn, finds affirmations in *Macbeth* but of a complex and paradoxical kind which spring from an inextricable mixture of energy and evil.

WILBUR SANDERS

In 'The "Strong Pessimism" of *Macbeth*', first published in the *Critical Review* in 1966, and later incorporated, with alterations, into *The Dramatist and the Received Idea* (1968), Sanders challenges those interpretations of the play 'in which evil is somehow *subordinated* to the good and to the natural, and the military victory of Malcolm's forces is seen as the *elimination* of the Macbeth-evil'.[62] As we have seen, both Wilson Knight, who seems to have coined the phrase 'the Macbeth-evil', and L. C. Knights, who used a very similar phrase ('the *Macbeth* evil'), produced such interpretations. In Sanders's view, these readings simplify and reduce a play in which 'good is the after-image of an evil long and steadily contemplated'. *Macbeth* could better be seen, Sanders suggests, as an example of what the German philosopher Friedrich Nietzsche (1844–1900), in *The Birth of Tragedy* (1872), called 'strong pessimism': a pessimism which is not a sign of weakness and decadence, but a 'penchant of mind for what is hard, terrible, evil, dubious in existence, arising from a plethora of health, a plenitude of being'.[63]

While this idea may seem to belong to the 1960s appropriation of Nietzsche, and thus to be more 'modern' than the interpretations of Wilson Knight and L. C. Knights, Sanders is more 'traditional' in the sense that he focuses, not on patterns of imagery as Wilson Knight and Knights do, but on the characters of Macbeth and Lady Macbeth, as Bradley did – indeed, as we shall see, he quotes Bradley with approval. Sanders does, however, point to the way in which the ambivalence of these characters is the result of a key characteristic of Shakespeare's *language*: its capacity 'to *imply* judgement without being constricted by it';[64] he also relates their ambivalence to a larger ambiguity in relation to ideas of 'good' and 'evil'.

Sanders traces the development of Macbeth from the moment he decides to grasp his deed – the murder of Duncan – to the end of the play. He sees Macbeth's lines near the end of the murder scene as a turning point: 'To know my deed 'twere best not know myself' (2.2.71). Sanders takes these lines to mean that Macbeth must reject his former self – the loyal and honourable subject, with qualms about killing his king – and sees them as marking the start of 'the construction of a new "self" whose premise is murder'.[65]

What follows could be seen – and often has been seen – as a drama of deepening moral collapse, as Macbeth steps further and further into blood. Sanders acknowledges the murderous brutality of Macbeth as he pursues 'total insensibility', and tries to numb 'that inner sensitivity which is his greatest torment'[66] by 'a willing embracement of evil';[67] but that is not the whole picture:

■ the sequence in which the evil sensibility is most clearly envisaged and enunciated – Macbeth's late-night colloquy with his wife (3.4.121–43) – is also one of the points in the play where we are most conscious of Macbeth's barbarian energy and courage. 'What a frightful clearness of self-consciousness in this descent to hell,' writes Bradley, 'and yet what a furious force in the instinct of life and self-assertion that drives him on!'[68] Improbable though it may seem, that word *life* is the right word. No interpretation which fails to reckon with the essential ambivalence of our reaction to the 'criminal' Macbeth can hope to do justice to the depth and subtlety of Shakespeare's conception.[69] □

This essential ambivalence is generated by Shakespeare's verse itself. As an example, Sanders considers the following lines:

■ I am in blood
　Stepp'd in so far, that, should I wade no more,
　Returning were as tedious as go o'er. □　　　　(3.4.136–7)

Sanders suggests that both the imagery and the movement of the verse contribute to the complex realization of Macbeth's position. The image is that of wading into a stream, where it is necessary either to go back to the bank one has left or forward to the opposite bank – or be swept away by the current; and the matter is more complicated because this stream has the thickness, the resistance, of blood and its guilty and murderous symbolism. The line-break after 'more' momentarily suspends a conditional clause which might also be a question – 'Should I wade no more' could be 'Should I wade no more?' – and the next line presents two alternatives, 'returning' or 'continuing', which seem evenly balanced and between which Macbeth could in principle, choose; but the fact that 'go o'er' falls at the end of the line and takes the final emphasis weighs the balance towards going on. As Sanders puts it: 'choice presents itself in such a form that there seems no choice – and yet the choice is real and damnable'. Sanders rejects what he sees as the attempt to resolve 'the complex reality of this verse' by 'the ready-to-hand explanation that Macbeth's freedom has been impaired by his violation of the "natural law" engraved in his own nature' (here he offers a reductive formulation of Knights's argument in *Some Shakespearean Themes*, considered earlier in this chapter). The lines do show this, but it is not all that they show; they work in a way which is typical of the most powerful passages in *Macbeth*, in that they assimilate our tendency to judge Macbeth into 'a larger act of imaginative recognition, which says, "Yes, it is so. That is the way of Mind. This man comes of our stock" '. Macbeth embodies the unresolvable 'mystery of will' which lies 'at the heart of experience': the will can initiate action but is also constrained in complicated and finally unknowable ways.

The capacity of Shakespeare's verse to suggest but suspend judgement makes it possible to show Macbeth as both damned and as possessing 'a positive energy of life'. His pursuit of 'sensibility' can also be seen as 'a quest for perfection', an attempt to integrate 'the divisive forces his own act has released'[70] and to 'recover that integrity of impulse and action, that unobstructed discharge of personal energy in which life delights'[71] (this echoes the line from *America, A Prophecy* (1793, Plate 8, line 13), by the Romantic poet William Blake (1757–1827), to which, interestingly, L. C. Knights also alludes in *Some Shakespearean Themes*:[72] 'For everything that lives is holy, life delights in life'). Even when Macbeth becomes a hardened killer, this energy remains and exemplifies an essential and vital element of human existence. Sanders does not deny the Christian aspect of Shakespeare, but highlights another aspect that is akin to Nietszche or D. H. Lawrence:

> ■ It is as if the Shakespeare who knew that the meek must, and do, inherit the earth, also saw from a different point of view (Nietzschean, Lawrencian) what a disaster it would be for the earth if they did, and preserved at the very core of his conception of evil an awareness of dynamism and power.[73] □

It is this sense of 'dynamism and power' that is crucial to understanding the effect, not only of Macbeth, but also of Lady Macbeth, who has 'a kind of validity and potency, even at those points where she most directly affronts all conventional notions of the feminine or even the human'.[74]

Validity and potency are also evident, for Sanders, in the 'Tomorrow and tomorrow and tomorrow' speech. We have seen that both Bradley and L. C. Knights, for all their differences, acknowledged the power of this speech but were concerned to deny it any status as a valid view of human existence. Sanders argues, however, that it could be seen as a strenuous and rigorous imaginative vision – an example, we might say, of 'strong pessimism' – and aims 'to avoid separating the act of judgement which *sees through* Macbeth, from the act of imagination which sees the world *with* him'. In Sanders's perspective, Macbeth's vision is not 'placed' by the positive movement of the last act as firmly as L. C. Knights would like, and he questions Knights's view – and that of many other critics – that the play ends affirmatively. 'Viewed from a certain angle, the victory of Malcolm and Macduff is a triumph, and a necessary one. But at close range, the killing has the disturbing ambivalence of all acts of violence'.[75] Malcolm's final speech, with its references to 'plant[ing] newly', 'loves', 'kinsmen', 'friends' and 'the grace of grace' (5.11.26–41) is a 'muted counterpoint' to the violence[76] and cannot annul 'an awed sense of the overwhelming potency and vitality of evil'.[77]

Like Kott, Sanders mounts an important challenge to those views of Macbeth – stretching from Wilson Knight in 1930 to L. C. Knights in 1959, and beyond – which see it as a play in which evil and good are sharply opposed and in which good finally and unequivocally prevails. Sanders highlights the issue of the possible ambivalence of the ethical and philosophical dimensions of *Macbeth* and argues that ambivalence is generated, above all, by a characteristic aspect of Shakespeare's language – its capacity to imply judgement but also to subsume it within a larger perspective. In their respective ways, both Kott and Sanders complicate the straightforward moral pattern of the play. As the next chapters of this Guide will show, critics in the later twentieth century would multiply these complications, producing interpretations of *Macbeth* which would make the 'indivisible unity' that L. C. Knights had praised in 1933 seem ambivalent, contradictory, fractured, fissured and incorrigibly plural.[78]

CHAPTER FIVE

The Later Twentieth Century: Politics, Violence and Ideology

In the later twentieth century, large changes came over literary criticism. The sense that the interpretative approaches which had emerged in the 1930s had outlived their usefulness and were producing largely repetitive readings, the development and dissemination of literary and cultural theory, and the entry of a new generation into university teaching, all combined to bring about a revolution in the ways critics understood literary texts. From the 1980s, critics would draw on a rich variety of perspectives – structuralist, historical, anthropological, political, post-structuralist, psychoanalytical, feminist and new historicist – as they scrutinized *Macbeth* for its contradictions and ambivalences, for the points at which its apparently secure value structure broke down. A pioneering example of such scrutiny was provided by Harry Berger Jr. at the start of the 1980s.

HARRY BERGER JR.

In 'The Early Scenes of *Macbeth*: Preface to a New Interpretation' (1980), Harry Berger begins by summarizing the view of the play which had become dominant in the mid-twentieth century: that it shows the disruption of order by evil and the eventual restoration of harmony. Berger contends that this view is not only the province of literary critics; it is shared by all the 'good' characters in the play and 'they justify themselves and their society by appealing to it'. The play also, however, 'subtly but persistently criticizes' this view. For Berger, *Macbeth* is centrally concerned with 'dramatizing failures or evasions of responsibility correlated with problematic structural tendencies that *seem* benign because it is in the interest of self-deceiving characters to view them that way'.[1]

Evidence of these problematic tendencies surfaces early, in 1.2, which shows the instability of the Scottish state, threatened by rebellion from within and invasion from without. Macbeth's killing of Macdonald anticipates Macduff's killing of Macbeth and raises the possibility that

Macduff, in his turn, may kill Malcolm – since he has after all, in killing Macbeth, killed a duly appointed king, become a regicide, and he has also led an English army to invade Scotland, as Cawdor helped Norway's invasion. From the start, Berger suggests, there is something rotten in Scotland which '*precedes*, rather than *follows from*, the horrors perpetrated by the Macbeths';[2] 'something intrinsic to the structure of Scottish society, something deeper than the melodramatic wickedness of one or two individuals, generates these tendencies towards instability, conflict, sedition, and murder'.[3]

In seeking to identify this 'something', Berger offers an especially close and interesting analysis of the sergeant's account of the combat between the loyalists, invaders and rebels and of Macbeth's slaughter of Macdonald. Acknowledging a debt to the discussion of this passage in Lawrence Michel's *The Thing Contained* (1970), Berger starts by considering the simile of the 'two spent swimmers', who represent the two parties to the conflict, and highlights its ambiguity: 'are these two fighters (or armies) trying to destroy each other or two swimmers trying to save each other? ... The simile projects a situation in which enemies cling together as friends, and friends as enemies'. The language in which Macbeth's assault on Macdonald is described switches the relationships between persons and personifications back and forth: ' "like Valor's minion" echoes "like a rebel's whore" but Fortune is the whore and Macbeth is the minion'. 'Minion' can mean 'favourite' or 'darling' but its further meaning of 'servant' associates it with 'slave' in the following line. Berger sees these complex relationships between persons and personifications as raising the questions of what it means to be Valor's servant or favourite, of whether Valor is a male or female personification, of what actual master or mistress the personification might conceal, and of whether serving Valor, rather than serving Fortune, is 'a way of legitimizing impulses which might otherwise discharge themselves in questionable or unlawful causes'.[4] Berger also presses the issue of whether the sergeant's evocation of Macdonald's weakness makes Macbeth's violence – even though the sergeant himself appears to approve of it – seem excessive, a kind of 'overkill'.

The sergeant goes on to warn that the battle remained uncertain; Berger takes issue with Roy Walker's interpretation of this warning, in *The Time is Free* (1949), as indicating simply the untrustworthiness of Macbeth:[5] rather, Berger suggests, it indicates, more generally, the danger of the very warrior spirit that Duncan's state requires for its survival. 'The danger to a king is a structural component of his social order, inextricable from the positive energy that sustains the order'.[6] The sergeant's final speech about the way in which Macbeth and Banquo fought off the fresh assault reinforces this danger, suggesting a violence that is almost out of control and that might not be fully discharged in defeating the enemy.

Ross's combat report, which follows soon after, raises further questions and contains more ambiguities. Berger calls the image of Macbeth as 'Bellona's bridegroom, lapp'd in proof' (1.2.54), 'a nightmare amplification of "Valor's minion" ' and finds it paradoxical because Bellona, 'the archaic goddess of war', was 'a fierce unyielding virgin' who would have been nobody's bridegroom and because 'lapp'd' suggests being wrapped or swaddled, perhaps like a baby, in fabric or waves. Violence, giganticism, eroticism and infantilism all play through the image. As the passage goes on, the difference between the two Cawdors breaks down; again, this could be seen, as Roy Walker suggests, as an example of dramatic irony which foreshadows the way in which Macbeth, once he is Thane of Cawdor, will betray the king, as the previous Thane of Cawdor did;[7] but there is also what Berger calls 'a structural irony': 'What Cawdor has lost and "noble Macbeth hath won" is a set of possibilities – for treachery as well as valour – built into the very role of thane, or into the promotion from a less to a more eminent thaneship that brings one politically closer to the king'.[8] Scotland is not troubled merely by 'a future harm' but by 'a settled instability'.[9]

Berger also considers the representation of Duncan in the early scenes of the play, arguing that the play presents Duncan as a thing and symbol, but also as a man – and that his predicament lies in the disjunction between these two aspects. His extravagant expressions of gratitude to Macbeth and Banquo after their success in battle show his '[f]ear of lack of control' and of the danger that comes 'from the excessive and hyperbolic achievements of his heroic subjects: these are structurally [his] chief concerns within the Scottish social order'.[10] The elaborate courtesy of his words to Lady Macbeth when he arrives at Dunsinane Castle is strained 'because he feels himself to be in a contest, a race, with Macbeth'.[11] Duncan's predicament is that 'the more his subjects do for him, the more he must do for them; the more he does for them, feeding their ambition and their power, the less secure can he be of his mastery ... the stronger he makes them, the weaker he makes himself'.[12]

Berger compares the Duncan scenes to the primitive forms of exchange which the anthropologist Marcel Mauss (1872–1950) analyses in *The Gift* (1925): 'To give is to show one's superiority ... To accept without returning or repaying more is to face subordination'.[13] It involves competition, and competition pervades 'all the expressions and relationships' in *Macbeth* – 'love, friendship, hospitality, homage, bounty, conversation, even the delivery of news and messages'. In this perspective, *Macbeth* does not portray a harmonious social order which is disrupted by Duncan's murder, but a highly competitive society in which the bestowal of favours and the expression of gratitude are aspects of the competition. On both a literal and a symbolic level, 'the natural basis of this warrior society is blood'. Blood provides 'the organizing principle of social relations, the foundation of kinship and lineage, place and name', but it is also 'the principle of individual self-assertion; the source of vital function, of courage, passion, and excitement and ... of aggression'. Duncan's gentleness makes him ill-adapted to this world and gives him, for Berger, a 'vaguely androgynous ... personality ... which reinforces the structural androgyny of his kingly function';[14] he has to be both father and mother, supplier of both blood and milk, but it is the milky quality which is most evident in him and which makes him vulnerable to those upon whom he relies for protection. They include the supposedly loyal subject Banquo, whose 'temple-haunting martlet' speech when Duncan arrives at Macbeth's castle can be seen as softening Duncan up still further, allaying a suspicion of Macbeth which Banquo himself feels. The speech contrasts hard and gentle terms, war and procreation, the weighty terms of defensive architecture and the lighter images of summer and nature, haunting and breeding. The name of the God of war, 'Mars', is audible in the term 'martlet' but reduces him to a small bird, and this is characteristic of the way Banquo's speech tries, without complete success, to soften the threatening aspects of the words and images he employs. ' "Breed" gives way to "haunt"; "the air is delicate" trembles between its summery and precarious senses" '. Berger suggests that this passage provides, among other things, 'a diffuse displacement of Banquo's situation with relation to Macbeth and Duncan': Banquo is 'the war-bird who makes his home as a kind of parasite in Macbeth's castle and Duncan's kingship', who 'has a bed hanging from either or both where he hides and watches from his secure coign of vantage', who 'will soon rise to haunt Macbeth' and whose 'procreant cradle' will be the source of the future kings of Scotland. He is 'in a special position which acutely focuses the general psycho-structural dilemma of Scotland'.[15]

Berger's analysis complicates any account of the play as a battle between good and evil, order and disorder, since it suggests that the instability of the Scottish state cannot be focused in Macbeth – or for that matter in Duncan, the 'good scapegoat' to Macbeth's 'evil scapegoat' – but is inherent in that state's unstable structure. And this instability is evident in the *language* of the play. In this close attention to language and its capacity to trouble binary oppositions, Berger anticipates deconstructionist and post-structuralist approaches, while his point about Duncan's personal and structural androgyny opens up a field which feminist critics, especially Janet Adelman, will explore further. In the meantime, further complications would be introduced into the interpretation of *Macbeth* by considering the play in historical terms, as the historian Michael Hawkins does in a key essay published in 1982.

MICHAEL HAWKINS

In 'History, politics and *Macbeth*', Michael Hawkins first of all sounds a sceptical note in relation to the idea that *Macbeth* is about 'evil'. Critics who hold this view, Hawkins charges, tend to take an abstraction and endow it with concrete properties, so that it becomes a force in its own right (this is epitomized by the references which we have seen to 'the Macbeth-evil' in Wilson Knight and 'the *Macbeth* evil' in Knights). Considered historically, the application of the term 'evil' can change: the murder of a political leader, for example, has not always, historically or in the later twentieth century, necessarily been regarded as wholly evil. Hawkins also questions an approach which tries to set Shakespeare in his historical context by arguing that his plays illustrate the commonplaces of contemporary political, philosophical and religious discourse: the dangers of ambition, the morally debilitating wages of sin, the importance of order, the cyclical nature of history or the operation of divine providence; Hawkins asserts that, if this is all that Shakespeare's drama is saying, it does not amount to very much.

Hawkins's own approach to historical contextualization seeks to relate *Macbeth* to the political questions that concerned Shakespeare's contemporaries. Perhaps the first of these was whether to engage in political life at all, and here *Macbeth* portrays a world of political activism: 'All the major characters are participants, fully committed to the [active life]',[16] and their actions have widespread consequences, for good and bad – Macbeth's tyranny brings loss and suffering to Scotland, his overthrow frees the time. Tranquility comes not from withdrawal from political life, but from its proper conduct: the insomnia of the Macbeths after they gain power by Duncan's murder contrasts with the peace that supposedly prevailed at Duncan's court and that, in the play, still prevails, to a greater degree, at the court of Edward the Confessor in England.

Hawkins suggests that the Elizabethans and Jacobeans were aware of four forms of political organization. The earliest was pre-feudal: a politics informed by blood and kinship relations. The next was feudal, where personal obligation was still fundamental but extended beyond family relationships. The third, and the most important one in Shakespeare's era, was monarchy, and the fourth, which was developing in that era, was institutional: the monarchy itself became an institution and there was an expansion of bureaucratic modes of running the state – collecting taxes, administering justice, maintaining order. Of these four forms, the institutional one is almost absent from *Macbeth* – the selection of Macbeth as king occurs offstage, and while Malcolm at the end of the play mentions 'the cruel ministers / Of this dead butcher' (5.9.34–5), 'ministers' here has the meaning of 'agents' – that is, those who act on Macbeth's behalf, rather than its modern sense of 'head of a government department' (COD). We never see Macbeth working at the business of government with his thanes; he looks very isolated, and this relates to the play's emphasis on personal links as a way of judging and resolving political questions. The pre-feudal, feudal and monarchical forms of political organization are all apparent in the play, however, and are summed up in Macbeth's triple relationship with Duncan as he himself expresses it in 1.7.13–14 – he is Duncan's kinsman (pre-feudal), host (feudal) and subject (monarchical).

In *Macbeth*, these forms mix together in complex ways. By murdering Duncan, Macbeth murders a blood relative – his cousin – and his killing of Macduff's wife and family would justify a vendetta, which Hawkins calls 'the classic solution of a blood feud'.[17] But *Macbeth* does not suggest that private revenge is an adequate motive in itself: it is assimilated into the broader aim of killing a usurping tyrant. It is through fulfilling this broader aim that Macduff takes his revenge for the killing of his wife and family and that Malcolm avenges the killing of his father. In exploring the interaction of family relationships and politics, the play vividly portrays the political dangers of wifely domination and childlessness. Macbeth is dominated by his wife, even if her ambitions are for him rather than solely for herself, and his lack of children means that he cannot hope to pass on the throne to his descendants – a matter of crucial importance in 'an age in which all kinds of authority and possessions, including kingship, property, public office and honours, could be inherited and in which efforts were made to strengthen the principle despite the bureaucratisation of public life'.[18] Macbeth's lack of children also resolves one further issue at the end of the play, as he has no son to try to take revenge on his behalf and perpetuate a blood feud.

The feudal dimension of *Macbeth* is evident, Hawkins argues, in its dramatization of a key dilemma for feudal society. Such a society required a military elite, drawn from the nobility – the thanes, in this play – who could wage war vigorously against the enemies of that society; but their military capacity also made them a potential threat, especially when the ostensible aim of their fighting – peace – was achieved. This dilemma is embodied in Macbeth, whose capacity for atrocious violence against the king's enemies ('unseamed him from the nave to th' chops' (1.2.22)) is turned against the king himself. Hawkins argues that Macbeth never becomes a wholesale coward or butcher; he provides 'not a caricature of manhood [but] one dangerous manifestation of it' and also demonstrates that 'manliness may be inseparable from fear'.[19] The problem of martial energy turning against the social order which employs it was not, however, confined to the feudal world, but was evident in Shakespeare's own: 'Macbeth, in one sense, presents the problem of the newly unemployed soldier which the *Calendar of State Papers Domestic* shows was so familiar to the Elizabethans'.[20]

Feudal society tried to contain the threat from the military elite by seeking 'to bind [its] members ... to agreed standards of behaviour'[21] through a range of ritual practices – statements of unity, oaths, initiation rites, ceremonial feasting. Hawkins remarks that 'such ceremonies would not have been stressed had these standards been naturally accepted',[22] an interesting point to consider in relation to those interpretations, most notably by Wilson Knight and Knights, which argue that the play shows a violation of a natural order that is exemplified by Macbeth's relationship of 'trust' to Duncan and by ceremonies like feasting; in Hawkins's perspective, such an order is not 'natural' but a particular and unstable form of political organization.

Hawkins sees Macbeth's banquet as 'the most significant affirmation of feudal unity in the play' and stresses that it is not only 'a symbol of fellowship' but a display of superiority and power – ultimately, the power to control food supplies. To refuse hospitality was to insult and call into question the superiority of the host; Banquo's particular way of refusing hospitality – by appearing, but as a ghost – throws Macbeth into a distress which reveals, not so much his guilt, but his failing power.

The monarchical aspect of *Macbeth* is concerned with three issues, what makes a good king, how is the royal succession to be decided and when is rebellion justified? In regard to the first issue, we can take up a question which we raised in the previous chapter: if, as Tillyard claims, Malcolm is Shakespeare's ideal king, how are we to judge Duncan? Hawkins suggests that Duncan, while portrayed as saintly, is also subtly shown to lack in some of the qualities which, in Elizabethan terms, would have been seen as required for successful kingship. Here the historical perspective links up with Wilbur Sanders's Nietzschean approach; Hawkins in fact quotes Sanders's remark that 'the Shakespeare who knew that the meek must, and do, inherit the earth, also saw from a different point of view ... what a disaster it would be for the earth if they did'.[23] At the start of the play, Duncan's kingdom is hardly a peaceable one; it is under internal and external threat from rebels and invaders, who presumably think they have a fighting chance of defeating him – and who might, indeed, have defeated him, had it not been for the military prowess – and the capacity for extreme and lethal violence – of Macbeth. As Malcolm Evans points out, Duncan is the only king in Shakespearean drama, apart from Henry VI, who does not lead his men into battle[24] – he needs Macbeth, Macduff and others to do his fighting and killing for him (in this respect, of course, he is much more like twentieth- and twenty-first-century heads of state). His saintliness is accompanied by a dangerous naivety; he places 'absolute trust' in those thanes who are his chief enemies – first Macdonald, Thane of Cawdor, and then the Thane who inherits Cawdor's title, Macbeth – and in this contrasts sharply with his Machiavellian son, Malcolm, the man who would be king, who carefully tests Macduff before deciding to trust him. The wisdom of Duncan's public nomination of his eldest son as his successor is open to doubt – even if Duncan trusted Macbeth, and even if Duncan's age made the issue of succession an urgent one, should he not have been aware that this could seem like a public and potentially provocative snub to the hero who had just visited violent death upon the king's enemies?

Duncan's nomination of his successor relates not only to his possible weakness as a ruler but also to the second issue regarding monarchy with which *Macbeth* deals – how is the royal succession to be decided? The play does not portray a political order in which primogeniture wholly prevails and in which the eldest son of the king is therefore *automatically* his father's successor; if Malcolm were, it would not have been necessary for Duncan to nominate him as such. Indeed, as Hawkins points out, some critics, most notably Elizabeth Nielsen, have argued that it would have been possible for Duncan to nominate Macbeth under 'the Scottish law of tanistry, under which the succession varied, at the choice of the baronage, between the main lines of the royal house, depending on suitability and political power'.[25] Hawkins rejects this argument, citing Roy Walker's point, in *The Time is Free*, that tanistry is not mentioned in *Macbeth*,[26] but he does emphasize the uncertainty in the play surrounding the *process* of succession, and its representation of two different ways in which succession may be legitimately decided. *Macbeth* starts by showing a situation in which the royal succession is legitimated by nomination and moves on to show one in which it is legitimated by hereditary right (Hawkins infers that the barons set aside Malcolm's nomination, mainly or wholly because they believe he has murdered Duncan, and choose Macbeth as King because they think he is the most suitable candidate; Malcolm then bases his own claim to the throne on hereditary right rather than nomination). *Macbeth* can be seen to show the vulnerability of nomination as a means of deciding succession and the possibility that an inadequate king may cause instability by the way in which he employs that means.

This brings us back again to the issue of how adequate a ruler Duncan is and links with the third issue relating to monarchy explored in *Macbeth*: when is the removal and murder of a king justified? Given the doctrine of divine right, it was clearly a sin to kill a king, but this might also mean that it was a sin to kill a king who, like Macbeth, had become king by killing the previous king. In other words, removing and killing a king was not necessarily justified because that king was an usurper; after all, Macbeth seems to have been chosen and crowned in the proper way and his rule seems to be generally accepted by his fellow-thanes, apart from Macduff; and it could be argued that the divine will was working itself out in his accession. In Shakespeare's sources, Macbeth was not removed and killed because he was an usurper, but because, after ruling effectively for ten years, he became a tyrant; in departing from its source to make Macbeth's tyranny follow immediately upon his usurpation, the play introduces an ambiguity into the justification of his fall: was it primarily because he was an usurper, or primarily because he was a tyrant? In Shakespeare's time, there was an argument that even the fact that the king was a tyrant did not necessarily justify removing and killing him, since his tyranny could be regarded as a test, sent by God, of the Christian humility of his subjects. Indeed, James I held this view. But in Shakespeare's play, it is Macbeth's tyranny that becomes the most prominent justification for removing him; even if one suspected, today, that Macduff's depiction of a sorrowing Scotland (4.3.4–8) might smack of the spin doctor, the play provides no evidence that Macbeth is a benign ruler or that his reign has been in any way beneficial (by contrast, as Hawkins points out, Claudius in *Hamlet*, although an usurper, can be seen as quite a competent king). In this respect, *Macbeth* returns again to the question of what makes a good ruler. It is not only a question of acquiring power but also of maintaining it; and maintaining it will be easier if it has been gained in a legitimate way – this is a point Machiavelli makes. Even so, a capable ruler might be able to maintain power even if he had gained it by usurpation (as Shakespeare's Henry IV does, though admittedly he has a son to help him, as Macbeth does not). Hawkins points out that Macbeth does in fact get away with the murder of Duncan: what he cannot get away with is 'incompetent rule': 'there is not only moral degeneration but political incapacity'.[27] Macbeth 'is unable to make the transition from a good "second in command" to that of chief politician; from the frenetic activism of his military role to the preservation of peace and order'.

By contrast, Malcolm is able to make the transition from military activist to a chief politician who seems equipped with the relevant skills and virtues and who at least promises peace and order. But Hawkins points out that if Malcolm is, as Tillyard suggests, 'Shakespeare's ideal king', he is an ambiguous figure. He has, as Tillyard puts it, 'subordinated all personal pleasures, and with them all personal charm, to his political obligations';[28] he has shown himself, in his testing of Macduff, fully capable of convincing deception, even if in a good cause; and he sheds the blood of others – young Siward, for example – in order to free the time. We can relate Hawkins's points about Malcolm here to Wilbur Sanders's observation that Malcolm's victory is a muted one.

Hawkins's essay mounts a significant challenge to the view of *Macbeth* as a play about 'evil' which makes a clear-cut distinction between evil and good and shows the eventual triumph of the latter. In his perspective, the play emerges as much more ambiguous and equivocal – much more an exploration of perplexing political questions than an affirmation of absolute ethical and metaphysical values and polarities. As we shall see, this sense of the play's ambiguities will be richly and energetically pursued in the later part of the twentieth century, not only in historically-orientated criticism but also by post-structuralist, deconstructionist and feminist-psychoanalytical critics. One of the first fruits of a mixture of historical and proto-feminist perspectives was offered in 1982 by Peter Stallybrass.

PETER STALLYBRASS

In his essay '*Macbeth* and Witchcraft' (1982), Peter Stallybrass applies to the play a functionalist perspective on witchcraft drawn from sociology and anthropology. In such a perspective, the belief in witchcraft is regarded as a means of reinforcing distinctions and definitions which are important to a specific social and political order; witchcraft accusations are one way of stigmatizing those who, explicitly or implicitly, challenge that order. According to Stallybrass, a concern that occult practices – sorcery, prophecy, astrology – might threaten the monarchy goes back at least to 1300, but James I's interest in witchcraft had developed after the witch trials of 1590, and it linked up with the interest in kingship and religion which he already held. Stallybrass suggests that witchcraft provided James with a way of strengthening the exalted view of the king's role that he wished to promote. If the King were, as James argued, God's representative on earth, then he was both especially vulnerable to the work of the devil and especially important in keeping the devil at bay. James's ideology of kingship provides a series of analogies and antitheses which shares and helps to determine the ideological ground on which *Macbeth* works: there are analogies between, in descending order of magnitude, God's rule over the earth, the king's rule over his subjects, the father's rule over the family, and the head's rule over the body; opposed to these are the devil's rule over the earth, the people's rule over the king, the woman's rule over the family, and the body's rule over the head.

Like James's ideology of kingship, *Macbeth* also employs antitheses, and Stallybrass discusses the way in which its amendments to Holinshed help to sharpen its antithetical structure. In Holinshed, Macbeth is seen as usurping the throne of an ineffectual king who has, he feels, defrauded him of his rightful succession, and he tells Banquo in advance what he intends to do; once he becomes king he carries through a programme of reform, makes 'commendable laws', and rules for ten years 'in equal justice' before turning into a tyrant.[29] In Shakespeare's *Macbeth*, Duncan is a virtuous king (although it may be, as Michael Hawkins argues, that he is represented in such a way as to make him open to criticism on certain counts); Banquo does not know of Macbeth's plan to kill the old king; and Macbeth's reign falls almost instantly into tyranny. This creates a much sharper contrast between the good and bad king and this contrast is clearly important in those critical interpretations, such as Wilson Knight's and L. C. Knights's, which see *Macbeth* as a play about evil. In terms of *Macbeth's* concern with witchcraft, however, the play's most significant change to Holinshed is that it makes the weird sisters more definitely demonic. In Holinshed, they are first described as 'three women in strange and wild apparel, resembling creatures of elder world',[30] and slightly later two alternative possible identifications are provided: 'the common opinion was, that these women were either the weird sisters, that is (as ye would say) the goddesses of destiny, or else some nymphs or fairies, endued with knowledge of prophecy by their necromantical science'.[31] Both these alternatives have benign connotations: goddesses of destiny could be spiritually elevated, and nymphs and fairies could be charming, playful and mischievous (as in *A Midsummer Night's Dream*). Such connotations are absent from the weird sisters of *Macbeth*.[32]

The witches in *Macbeth* remain ambiguous, however. In some respects they seem petty figures who typify the English village 'witch' as she emerges from folklore and witch trials; they are old – 'withered' with 'choppy [chapped] finger[s]' and 'skinny lips' (1.3.38, 42, 43) – and some of their activities look trivial – asking a sailor's wife for chestnuts, killing swine. But in other respects they are impressive; they are mysterious, 'look not like th'inhabitants of o'th' earth' (1.3.39), and give symbolically complex, potentially misleading but ultimately accurate prophecies about the future of kings. Stallybrass suggests that this ambiguity enables the play to offer a double perspective on evil, in which it is both reductive, consuming itself to nothingness – Macbeth dwindles to 'a dwarfish thief' (5.2.22) and finally to a bodiless head – and expansive, a terrifying metaphysical force that could turn the world back to chaos unless it is countered by metaphysical good.

Macbeth further strengthens its antithetical structure by linking witchcraft, and social, political and metaphysical disorder with unnatural femininity, as represented by Lady Macbeth. As Stallybrass puts it: 'Lady Macbeth is shown in the very attempt of overthrowing a norm inscribed in her own body. "Remorse", "compunctious visitings of Nature", and the "milk" of "woman's breasts" ' (1.5.42–5) are established as the "feminine" virtues even as Lady Macbeth negates them'. Lady Macbeth proclaims herself 'as mother/lover of the spirits' and thus 'implicitly subverts patriarchal authority in a manner typically connected with witchcraft'. She also subverts it in her husband by impugning his manhood. The threat to patriarchy that Lady Macbeth embodies is countered by the introduction of Lady Macduff and her family in 4.2, a scene with no basis in Holinshed. It is worth noting, however that this scene might also be seen, at least temporarily, as putting patriarchy into question, as it focuses on Macduff's apparent desertion of his wife and children, even though it could seem that a patriarchal norm is reinforced when Lady Macduff characterizes his behaviour as 'unnatural' ('he wants [lacks] the natural touch' (4.2.9)). Stallybrass points out, however, that Lady Macduff appears late in *Macbeth*, and proposes that the play offers another 'good' alternative to the 'bad' Macbeths – a family without women: Duncan and his sons, Malcolm and Donalbain; Banquo and his son Fleance; even Siward and his son Young Siward:

■ On the one hand there are the (virtuous) families of men; on the other hand, there are the antifamilies of women'. And here, the notorious question 'How many children had Lady Macbeth?' is not entirely irrelevant. For although Lady Macbeth says, 'I have given suck' (1.7.54), her children are never seen on the stage, unlike the children of Duncan, Banquo, Macduff and Siward. Are we not asked to accept a logical contradiction: Lady Macbeth is *both* an unnatural mother *and* sterile? This links her to the unholy family of the Witches, with their familiars and their brew which includes 'Finger of birth-strangled babe' and the blood of a sow which has eaten its own litter (4.1.30, 80–1). Like the Witches, Lady Macbeth and her husband constitute an 'unholy' family, a family whose only children are the 'murdering ministers' [whom Lady Macbeth invokes to come to her 'woman's breasts'].[33] □   (1.5.45–6)

Lady Macbeth does not function as the representative of unnatural femininity throughout the play, however. She starts to turn into her own antithesis even before the murder when she is unable to kill Duncan herself because he looks like her father (2.2.12–13). In the words of Stallybrass: ' "Nature" is reasserted through her in its most compelling guise – the Law of the Father which, in this society, founds and is founded by the Law of the King'.[34] By the last act of the play, Lady Macbeth is the sleepwalker horrified at the quantity of the old man's blood (the blood of the father), aware of Lady Macduff's death, and solicitous for her husband. Her transformation can be interpreted in psychological terms but also functions to affirm, within one character, the antitheses of unnatural / natural wife and mother, and the eventual triumph of the 'natural'.

Like Lady Macbeth, the witches also turn into their own antitheses, not in psychological terms but in terms of the truth of their prophecies. If at first they are 'imperfect speakers' (1.3.68) whose words are equivocal, the visions that they later summon are, Stallybrass contends, more and more definite – from 'the armed head' to the 'bloody child' to the 'child crowned' to the 'show of eight Kings, the last with a glass in his hand, Banquo following' which 'stretch out to th' crack of doom' (4.1.133) – the show of eight kings which culminates in James I, whose occupancy of the throne – and perhaps actual presence at the play, in the case of a court performance – serves as the confirmation of the truth of the prophecy. As the unsexed woman is resexed and thus reaffirms the patriarchal order and the antithesis which supports it, so '[c]ursed witches prophesy the triumph of godly rule'³⁵ (in this respect they do, of course, take on some of the more elevated and benign connotations which 'the weird sisters' have in Holinshed). While the witches and Lady Macbeth are separated from evil spirits as the play proceeds, Macbeth tries to invoke them himself, as in the 'Come, seeling night' speech (3.2.47), and to commune with them more closely, and he becomes increasingly isolated.

Stallybrass provides the following summary of his view of the role of witchcraft in *Macbeth*:

■ Witchcraft, prophecy and magic function in *Macbeth* as ways of developing a particular conceptualization of [way of thinking about] social and political order. Witchcraft is associated with female rule and the overthrowing of patriarchal authority which in turns leads to the 'womanish' (both cowardly and instigated by women) killing of Duncan, the 'holy' father who establishes both family and state. This in turn leads to the reversals in the cosmic order which the Old Man and Ross describe, and to the reversals in the patriarchal order, culminating in the killing of Lady Macduff and her [children]. The conclusion of the play re-establishes both the offended (and offending? [because of his desertion of his wife and family]) father, a father, paradoxically, 'not born of woman' (5.3.4) (does this imply that he is unnatural or untainted?), and the offended son/king. And the witches can simply disappear, their evil supplanted by the prophetic vision of Banquo's line and by the 'heavenly gift of prophecy' and 'miraculous work' (4.3.158, 148) of a legitimate king.³⁶ □

As this summary shows, Stallybrass does not deny that the play contains the kind of 'symbolic ordering' that critics from Wilson Knight and L. C. Knights to Irving Ribner and Kenneth Muir have found in it; but he wants to relate these symbolic orderings to 'particular manoeuvres of *power*', to see them as ways of looking at and thinking about the world that help to confirm certain social relations. He aims 'to analyse, rather than repeat, the terms of the play itself'.³⁷ But we have already met the argument, for example in Wilbur Sander's account, that 'the terms of the play' are not necessarily as clear-cut as critics such as Wilson Knight would argue; and this view can also be found in Stephen Booth's thoughtful, exploratory book of 1983, which discusses *Macbeth* in the light of a theory of tragedy as indefinition.

STEPHEN BOOTH

In *'King Lear', 'Macbeth', Indefinition and Tragedy* (1983), Stephen Booth contends that 'the response we record when we label an event tragic is a response to the fact of indefinition ... [the] literary works we call tragedies have their value as enabling actions by which we are made capable, temporarily, of enduring manifestations of the fact that nothing in human experience is or can be definite'.[38] *Macbeth* 'puts us through an actual experience of the insufficiency of our finite minds to the infinite universe'.[39] While it seems to have a beginning, a middle and an end, its beginning and end, on closer examination, do not provide a clear sense of origin or closure: the play is 'all middle'.[40] Throughout the play, finality is never attained: the murder of Duncan is never over, Banquo comes back as a ghost within the play, and, as the supposed ancestor of the line of Stuart kings, extends into the time of Shakespeare's contemporary audience. The characters want closure but cannot find it, for example in the matter of murder ('The time has been / That, when the brains were out, the man would die / And there an end' (3.4.77–9)) and in the matter of sleep, which Macbeth cannot achieve and which provides his sleepwalking wife with no relief. Beginnings are also elusive – what happened to Lady Macbeth's child, how was Macduff (not) born of woman? Cause and effect are not clearly apparent in the play. No closed category can be maintained – in the Captain's combat report, for example, 'the doers of good sound either like or worse than the evildoers'.[41] As the play unfolds, it is often hard to distinguish between Macbeth and his Lady, and in this they resemble other characters in the play 'who are regularly in doubt about their own and other people's sexes'.[42] Words, particularly the word 'man', also elude final definition.

Booth argues that the 'most obvious examples of the insufficiency of limits are the equivocations that are one of the play's recurrent topics' and claims that *Macbeth* itself, as a whole, is 'a kind of equivocation between the fact of limitlessness – indefinition, tragedy – and the duty of art to limit and define'.[43] The play is great because it gives full scope to both these poles. A microcosm of the whole drama is Macbeth's 'If it were done ... ' soliloquy in 1.7. Everything in this soliloquy refuses fixity; for example, in 'catch with his surcease success', the word 'success' 'is emblematic of the speech and the play', suggesting 'both triumphant final achievement' and 'that which follows', 'succession'. In the lines 'He's here in double trust: / First as I am his kinsman and his subject, / ... then as his host' (1.7.12–14), the 'two' suggested by 'double trust' turn into three (kinsman/subject/host), exemplifying the 'process by which pairs turn into trios in this baby-ridden play' (Booth sees the largest example of this process as the inexplicable appearance of the third murderer in 3.3). In the last sentence of the soliloquy, 'I have no spur / To prick the sides of my intent, but only / Vaulting ambition, which o'erleaps itself / And falls on th' other' (1.7.25–8), the image of spurring occurs *before* the image of mounting (if we take 'vaulting' to mean 'vaulting into the saddle'), and this reversal of sequence suits the sentence itself (which breaks off unfinished when Lady Macbeth enters) and the inconclusive, indefinite nature of the whole play. But if the soliloquy refuses fixity, it is also given an orderly form by the very terms which promote the sense of limitlessness: the juxtaposition of 'surcease' and 'success', for example, links the two words by sound and helps to bind together the soliloquy.

Booth argues that the tragedy of *Macbeth* occurs, not in the character of Macbeth or onstage, but in the 'failure of categories' that takes place in the audience.[44] The audience ought to categorize Macbeth as evil and Malcolm as good; but it continues to see the action of the play from Macbeth's viewpoint, sharing imaginatively in both his consciousness of evil and his perpetration of it, and in his sense of 'the magnitude of the situations and events the play presents'.[45] Apart from Lady Macbeth when she is sleepwalking – and possibly, Booth suggests, 'the comically philosophical Porter'[46] – none of the other characters are on the same scale; for example, 'Banquo and Duncan sum up their radical blandness in their slow, luxuriously fatuous commentary on the salubrious climate at Macbeth's castle'[47] – a challenging alternative view of a passage which has been seen by critics such as Wilson Knight and L. C. Knights as epitomizing the positive values of the play. But it is Malcolm whose sense of the size of events is the most inferior to Macbeth's and who most notably fails to win the audience's sympathy away from Macbeth. Earlier in the play, when he greets the bleeding sergeant who had saved him from being captured, and when he gives the noble and generous account of Cawdor's death, Malcolm looks as if he might become Macbeth's equal; but his response to Macduff's announcement that 'Your royal's father's murdered' – 'O, by whom?' – sounds like silly 'small talk'[48] and his further comments in the scene are feeble. It is in 4.3, however, that Malcolm's lack of stature is most fully evident, and it comes across, above all, in his *language*: it is sometimes bombastic and padded – 'What I believe I'll wail; / What know, believe; and what I can redress, / As I shall find the time to friend, I will' (4.3.8–10) – and sometimes 'elliptically foreshortened', as when 'wisdom' is substituted for 'it may be wise' in 'and wisdom / To offer up a weak, poor, innocent lamb' (4.3.15–16). His apparent self-accusations show a 'contorted' syntax and a 'tortuous' pace; Booth suggests that it is difficult, for Macduff and for the audience, to be quite sure who he is talking about when he says:

> ■   But for all this,
> When I shall tread upon the tyrant's head
> Or wear it on my sword, yet my poor country
> Shall have more vices than it had before,
> More suffer, and more sundry ways, than ever,
> By him that shall succeed.

Macduff: What should he be?
Malcolm: It is myself I mean. ☐   (4.3.45–51)

When Ross enters, there is considerable delay before he tells Macduff what has happened to his wife and children, and while this generates 'theatrical energy' it is also disagreeable, very much like any scene that drags. This further reduces the stature of Malcolm and of Macduff, and three more scenes which involve them – 5.2, 5.4 and 5.6 – also fail to win the audience over to the play's ostensible heroes. They delay our movement towards the conclusion, are slow even when short (5.6 is only ten lines), and the military action seems 'dramatically irrelevant to a climax for which the terms have been firmly established as supernatural'.[49]

The failure to categorize Macbeth as evil and his opponents as good might seem likely to provoke discomfort in an audience; but, Booth argues, it does not do so because 'the clash between two powerful, urgent, differently based sets of judgements remains only potential' and thus gives the audience 'a token experience of being able to cope with conflicts comparable to those our minds cannot cope with, those that cannot be placed and managed in a single frame of reference'.[50] Nonetheless, this clash means that 'the experience of seeing or reading *Macbeth* is experience of an object that is under constant pressure from within – an object full of volatile elements always ready to meet and explode'.[51] For Booth, however, *Macbeth* never explodes but enables the audience to experience and apparently to cope with the failure of categories and the absence of final definition: and it is this indefinition which constitutes tragedy. In a vivid, tightly-packed book published two years after Booth's, James L. Calderwood is also interested in the way in which *Macbeth* challenges categories and in its relationship to theories of tragedy; and he is concerned, moreover, to compare and contrast it with *Hamlet* and to explore the way in which it dramatizes the interfusion of violence and culture.

JAMES L. CALDERWOOD

In *If It Were Done: 'Macbeth' and Tragic Action* (1986), James L. Calderwood looks at *Macbeth* in three ways – as 'a kind of counter-*Hamlet*' which 'almost systematically' opposes the 'modes and structures of presentation' of the earlier play; as 'a tragedy about the nature of tragedy'[52] which subverts 'the Aristotlean principles of wholeness, completeness and limited magnitude, even of beginning, middle and end'; and as 'a sort of psycho-sociological study of violence and culture'.[53] Calderwood first of all considers *Macbeth* in the light of concepts, such as 'time, action, and mediation', that 'play a prominent role in *Hamlet* '.[54] Taking *Macbeth* as a 'counter-*Hamlet*', he observes that, whereas the key action in *Hamlet* – killing Claudius to avenge his father's murder – is postponed for a long time, the key action in *Macbeth* – killing Duncan – occurs early and quickly. While *Hamlet* is characterized by 'inbetweenness', in which the gap, the middle, the channel of communication or cause and effect between two persons or events is often blocked – particularly between Hamlet and Claudius, and between the Ghost's injunction to revenge and Hamlet's enactment of it – the gap or middle in *Macbeth* is much narrower. For Hamlet, imagination interferes with action; for Macbeth, it is the source and means of action: 'Duncan's murder takes place in the mind before it occurs in the castle, and the route from the subjunctive "If it were done" (1.7.1) to the indicative "I go, and it is done' (2.1.62) is paved by murderous fancies'. The 'dagger of the mind' (2.1.38) quickly forges a lethal dagger of steel. But the imagination in *Macbeth* is not quite as simple as this: it is, as Calderwood puts it, 'both a get-between and a go-between for action'.[55] While it can lead quickly to action, as with the 'dagger of the mind', it can also retard the desire to act, as in the 'If it were done' soliloquy where Macbeth imagines multiple objections to killing Duncan. But this inhibiting aspect of the imagination becomes less prominent as the play proceeds.

Where Hamlet is reactive, Macbeth initiates action. Hamlet is fixated on the past, which is appropriate to a tragedy concerned with revenge; Macbeth looks to the future. The Danish play is retrospective, the Scottish Play 'prophetic and premeditative':[56] in *Hamlet* 'future action is repeatedly deferred and frustrated'; in *Macbeth*, 'it is constantly anticipated and impending'.[57] But Macbeth cannot escape the past and – this is the point made earlier by Stephen Booth – his deeds can never achieve closure. It is ironic but fitting that, in the end, the future seems meaningless as his past catches up with him: tomorrow is merely weary repetition.

In *Hamlet*, sleep and dream are linked with a procrastinating subjectivity which internalizes all external concerns; it is a sleep from which he must awaken to act and to end the play of which he is the protagonist. By contrast, in *Macbeth*, dreamlike subjectivity quickly leads to action – the 'horrid image' that comes upon him leads to Duncan's murder, the hallucinatory dagger is replaced by a real one – and sleep departs to leave him in a waking nightmare. Hamlet, faced with the perplexing problem of killing a king in a corrupt world without being corrupted himself, delays action by changing it into '"act" – into madplay, wordplay, and finally a stage play' – *The Murder of Gonzago*; but he must finally move from 'acting to action'. There are scant references to plays and theatre in *Macbeth*, but Calderwood suggests that the ones that do exist are significant. When Macbeth learns that he is now Thane of both Glamis and Cawdor, he says: 'Two truths are told / As happy prologues to the swelling act / Of the imperial theme' (1.3.126–8), and thus implies that the witches' prophecies are part of an unfolding play in which he is acting a part. In doing this, he conforms to Lady Macbeth's description of him as one who 'wouldst not play false, / And yet wouldst wrongly win' (1.5.20–1). Developing the idea of Macbeth as a player or actor, Calderwood sees him as taking on different roles as he perpetrates the murder of Duncan. In 2.1, he turns himself from loyal subject, kinsman and host into 'an extreme version of the stage villain': 'withered murder, / Alarumed by his sentinel, the wolf / ... With Tarquin's ravishing strides, towards his design / Moves like a ghost' (2.1.52–5). In contrast to 'The Murder of Gonzago' in *Hamlet*, however, 'The Murder of King Duncan' is, within the play of *Macbeth*, actual and bloody; the role has become reality and though Macbeth quickly adopts other roles when Macduff and Duncan arrive, he cannot escape the truth of his deed. '[S]tage-play in *Macbeth* – the hero's imaginings, the Witches' prophecies – turns into reality in Scotland. For all its witches and demonism, *Macbeth* is a positive and ultimately realistic play, whereas *Hamlet* negates its realities again and again with a self-frustrating vengeance'.[58]

While action in *Hamlet* is 'external to the hero', perhaps because the public sphere is corrupt, it 'originates within the hero' in *Macbeth*, perhaps because the corruption lies in the protagonist's imagination. Where *Hamlet* moves towards meaning, *Macbeth* moves away from it, finally reaching a nadir of meaninglessness with the 'Tomorrow and tomorrow and tomorrow' soliloquy. Hamlet inherits corruption, Macbeth brings it into the world (this view, which chimes in to some extent with earlier twentieth-century interpretations of the play, has, of course been challenged by some of the critics considered in this chapter who see the state of Scotland which exists at the start of the play as violent and unstable, not at all a pure and uncorrupted kingdom). Hamlet's identity is negated by his failure to kill the king, making him primarily defined by what he is not – a revenger; he is 'a poststructuralist with an undecidable text' who cannot make up his mind about the correct inter-pretation and the appropriate action that would issue from it. Macbeth, by contrast, is 'something of an existentialist' who defines himself by the choices he makes and the actions he performs.

In *Hamlet*, negation works to evoke vividly that which is supposedly negated, most notably near the end of the closet scene. Thus Hamlet says 'Not this, by no means, that I bid you do' (3.4.165) – in other words, he provides a negation – and then goes on to offer a powerful description of Gertrude betraying him to the 'bloat King' (3.4.166) which, so to speak, negates the negation, making it impossible for us to forget it even while it is supposedly confined to the negative realm. Calderwood contrasts this scene with Malcolm's testing of Macduff in 4.3 of *Macbeth*, where Malcolm confesses to evils but then negates his confession, saying that it consisted of falsehoods (it is, in fact, open to question whether they are entirely negated in terms of what they reveal about Macduff – for example, his apparent willingness to tolerate Malcolm's covert satisfaction of his supposedly insatiable lust with Scottish women overawed by the glamour of power). Calderwood asserts that in *Macbeth*, 'negation is genuinely negative. It erases its subject instead of foregrounding it while pretending to erase it as in *Hamlet*'.[59]

Calderwood's contrasting of *Hamlet* and *Macbeth* comes finally to 'the issue of time and form',[60] and this links up with his earlier claim that Hamlet, the character, looks back, while Macbeth, the character, looks forward. The opposing orientations of the two protagonists are echoed in – or, perhaps, produced by – the form of the play. The form of *Hamlet* is retentive and does not proceed in a straightforward way but, rather, constantly dilates and delays; *Macbeth* is protentive, moving steadily towards the future (protentive is an adjective derived from 'protension', a term used in the phenomenological philosophy of Edmund Husserl (1859–1938) to mean an 'extension of the consciousness of some present act or event into the future'. (*The New Shorter Oxford English Dictionary*, 1993)). Macbeth's soliloquies, in contrast to Hamlet's, are not self-explorations which hold up the action, but 'incitements to dangerous deeds';[61] these deeds, however, fail to deliver the future that Macbeth desires. But if Macbeth does not get what he wants, the audience does, finding 'gratification in Shakespeare's conversion of ambitious desire on Macbeth's part into prophetic form in *Macbeth*'. The play keeps its promises, moves towards the fulfilment of predicted events.

Calderwood then turns to consider *Macbeth* as a tragedy about the nature of tragedy. The play is pervaded by a concern with the tragic action of the protagonist, his 'doing', and with the tragic action that is the play in which he has the lead role. There is no other play in which the occurrence of the words 'do' 'done' and 'deed' is so frequent or so central and the play can be seen as a completed action with a beginning, middle and end, in accordance with Aristotlean criteria. But it is not quite so simple: the action is 'undone' because it is never wholly complete, because it is contaminated by erotic metaphors, and because it is not shown directly to the audience. Like Stephen Booth, Calderwood finds it difficult to locate precisely the start and finish of the action of the play. For example, its first line, 'When shall we three meet again?', seems like the end rather than the beginning of a meeting and postpones making a start until the next encounter of the witches. Conversely, it soon becomes clear that part of the action – the 'hurly-burly', the conflict – has already begun. So the play opens with what Calderwood calls an 'unbeginning' rather than a 'beginning'. And arguably it concludes, or fails to conclude, with an 'unending', where the similarities between Macduff's position at the end of the play and Macbeth's at the start raise the possibility that closure has not been achieved and that the cycle of violence could start again.

Focusing on Macbeth's words after he has killed Duncan – 'I have done the deed' (2.2.14) – Calderwood suggests that this carries a sexual implication and that 'the murder of Duncan is a metaphorically displaced act of copulation between Lord and Lady Macbeth'.[62] He links this to a range of other examples which seem to link sex with killing; for example, the way that Lady Macbeth prepares for murder by invoking the spirits to 'unsex me here' – thus rechannelling her 'libidinous energies ... into violence';[63] her goading of Macbeth to murder by casting aspersions on his manliness; her highly charged words when she says of the grooms: 'That which hath made them drunk hath made me bold. / What hath quenched them hath given me fire' (2.2.1); and Macbeth's comparison of himself, as he approaches Duncan's chamber, to Tarquin moving with 'ravishing strides' towards the rape of Lucrece. As Calderwood vividly puts it: 'The imagery of sexual impotence, stimulation, and performance constitutes an erotic metaphor for murder, a kind of intermittent flashing onto the regicidal screen of a subliminal image of the sexual act'.[64] This 'undoes' the murder of Duncan in the sense that it prevents it from being a whole, complete action; it is monstrous and unnameable, and it brings forth monsters.

Calderwood's third topic is *Macbeth* as a psycho-sociological study of violence and culture, and here he draws upon the ideas of René Girard in *La Violence et le sacré* (1972; trans. as *Violence and the Sacred*, 1977). He also acknowledges that, in regard to this aspect of the play, his views have much in common with those of Harry Berger Jr, and he credits Jan Kott with 'one of the earliest attempts to give violence its due in *Macbeth*'.[65] In the opening battle of *Macbeth*, Calderwood argues, violence both undoes cultural differences – we can think here of the way in which the combatants become confused in the captain's account – and provides cultural meanings: the battle is 'a sacrificial bloodletting that charges men's lives with value', above all the life of the King; 'victory reaffirms his sacred status' but also creates differences that can be the source of further violence which undoes those differences again. The treacherous Thane of Cawdor survives in Macbeth; Lady Macbeth blurs 'the distinction between maternal child-nourisher and defeminized child-killer'; both the Macbeths 'confuse the differences between beast and man'; and all this results in 'a deed of darkness', the murder of Duncan, which 'grotesquely fuses king-subject, host-guest, father-son, mother-wife, and Creator-creature in what is at once an incestuous regicide-deicide-parricide': the killing of a king, a god, and a father.[66]

Macbeth's slaughter of Duncan releases a wave of violence that engulfs the whole of Scotland and breaks down all cultural distinctions in what Girard calls a 'sacrificial crisis' which has to be cured by means of a scapegoat, or *pharmakos* – and Macbeth fulfils this role, though he is not merely a *pharmakos*; his capacity to recognize his crimes and losses elevates him to tragic stature. Calderwood cites the argument of Jacques Derrida (1930–2004), in *Dissemination* (1972; trans. with same title, 1981), that the etymology of the word *pharmakos* includes the ideas of both 'medicine' and 'poison', and argues that Macbeth incorporates both these meanings: he is 'both the disease of violence his community suffers from and its cure'.[67] But how complete and permanent is the cure? Calderwood suggests that 4:3, in which Malcolm appears, as in a ritual, temporarily to assume and indeed magnify the evils of Macbeth in order to purge them, could be seen to reflect, on a miniature scale, the whole action of the play – and also to imply that the cure may be a carrier of the disease. In his attempt to highlight the difference between himself and Macbeth, Malcolm has to forge a temporary identity with Macbeth, and we can ask whether he can then wholly shed this identity, and whether the new differences he creates at the end of the play, when he converts his thanes and kinsmen to earls, might not lead to the further violence that would, once again, undo difference.

Calderwood's consideration of violence and culture in *Macbeth* rarely focuses on the specific historical context of Jacobean England in which the play emerged, but there is one particularly interesting moment when he does make the connection, suggesting that not only Macbeth, but also the play of which he is the protagonist, is a *pharmakos* that served as a medicine to the times. 'The violent impulses of Jacobean England – with its religious and political paranoias in the aftermath of the Saint Bartholomew Massacre, the Essex Rebellion, and the Gunpowder Plot – are apparently funneled into this play, much as the evils of Scotland are funneled into Macbeth, and are then purged by the violent action of ritualized drama'.[68] But if the purging of Macbeth fails wholly to cure the violence and may indeed set the scene for its reawakening, so the purging effected by *Macbeth* will not be wholly successful; the play cannot completely absorb the violence that it seeks to assimilate. This opens up the possibility of more historically specific readings which relate that violence to the ideological and political conflicts of the Jacobean era – and this is the kind of reading Alan Sinfield offers in a highly influential essay which appeared in the same year as Calderwood's book.

ALAN SINFIELD

In '*Macbeth*: History, Ideology, and Intellectuals', Alan Sinfield, like Michael Hawkins, questions whether the play is about 'evil' and suggests that it tries to make a distinction between the supposedly legitimate violence of the state and the supposedly illegitimate violence of those who dissent from or oppose its authority; it is this illegitimate violence that the play seeks to label as 'evil'. This distinction is fundamental to the development of the modern state as it emerges from feudalism, and it was a crucial part of what Sinfield calls 'Jamesian ideology' – the ideas about kingship which James I held and wrote about. Jamesian ideology, Sinfield charges, has also been endorsed by those critics of *Macbeth* who have interpreted it as a play in which evil disrupts but is finally defeated by good. Sinfield contends, however, that an alternative ideology which saw violence against the state as a sometimes permissible response to bad rulers can be found in *De jure regni* and *History of Scotland* by George Buchanan, that this ideology is also active in the play, and that the politically radical critic can draw on it to produce a reading of *Macbeth* which challenges the distinction between legitimate and illegitimate violence in James's time and in the present.

To suggest the way in which the play endorses state violence, Sinfield starts by quoting the Captain's account of Macbeth's slaughter of the rebel Macdonald – 'he unseamed him from the nave to th' chops' – and Duncan's approving comment: 'O valiant cousin! worthy gentleman!' (1.2. 22, 24): 'Violence is good, in this view, when it is in the service of the prevailing dispositions of power; when it disrupts them it is evil'.[69] We saw in Chapter 4 that Wilson Knight's 1931 analysis in *The Imperial Theme* exemplifies this position. Of course, earlier critics have not always seen the violence evoked in the opening scenes as wholly good, as we also saw in Chapter 4: William Empson suggested in 1930 that Ross's description of Macbeth as 'Nothing afeard of what he himself did make / Strange images of death' could be seen to imply a similarity between killing in battle and murder. Roy Walker's *The Time is Free* certainly sees the play as being about the triumph of good over evil but nonetheless called the battle a 'foul enough bloodbath';[70] and Sinfield himself cites G. K. Hunter's comment, in his introduction to the 1967 Penguin edition of *Macbeth*, on the 'violence and bloodthirstiness' of Macbeth's killing of Macdonald'.[71] But even where Macbeth's violence on behalf of Duncan has not won wholesale approval, it has often been strongly distinguished from Macbeth's violence *against* Duncan. But it is his violence on behalf of Duncan that also makes him a threat to Duncan.

In this respect, *Macbeth* dramatizes one of the structural problems which, according to Sinfield, faced the early modern state in its development from feudalism – the potential split between legitimacy and power: the legitimate monarch might not be the most powerful person in the realm. This is Duncan's situation after the victory over the rebels and invaders; Macbeth amply acknowledges, in his soliloquy at the start of 1.7, that Duncan's legitimacy is divinely sanctioned, for example by angels and cherubim; but the power lies in the hands of the leading soldier, Macbeth, who has played a crucial part in saving Duncan from deposition and who could therefore aspire to the throne.

The second and more persistent problem that faced the early modern state was distinguishing between monarchical rule and tyranny. The St Bartholomew's Day Massacre of Huguenots in France in 1572, the persecution, torture and execution of many 'witches' in Scotland in 1590–91, the arrest, fining, imprisonment, torture and killing of Roman Catholics in England since Henry VIII's break with Rome, were all examples of state violence that brought home this problem. As Sinfield puts it in relation to *Macbeth*: 'what is the difference between Macbeth's rule and that of contemporary European monarchs?'[72] James I affirmed a clear distinction between 'a lawful good king' and 'an usurping tyrant' and argued that the 'lawful good king' acknowledges himself to be 'ordained for his people' because he has received his 'burden of government' from God, to whom he must be accountable; the 'usurping tyrant' thinks that his people are ordained for him. Since the ends of the 'lawful good king' and the 'usurping tyrant' ends are 'directly contrary', their means necessarily are as well.[73] Sinfield suggests that this perspective effectively makes all the actions of the 'lawful good king' legitimate, characterizes any challenge to his power as a challenge to God and his people, and justifies any violence used to defend that power (though eventually, as Peter Stallybrass had pointed out in 1982, James would regard any challenge to the power of a tyrant, as well as to a 'lawful good king', unacceptable).

Sinfield acknowledges that *Macbeth* 'seems organized to validate James's contention that there is all the difference in this world and the next between a usurping tyrant and a lawful good king' and that '[a]n entire antithetical apparatus of nature and supernature – the concepts through which a dominant ideology most commonly seeks to establish itself – is called upon to witness against him as usurping tyrant'.[74] But this does not mean that a 'Jamesian reading' of *Macbeth* is inevitable, since the play can also be related to Buchanan's theory of sovereignty in *The Powers of the Crown in Scotland* and to his *History of Scotland*, a book which illustrates that theory and justifies the removal of a legitimate monarch who could also be judged a tyrant – who, in other words, embodied the two types of ruler who were, in Jamesian ideology, wholly distinct. This monarch was James's mother, Mary Queen of Scots, who was deposed in 1567. What Sinfield calls 'the Buchanan disturbance' thus highlights the problems in Jamesian ideology and in *Macbeth* itself.

Sinfield recognizes that earlier critics have noted many of these problems, even if they have tried to resolve them into a unified interpretation of the play: there is, as already mentioned, the extreme violence with which the rebellion is suppressed and there are the points made by Harry Berger Jr and Michael Hawkins which we considered earlier in this chapter: the possible weaknesses of Duncan as king, the uncertainty about whether the succession was hereditary or elective. Sinfield also highlights the ambiguous positions of Banquo after the murder and of Macduff at the end of the play. Banquo suspects but does not explicitly oppose Macbeth; he tells no one else about the witches' prophecies and still wonders if they may be a source of hope for him. Macduff, by the end of the play, 'stands in the same relation to Malcolm as Macbeth did to Duncan in the beginning. He is now the king-maker on whom the legitimate monarch depends' and the state thus remains unstable, with Malcolm's power potentially open to violent challenge. The conversation between Malcolm and Macduff in 4.3 also blurs the distinction between true king and tyrant: Macduff initially believes what Malcolm tells him about his insatiable carnal desire but is still ready to accept him as a lawful king and indeed points out that he should be able to satisfy his lust with the 'willing dames' of Scotland while pretending to be indifferent (4.3.74); he is even prepared to accept a king whose 'avarice', by Malcolm's own account, would lead him to seize the property of his nobles and to pick unjust quarrels with them, even with 'the good and loyal' (4.3.84) in order to do so.

Macbeth can thus be interpreted in the perspective of James or Buchanan. The Buchanan disturbance cannot be explained away and is inevitably invoked through the play's attempt to tackle the problems in absolutist ideology – to deal with those problems, it must, to some extent, make them visible. Sinfield contends that most criticism, up to the time that he was writing, has supported the Jamesian position, but an alternative pro-Buchanan critical route is possible that would read *Macbeth* in such a way as to promote 'scrutiny ... of the legitimacy of state violence',[75] not only in the Jacobean era but also in our own. He speculates that this alternative route could become a central one.

Sinfield mocks the conservative critics of *Macbeth* who identify themselves with the supposed social and political order that the play can appear to endorse, and the liberal critics who see in the tragic protagonist a reflection of their own doomed attempt to find a place for their superior sensibility in a constraining world. Conservative critics, he suggests, are like the English doctor in *Macbeth* whose only lines are in response to Malcolm's question about whether the King is coming forth:

■ Ay, sir. There are a crew of wretched souls
That stay his cure. Their malady convinces
The great essay of art, but at his touch
Such sanctity hath Heaven given his hand,
They presently amend. □   (4.3.142–6)

Such critics, Sinfield suggests, 'encourage respect for mystificatory images of ideal hierarchy that have served the state in the past, and who invoke "evil", "tragedy" and "the human condition" to produce, in effect, acquiescence in state power'.[76] He compares liberal critics to the Scottish doctor who, invited to cure the sickness of Scotland – 'If thou couldst, Doctor, cast / The water of my land, find her disease' (5.3.52–3) – is reluctant to offer an analysis and wishes he were somewhere else – 'Were I from Dunsinane away and clear / Profit again should hardly draw me here' (5.3.63–4): 'the liberal intellectual ... knows there is something wrong at the heart of the system but will not envisage a radical alternative and to ratify this attitude, discovers in Shakespeare's plays "tragedy" and "the human condition" as explanations of the supposedly inevitable defeat of the person who steps out of line'.

This taunting of the ineffectual liberal humanist critic – which recalls Lady Macbeth's taunting of her milk-livered husband – was a recurrent note of the left-wing critical rhetoric of the 1980s, which promoted a heroic image of the critic who was ready to envisage a radical alternative and use the keen knife of analysis to slash through the mystifications of the body politic. The political transformation that was supposed to accompany this did not occur, but Sinfield's speculation that the kind of reading of *Macbeth* he promoted would become more central was realized. Sinfield's own approach, however, is not so much 'against the grain', as he claims, but above the grain; it operates at some distance from the text, removing itself from the pressures of its language and constructing a modified *Macbeth* which is closer to the kind of play Buchanan might have written than to Shakespeare – a play which is the occasion for a debate in which the legitimacy of state violence is scrutinized. Other radical readings of *Macbeth* aim to get rather closer to the text, combining a concern with history and ideology with theoretical perspectives which Sinfield does not employ, especially post-structuralism and deconstruction. In the next chapter, we shall look at key interpretations of *Macbeth*, by Catherine Belsey, Terry Eagleton and Malcolm Evans, which draw on such perspectives.

CHAPTER SIX

The Later Twentieth Century: Language, Subjectivity and Subversion

P ost-structuralism and deconstruction had emerged in France in the 1960s, but it was not until the 1980s that they began to impinge strongly on literary studies in the United Kingdom and the United States; as key works were translated, commentaries and explications appeared, and controversy raged. These two movements of ideas challenged cherished and often unexamined assumptions on which much literary interpretation – including the interpretation of Shakespeare – had proceeded until then. These assumptions included the notion that texts were organic wholes in which all apparent contradictions were eventually resolved; that language gave access to truth; and that human subjectivity was a unity. Instead, post-structuralism saw texts as montages of disparate elements, texts as constructing truth rather than revealing it, and human subjects, who were constituted in language, as split, while deconstruction held that any text would, necessarily, subvert itself, dissolve the grounds on which it was supposedly based. In many ways, these approaches were well suited to Shakespeare, whose texts were full of different discourses, whose elaborate language constructed and dissolved worlds with protean flexibility, whose characters, however much one wanted to treat them as 'real people', were constituted in language, and whose plays often seemed to undermine their own premises. Some critics who used post-structuralist and deconstructionist perspectives linked them with left-wing political radicalism of a socialist or Marxist kind; this was also helpful in Shakespeare criticism, since, with these perspectives, there was no need to try to prove that Shakespeare himself was a radical, or that his plays really carried a radical message; the radicalism lay not in any message that might be extracted from the play but in the way in which the play worked to subvert reactionary notions. A groundbreaking book in introducing post-structuralist ideas to a wider audience was Catherine Belsey's *Critical Practice* (1980), and she used *Macbeth* as one of her key examples.

119

CATHERINE BELSEY

In *Critical Practice*, Catherine Belsey draws on the theories of, among others, Jacques Lacan (1901–81) and Émile Benveniste (1902–76), and on Marxism, she argues that there is a split between the 'I' who speaks and the 'I' whom I speak of when I speak – what Benveniste calls the subject of the enunciation and the subject of the enounced – and that this split becomes especially evident at times of social crisis, when the mode of production is threatened or changing; this happens in the Renaissance, for example, when capitalism is increasingly displacing feudalism. It is exemplified by *Macbeth*, where 'the discontinuity of the ego and the explicit division of the subject' are 'a structural principle of the play':[1]

■ Here the ethical and ideological norms of loyalty, kinship and hospitality are set against the 'black and deep desires' of the protagonist, which seem to come to the surface at the beginning of the play and to escape rational control. Macbeth, loyal and unified *subject* [Belsey's italics emphasize the way in which, in her perspective, the idea of being the 'subject' of a ruler is linked with believing oneself to possess a unified *subjectivity* and being *subjected* to a particular social order] of a king who stands for these ideological (and discursive) norms, becomes a regicide in defiance of his own discourse ('I have no spur ...' (1.7.25) and in the process destroys his own capacity to participate meaningfully in the symbolic order of language and culture. The imagery of the soliloquies themselves externalizes the desires, which seem to present themselves to consciousness as independent utterances inviting consent: 'why do I yield to that suggestion / Whose horrid image doth unfix my hair ... ?' (1.3.133–4); and the process of temptation explicitly destroys the unity of the self: 'My thought ... Shakes so my single state of man ...' (1.3.138–9). Macbeth consents to the suggestion, identifies with the perpetrator of his actions and cements the division of his own subjectivity: 'To know my deed 'twere best not know myself' (2.2.71). He becomes increasingly isolated from other people, and his discourse, confined to 'Bloody instructions' [1.6.9] is not able to give meaning to the world, which comes to seem 'a tale / Told by an idiot ... Signifying nothing' (5.5.25–7). He has refused the subject-positions offered him by the symbolic order, and in consequence meaning eludes him, he has fallen into non-meaning.[2] □

This offers an interesting way of looking at Macbeth, but it is worth noting three questions that arise in the context of Belsey's overall argument. One problem is that her interpretation does treat the play as in some sense realistic, as offering an illustration, in the portrayal of Macbeth, of a psycholinguistic truth: that the subject is split and the ego discontinuous. A second problem is that this split subject is also discussed at points as if it possessed a capacity for choice like the free and conscious subject of Sartrean existentialism: 'Macbeth *consents to* the suggestion, *identifies with* the perpetrator of his actions and cements the division of his own subjectivity. ... He has *refused* the subject-positions offered to him by the symbolic order' (italics added). This echoes the attempts of character criticism, such as Bradley's, to show Macbeth has free will, that he is a freely choosing agent despite the apparent compulsions, for example of the weird sisters, to which he is subjected. A third problem is that this interpretation bears an uneasy relationship to Belsey's view that the gap between the 'I' that speaks and the 'I' that is represented in speech is 'the source of possible change', with the implication that the 'possible change' is desirable; if *Macbeth* is regarded as a play about the discontinuity of the ego and the division of the subject, however, it suggests that such discontinuity and division – or at least, an awareness of it – is, to say the least, a highly troubling condition that can lead to disaster; that Macbeth might have been much better off with an apparently unified subjectivity, even if it were of an illusory kind.

In *The Subject of Tragedy*, Belsey draws further examples from *Macbeth* in considering the ways in which the development of the soliloquy in Renaissance drama offers a way of trying to present a supposedly unified and autonomous individual in which elements that in morality plays might have been represented by personifications (good, envy, etc.) are internalised as inner conflicts. But the Renaissance soliloquy does not quite succeed in doing this, partly because it bears the traces of earlier allegorical modes, and partly because it is impossible anyway. This sense of the split subject can be found, for example, in Lady Macbeth's 'Come you spirits ...' soliloquy (1.5.38–52). Lady Macbeth is the subject of the enunciation, the 'I' that speaks – we can see and hear her doing so on stage (though she is also an actor) – but the subject of the enounced, or, as Belsey puts it in this book, the subject of the utterance, is almost absent from the speech. The spirits, rather than Lady Macbeth, are the grammatical subject of the actions – and the moment that the subject of the utterance 'appears (as "me") in the third line of the text, it is divided into crown, toe, cruelty, blood, remorse, nature, breasts, milk' (although it is also worth noting, as Belsey does not, these are also linked with 'the subject of the utterance' and assembled into some kind of unity by the possessive pronoun 'my' – which is then, however, applied to the 'keen knife' which Lady Macbeth does not necessarily intend to wield herself). The soliloquy ends by opposing heaven and hell, repeating the morality pattern of the human being 'as a battleground between cosmic forces, autonomous only to the point of choosing between them'.[3]

Belsey also considers the 'Pity, like a naked new-born babe' speech and suggests two possible interpretations. She conjectures that a seventeenth-century audience familiar with emblematic imagery might have considered two major figures – pity, 'like a naked new-born babe' and pride, represented by the knight spurring on his horse until it throws him. The links between the elemental, human and supernatural images might show the hero's struggle as part of 'the cosmic struggle with which he is continuous and which is duplicated in his own being'. What Belsey calls 'humanist criticism' would fill the gap between 'the subject of the utterance confronting a moral choice, and the subject who speaks, who identifies in cosmic imagery the perils of his own ambition' by constructing 'the feeling, self-conscious, "poetic" Macbeth, a full subject, a character' ('poetic' here is perhaps an allusion to Bradley's idea of Macbeth as a 'poet', quoted in Chapter 3 of this Guide).

Belsey suggests, then, another way of reading *Macbeth* – neither as a play about character nor as a poetic whole, but as a much more fragmented work, in which soliloquies, in particular, open up the gap between the representation of 'character' and emblem and allegory, and between the subject of the enounced and the subject of the utterance. This idea of a fragmented *Macbeth* can also be found in Terry Eagleton's *William Shakespeare*.

TERRY EAGLETON

In 1967, Terence Eagleton – as he then styled himself – published a book called *Shakespeare and Society*, in which he devoted a chapter to *Macbeth*. The chapter remains interesting both in itself and by comparison with the interpretation of *Macbeth* he later offers in *William Shakespeare* (1986). *Shakespeare and Society* mixes the idioms of Jean-Paul Sartre (1905–80) and Raymond Williams (1921–88); it employs a quasi-existentialist vocabulary of 'authenticity' and 'inauthenticity' but also counters the individualist stress of existentialism by emphasizing that authenticity is achieved, not by isolating oneself from human community or by gratuitous acts, but through 'social responsibility'.[4] In his reading of *Macbeth*, Eagleton sees the play turning on the paradox of an act – the murder of Duncan – which is intended to provide a final and complete self-definition but fails to do so. The act makes Macbeth king but he cannot rest secure in that role: he has to fight 'to *become* what, objectively, he is'. The 'idea of a perfected, completely achieved act is insistent in the play', but Macbeth never realizes it. The fundamental reason for this is that it is impossible: 'any achievement involves a process of reaching and a process of results, and both processes can destroy what is attained'. In this respect, it seems that Macbeth makes a philosophical error which he could have made even if he had attained the crown by legitimate means. But by killing Duncan he also cuts himself off from human community and falls into 'the pure negativity of evil, the area of nameless deeds'. The 'community' in question in *Macbeth* is a quasi-feudal one and Eagleton seems to approve of this as much as Wilson Knight and L. C. Knights do, although he employs existentialist terms: 'Before the murder, Macbeth's authentic life consists in serving Duncan, and the service is not an external, mechanical obedience but a living self-expression ... In destroying Duncan he is being inauthentic, less than himself'.[5]

In Eagleton's view, Lady Macbeth also makes a philosophical error in failing to see that limits create rather than constrain humanity and in urging Macbeth to transgress boundaries in order to achieve what he wants. She believes in 'gratuitous commitment': Macbeth has decided to kill Duncan and so he should do it; in her eyes, he is 'inauthentic' because he will not act to attain his desires. She shows no sense of social responsibility and no concern for the harm he may do. Although Macbeth resists her at first, he himself comes increasingly to exemplify 'gratuitous commitment', reaching a point at which he gains a kind of strength from openly acknowledging absurdity, chaos and meaninglessness and devoting his energy to fighting to the death. But this is not a final answer: Macbeth 'undoes himself in rejecting social responsibility, and whatever value can be forcibly created from this rejection must be inevitably marginal'.[6] The play presents 'a kind of energy which is formidable in its human strength, but negative at root'.[7]

In the reading of *Macbeth* which opens his *William Shakespeare*, published nineteen years later, three figures who are mentioned only twice in the *Macbeth* chapter of *Shakespeare and Society* move to centre stage and become, in their marginality, the source of 'positive value': the witches. Eagleton asserts, provocatively, that '[t]he witches are the heroines of the [play]', although he acknowledges that *Macbeth* itself, and most critics, work to deny this; he turns them into an anarchic female commune who, by their ambiguous appearance and poetic, riddling use of language, 'strike at the stable social, sexual and linguistic forms which the society of the play needs in order to survive'. They arouse ambitious desires in Macbeth and thus reveal the social order which, according to *Shakespeare and Society*, provided him with 'his authentic life' and 'a living self-expression' as 'the pious self-deception of a society based on routine oppression and incessant warfare'.[8] The view that Eagleton himself expressed in *Shakespeare and Society* – that limits should be seen as creative rather than constraining – is attributed to Macbeth in *William Shakespeare*: Macbeth 'fears the troubling of exact definitions: to be authentically human is, in his view, to be creatively constrained, fixed and framed by certain precise bonds of hierarchical allegiance ... To transgress these determining bonds, for Macbeth, is to become less than human in trying to become more.'

It might therefore seem that Lady Macbeth – who, after all, rejects the bonds that cement an oppressive, martial society – could also, like the witches, be a kind of heroine; could it not be said that she, like the witches, strikes 'at the stable social, sexual and linguistic forms which the society of the play needs to survive'?[9] But if, for Eagleton, the witches have flipped from foul to fair in *William Shakespeare*, Lady Macbeth becomes fouler than ever. In the earlier book, she was an exemplar of gratuitous commitment, which might at least connote a certain existential daring of the kind associated with the French writer André Gide (1869–1951): now, she is 'a bourgeois individualist'[10] who regards rank and kinship not as determinants of identity but as restrictive practices to be swept aside in the quest for personal goals, and a ' "bourgeois" feminist'[11] (the quote marks round 'bourgeois' are Eagleton's) who tries to become more masterful and manly than the patriarchal system which keeps her in her place. In contrast, the witches 'live in community ... and they are indifferent to political power because they have no truck with linear time, which is always, so to speak, on the side of Caesar'.[12] This, however, does not take account of the point made by Peter Stallybrass in 1982: that, as the play advances, the witches' prophecies become increasingly aligned with political power, and – in the line of kings that stretches out to the crack of doom – show that power as perpetuating itself in linear time. Eagleton acknowledges that the kind of subversiveness that the witches represent can be appropriated by a political system in a way which reinforces that system, but he does not engage with the extent to which the witches are shown to be on the side of Caesar. It could also be pointed out that their alliance with earthly powers also emerges in their desire to persecute the powerless – the 'rump-fed runnion' and her sailor husband (1.2.3–23) – and their racism and religious bigotry as they throw into their gruel 'Liver of blaspheming Jew', 'Nose of Turk and Tartar's lips' (4.1.26, 29).

While Eagleton celebrates the witches' ambiguous use of language insofar as it calls into question a perfidious social order, he also seems to feel that ambiguity has its limits, that language can lose touch with material reality – especially the reality of the body – to a degree where it becomes destructive. Indeed, he interprets the disintegration of the Macbeths as a process in which language and desire become increasingly detached from material and bodily reality:

■ Macbeth will end up as a bundle of broken signifiers, his body reduced to a blind automaton of battle; his sleepwalking wife disintegrates into fragments of hallucinated speech and mindless physical action. ... The Macbeths are finally torn apart in the contradiction between body and language, between the frozen bonds of traditional allegiance and the unassuageable dynamic of desire.[13] □

It is interesting to observe here that Eagleton speaks as if the Macbeths were realistic characters, and even endows them with bodies, whereas it could be argued that they have been 'bundles of signifiers' all along and that Lady Macbeth was never 'integrated'; the term 'disintegration' implies a previous 'integration', a unified subjectivity, of the kind which Catherine Belsey questions. If the witches subvert an oppressive order by their ambiguous use of language, why could it not be said that the Macbeths do the same when they themselves become 'imperfect speakers'? Are they still bourgeois individualists when they have lost control over language to this extent, or is their fate a monitory warning of the dangers of bourgeois individualism? The final difference, for Eagleton, between the relationship of the witches to language and the relationship of the Macbeths to language seems to be that the witches have changeable bodies that can move in and out of material shape, whereas the Macbeths are split between language, desire and the unbearable weight of human being.

While Eagleton's interpretation of *Macbeth* in *Shakespeare and Society* is a sober one which emphasizes that Macbeth destroys himself because he rejects 'social responsibility', his reading of the play in *William Shakespeare* is exciting and excitable, stressing the social irresponsibility and subversiveness of the witches and the way in which the 'natural' necessarily invokes the 'unnatural'. But he also recognises the limits of the witches' subversiveness, the way in which it can be appropriated to reinforce political order, and he does imply that language should be in some kind of connection with material reality, especially the reality of the body. There is, in fact, a certain tension in Eagleton's reading between a deconstructionist sense of language as an unstable process that constitutes reality and a (historical) materialist sense of physical and political reality. Malcolm Evans, in *Signifying Nothing* (1986; 2nd edn, 1989), also brings a deconstructionist sense of language as an unstable process and a radical political awareness to *Macbeth*, but there seems to be less tension between these two approaches in his interpretation than there is with Eagleton's; Evans is a more thoroughgoing deconstrucionist.

MALCOLM EVANS

For Malcolm Evans, 'equivocation' is crucial to the play and it is seen both to exemplifying the true activity of language and to constitute a political challenge. He directs his fire against the kind of criticism which we have considered in Chapter 4 of this book, which presents a view of *Macbeth* as, for example, a 'vision of evil' (Wilson Knight) and 'a statement of evil' (L. C. Knights). Evans sees the equivocal operations of language in the play as unsettling such metaphysical certitudes and throwing them into crisis – or rather, disclosing that they are already in crisis.

In the early scenes of *Macbeth*, it is, Evans suggests, not only the witches who are 'imperfect speakers' (1.3.170); 'imperfect speaking' spreads across the text and upsets the hierarchies it seeks to affirm. Evans proposes that 'two basic linguistic modes' are evident in these scenes of *Macbeth*.[14] One is a single, unequivocal mode, applied to or employed by the 'good' characters, which seeks to suppress the constructive role of language and to present a questionable hierarchical ideology as if it were 'natural'; the other mode, most apparent in the words of the witches and Macbeth and Lady Macbeth, is an 'equivocal' one which challenges and invades the first form and draws attention to the material, constructive and heterogeneous aspects of language, the ways in which it makes meanings which its own operations constantly subvert and call into question.

For example, the captain's account of the battle asserts conventional hierarchies reinforced by images drawn from nature but also undermines them; Banquo and Macbeth are likened to eagles and lions repulsing the sparrows and hares of the Norwegian assault (1.2.35) but they are also, Evans suggests, implicitly compared to those who killed Christ when they seem as if they might be fighting 'to memorize another Golgotha' (1.2.41) – Golgotha, the 'place of skulls', was where the Crucifixion took place.

Macbeth's proclaimed status as a man well worthy of being called 'brave' is cast into doubt not only by the implication that he is (along with Banquo) a Christ-killer, and by the excessive language in which his supposedly legitimate violence is evoked, but also by grammatical ambiguities, as in the account of Macbeth's attack on Macdonald, the Thane of Cawdor who has rebelled against Duncan:

■ For brave Macbeth – well he deserves that name! –
   Disdaining fortune, with his brandished steel
   Which smoked with bloody execution,
   Like Valour's minion
   Carved out his passage till he faced the slave,
   Which ne'er shook hands nor bade farewell to him.
   Till he unseamed him from the nave to th' chops,
   And fixed his head upon our battlements. □   [1.2.16–23]

As Kenneth Muir points out in his Arden edition of the play, it is unclear whether 'which', in the clause 'which ne'er shook hands', refers to Macbeth, Macdonald or fortune. Evans sees this as a significant ambiguity which blurs the distinction between characters and categories and links with the image of displaying the head of Macdonald – an image which, of course, anticipates the display of Macbeth's head by Macduff near the end of the last act. It is worth noting here, however, that Evans does not mention Muir's suggestion that half a line, and possibly more, is missing after 'Till he faced the slave';[15] if that is the case, the syntactic ambiguity might be more an accident of textual transmission than an example of the inherent instability of language and of ideological categories; the missing text might have resolved this particular ambiguity, although the sense of an 'imperfect' attempt to give language a single, unequivocal meaning, of a conflict between two linguistic modes, could still be illustrated by other aspects of the speech.

Ross's report, in 1.3, of Duncan's response to news of the battle also exemplifies the conflict between an unequivocal and an 'equivocal' linguistic mode. Most editors since Nicholas Rowe in 1709 emend the phrase in lines 97–8 to 'As thick as hail / Came post with post', but Evans prefers to retain the Folio version: 'As thick as tale / Can post with post'. This version contributes to the sense of linguistic crowding and confusion which is crucial to Evans's argument, and it is therefore the version given in the following quotation:

■ The King hath happily received, Macbeth,
The news of thy success; and when he reads
Thy personal venture in the rebels' sight
His wonders and his praises do contend
Which should be thine or his; silenced with that,
In viewing o'er the rest o'th' self-same day
He finds thee in the stout Norwegian ranks,
Nothing afeard of what thyself didst make,
Strange images of death. As thick as tale
Can post on post, and every one did bear
Thy praises in his kingdom's great defence,
And pour'd them down before him. □   [1.3.87–98]

According to Evans, the first, unequivocal linguistic mode is evident in Ross's attempted portrayal of a gratified, thankful king and his bold defender; but this is challenged by the other, equivocal mode, which generates ambiguities and gives a sense of the instability of language and of a hierarchy in which subjects occupy fixed positions. 'He finds thee in the stout Norwegian ranks' means, on the unequivocal level, that Duncan hears of Macbeth pitching boldly into the Norwegian ranks to fight *against* them and *for* Duncan; but it could also mean that Duncan hears that Macbeth is fighting *alongside* the Norwegian ranks and *against* Duncan. Similarly, 'Thy personal venture in the rebels' sight' (or 'fight') refers, on the unequivocal level, to Macbeth visibly putting his life on the line, in full view of the rebels, to fight *against* them; but it could also mean that he is visibly risking his life, in full view of the rebels, to fight *for* them. When Duncan 'reads' of Macbeth's 'personal venture', 'his wonders and his praises do contend / Which should be thine or his'; he seems to become identified with Macbeth and with the story of his exploits to such an extent that he loses control of his responses, and his astonishment and admiration take on a combative life of their own, fighting with each other over which of them constitutes the most appropriate response, and over whether it is Macbeth or Duncan who most deserves that response: this conflict leaves Duncan at a loss for words ('silenced with that'). Macbeth himself then becomes a reader, like Duncan, and an author, confronting the 'Strange images of death' that he himself makes ('maker' was a medieval word for 'poet'). In this passage, fixed positions – king, thane, protagonist, author, reader – are revealed as unstable by the ambiguities of language itself when it works in the second, 'equivocal' mode.

Evans argues that the unequivocal and 'equivocal' linguistic modes co-exist and contend throughout the play and are never fully fused into a unity; Malcolm's assertion of the first form of discourse at the end is reductive (Evans here provides another explanation for Wilbur Sanders's sense that the ending is muted; it is an attempt to 'mute' the second, equivocal linguistic mode). And it is the 'equivocal' mode which not only highlights the unstable nature of language and hierarchy but also signifies the 'nothing' that the unequivocal mode seeks to deny. This 'nothing', however, 'is not merely an absence but a delirious plenitude of selves and meanings, always prior to, and in excess of, the self-naturalizing signs and subjects of the discourses it calls perpetually to account', and to call it 'evil' is 'to reprocess the text through a moral discourse it renders problematic'. Evans argues that even orthodox Christian doctrine holds that 'nothing', while it can be identified 'with sin or chaos', is also 'the ground of all creation' and that *Macbeth* 'signifies nothing in this paradoxically positive sense'.[16]

Evans thus recovers an affirmative and even metaphysical *Macbeth*: its affirmations do not lie in its portrayal of human potential (Bradley), of the triumph of good over evil (Wilson Knight, Knights) or of the energy inextricably intermixed with evil (Sanders), but in the activity of its language – especially in its 'equivocal' linguistic mode – which subverts fixed hierarchies and implicitly opens up the possibility of political change. Its metaphysical dimension lies not in its dramatization of metaphysical absolutes but in its exemplification of the creative nothingness which precedes and exceeds stable systems of meaning and identity. As we have seen, previous critics, such as L. C. Knights, have remarked on some of the ways in which *Macbeth* calls stable meaning into question, but they have tended to see it as bad, even nauseating – we may recall Knights's comment on the 'sickening see-saw rhythm' of

Macbeth's lines 'This supernatural soliciting / Cannot be ill, cannot be good' (1.3.129–30).[17] For Evans – as for Eagleton in *William Shakespeare* – the 'see-sawing' of the 'equivocal' linguistic mode is not sickening, but exhilarating and liberating. This depends, of course, on a privileging of the 'equivocal' mode as one that is closer to the 'truth', as Evans sees it, about language and about human society. But it remains the case that *Macbeth* associates the 'equivocal' linguistic mode with agonizing mental processes that few people would welcome and with forms of behaviour that no society would be likely to encourage, and Evans's interpretation does not take full account of this. Like Belsey and Eagleton, however, he does employ post-structuralist and deconstructionist theory and a scepticism about the metaphysical and political values the play ostensibly endorses to open up the play to new interpretations and highlight areas of energy and difficulty. Further ways of opening up *Macbeth* and highlighting areas of energy and difficulty were provided by feminism, sometimes allied with revised forms of psychoanalysis, and by new historicism, which situates literary texts within wider discourses that work to enforce and subvert social and cultural power. In the last chapter of this Guide, we shall consider crucial feminist readings by Coppelia Kahn, Marilyn French and Janet Adelman; a key interpretation by Stephen Greenblatt, usually identified as the leading new historicist critic, which argues, in an interesting departure from new historicist orthodoxy, for preserving a distinction between *Macbeth* and the wider discourses that worked to promote a belief in witchcraft; and an important exploration by Stephen Orgel of the witches in *Macbeth* and the way in which they open up a paradoxical space in the play for women.

CHAPTER SEVEN

The Later Twentieth Century: Men, Women and Witches

M any varieties of feminist literary criticism developed in the 1970s and 1980s, but one of the most powerful linked feminism with psychoanalysis. This was not a straightforward link; many elements of psychoanalysis could themselves be seen as open to feminist critique, as displaying sexist biases in their ideas of what constituted normative female and male sexuality and identity. Nonetheless, the link often proved enabling; and a combined feminist-psychoanalytic approach could seem, in many ways, well suited to *Macbeth*, a play which Freud himself had already tackled and which, especially through the figures of the witches and Lady Macbeth, raises key questions about femininity, and also – as Eugene M. Waith had noticed back in 1950 – about masculinity. The first major feminist-psychoanalytical reading of the 1980s came from Coppélia Kahn.

COPPÉLIA KAHN

In *Man's Estate: Masculine Identity in Shakespeare* (1981), Coppélia Kahn, adopting a psychoanalytic perspective strongly influenced by American ego psychology, sees *Macbeth* as a play about the failure to achieve a secure, fully individuated masculine identity. This failure, as focused in the character of Macbeth, has three components: one is Macbeth's dependency on women for his sense of identity, and particularly on destructive female figures – the witches and Lady Macbeth; a second is his rivalry with men which shows itself in his violent struggles with them – with the rebels at the start of the play, then with Banquo, then with Macduff; a third, closely related to his rivalry with men, is his exclusion from fatherhood, in contrast to Banquo; Macbeth's only children are the corpses of the ones he has killed. His lack of children is, for Kahn, 'a metaphor for his unfinished, not fully individuated identity',[1] for 'his failure to realize an authentic manliness that integrates his conscience and his feelings with his valour' and fosters rather than merely destroys life.[2]

Femininity, for Macbeth, is represented in the figures of the witches as 'a chaos of physical and moral elements, deviously inviting men to their destruction by confusion rather than direct attack'.[3] Images of solids, liquids and immaterial spirits signify the feminine, and figure as the opposite of the 'milk of human kindness'. The witches concoct a 'thick and slab' gruel and some of its ingredients – 'Finger of birth-strangled babe, / Ditch-delivered by a drab', 'sow's blood, that hath eaten / Her nine farrow' (4.1.30–2, 80–1) – link childbearing with infanticide, the feminine with death, in ways that relate to contemporary realities. Lady Macbeth is associated with the 'spirits / That tend on mortal [i.e. murderous] thoughts' (1.5.38–9) and with liquids – the drugged possets she gives to Duncan's grooms to make them drunk and soporific and the drink which provides the pretext for her to strike the bell that summons her husband to kill the king. It is thus 'a liquid feminine element' that provides the source of Macbeth's supposedly masculine act of murder and prevents it from being the means by which he becomes a man; which, like drink in the Porter's words, both 'makes' and 'mars', 'provokes the desire' but 'takes away the performance' (2.3.27–308).

The links, in Macbeth's world, between femininity and murder are also evident in the way the text plays on the idea of 'doing' as having sex and killing. Lady Macbeth implies an association between Macbeth's reluctance to kill and sexual impotence, for example when she asks: 'Art thou afeard / To be the same in thine own act and valour / As thou art in desire?' (1.7.39–41) or reminds him that he first broached the idea of killing Duncan and now seems to have backed away from it: 'When you durst do it, then you were a man ... Nor time nor place / Did then adhere, and yet you would make both. / They have made themselves, and that their fitness now / Does unmake you' (1.7.49–54). His response to Banquo's ghost provokes her to question his manhood again, but he takes refuge from her taunts by asserting that he could fight anything but Banquo's ghost – he would take on 'the rugged Russian bear, / The armed rhinoceros, or th' Hyrcan tiger', or the living Banquo; it would only be justifiable to impugn his manhood if he showed fear when faced with these dangers – then, indeed, he would accept being called 'the baby of a girl [a baby girl or a girl's doll]' (3.4.99–100, 105). Here, Kahn suggests, 'Macbeth's rhetoric shows how desperate he is to make himself into his wife's kind of man, if only in words'.[4]

If Macbeth fails to become a man in his wife's terms, he also fails to become a man by not becoming a father, and it is in fatherhood, according to Kahn, that the 'ultimate manly satisfaction in this play resides'.[5] The issue of fatherhood is especially focused in his rivalry with Banquo, 'Macbeth's ideal self-image', who combines courage, conscience, paternity and the possibility that his sons will be kings. In his soliloquy in 3.1.49–73,

Macbeth reflects that 'Under [Banquo] / My genius is rebuked', that his crown is 'fruitless' and his sceptre 'barren', that no son of his will succeed him, and that he has given his soul to the devil to make 'the seeds of Banquo' kings; Banquo thus has 'a kind of greatness and power in him forever denied Macbeth – the power to procreate and specifically, to have sons. Sexually and socially, in Shakespeare's world, fatherhood validates a man's identity.'[6] Macbeth personifies his lack of sons in an opponent whom he can fight and destroy – as, indirectly, he destroys Banquo; Kahn suggests that Macbeth displaces his own envy of Banquo on to the murderers whom he hires to kill his fruitful rival, when he tells them, immediately after the soliloquy which invokes 'the seeds of Banquo', that Banquo has held them 'under fortune' and refers mockingly to 'this good man' and 'his issue' whose 'heavy hand hath bowed you to the grave / And beggared yours for ever' (3.1.79, 90–2). When he is encouraging the murderers to feel in this way about Banquo, he is also, indirectly, talking about how *he* feels about Banquo.

Macbeth then moves from 'active enmity towards Banquo' to 'passive identification with the mysterious, evil feminine powers'. We saw in Chapter 5 that Peter Stallybrass argued that the witches and Lady Macbeth are separated from evil spirits as the play proceeds and that Macbeth tries to invoke them himself, as in the 'Come, seeling night' speech (3.2.47). Kahn suggests, however, that the association between evil spirits, Lady Macbeth and the witches persists in Macbeth's language in 3.2; he invokes 'Hecate' and 'night's black agents' and uses the passive voice to suggest that these evil agencies will do the necessary work: 'there shall be done / A deed of dreadful note' (3.2.44–5). He is both trying to satisfy Lady Macbeth by accomplishing a deed and evading his own responsibility for it, not merely by hiring others to do it, but by seeing it as part of a more general uprising of nocturnal evil over which the female goddess, Hecate, presides. Kahn asserts that Macbeth's language 'reveals his continuing dependence on [Lady Macbeth's] now internalized influence'.[7]

Macbeth's continuing dependence on feminine powers is also evident in his visit to the witches after the banquet. Kahn argues that the apparitions the witches conjure up, taken simply as visual symbols without the words which they utter, represent, in a complex way into which many elements enter, the conflicting demands that manhood makes on Macbeth. The first apparition, the armed head is an image of the adult warrior; the second, the bloody child, is 'the infant man, bloodied at birth when nature separates him from his mother', and the blood signifies 'his link with women' and his vulnerability and dependency which, like that of the 'naked new born babe' in Macbeth's soliloquy, is paradoxically powerful, able to move people to compassion and action;[8] the third apparition, the child crowned with a tree in its hand, represents the fatherhood that Macbeth lacks and that is enjoyed by a man like Banquo, who can 'refrain from action and wait for the seeds of time to grow'; the tree 'suggests a family tree, an organic union of male and female sustained from generation to generation'.

If the apparitions, in their visual significance, are images of different aspects of manhood, they resemble Lady Macbeth and the witches in their verbal performances, which 'pander to [Macbeth's] infantile need for magical reassurance and utter certainty' and which both make and mar him as a man, emboldening him at first but enervating him when their true meaning is revealed. Kahn attaches particular significance to Macbeth's response to the second prophecy, that 'none of woman born / Shall harm Macbeth' (4.1.96–7), which he echoes in the last act 'as if it were a charm to ward off the gathering army' (5.3.6–7) and which '[p]sychologically ... serves to make all other men seem effeminate compared to Macbeth' and 'sets him apart from women'.[9]

In contrast to Macbeth's confusions over his masculine identity, Macduff and Old and Young Siward are offered as 'touchstones' of a 'manhood' which is set 'in the context of procreation and the family'.[10] Macduff's flight from his family provokes Lady Macduff to produce, in her speeches, her own ideal of the family in which the male is protective and the woman dependent, as in a family of birds – an image which echoes Banquo's evocation of the breeding martlet in 1.6. This 'natural' relationship contrasts with the 'perverse' relationship of the Macbeths, where the husband is dependent on the wife. Kahn does not, however, address the problem raised by the way in which one of her 'touchstones' of manhood, Macduff, 'wants the natural touch' (as Lady Macduff puts it) and deserts his family; he seems, at this point in the play, a rather brittle touchstone.

It is in Macduff's response to the news of his wife and children's death, however, that he becomes a more durable 'touchstone' of manhood: Kahn cites his exchange with Malcolm in which 'Shakespeare sums up, with full impact and precise economy, the critique of masculinity expressed by the whole play':

■ *Malcolm*: Dispute it like a man,
  Macduff: I shall do so,
  But I must also feel it as a man.
  I cannot but remember such things were
  That were most precious to me. □   (4.3.221–5)

Macduff has to experience manly, paternal grief and then, 'with courage and pity fused', fight his opposite, Macbeth, 'who kills pity in the name of courage, who kills children'; in that combat, he is fighting, 'not only for honour or glory, not only to save his country or avenge his family, but ... to defend the continuance of human life itself as it devolves on love between men and women, procreation, nurturance, and pity'.[11] But there is a problem here which Kahn does not mention; Macduff's identity as a defender of family values has been cemented by his rejection of them: it is his desertion of his wife and family and their subsequent death which has made him a man. This seems to complicate his function as a touchstone of a manhood which is set 'in the context of procreation and the family'. Kahn's claim that the two Siwards function as such touchstones is also questionable, since their 'manhood' could appear to depend on the absence of women and of any 'feminine' grief or compassion. They could be seen to form one of the play's virtuous families without women, as Peter Stallybrass suggests, and if, as Kahn claims, Old Siward, satisfied that his son met a heroic death facing rather than fleeing his enemy, 'seems to attain through his child that sense of completion Macbeth can never know', it is an ironic completion in feminist, procreative and familial terms since it ends his son's life without any mention of his mother at all.

In the verbal combat between Macbeth and Macduff which precedes their fight to the death, Macbeth is still, Kahn suggests, regressively dependent on women, in the sense that he still has an infantile reliance on the magical guarantee of invulnerability provided by female sources – the witches and the apparitions they conjure up, who are 'female' because they speak in the same equivocal, misleading way as the witches and who have told him that 'none of woman born' can kill him. This guarantee dissolves, of course, when Macduff declares that he was 'untimely ripped' from his mother's womb and thus implicitly affirms a relationship which combines two aspects of masculinity that Macbeth has not been able to reconcile: a sense of independence from, and an acknowledgement of a bond with, the feminine; Macduff has emerged, though not smoothly, from his mother's womb, but he did have his origins there. Macbeth admits that Macduff's revelation 'hath cowed my better part of man' (5.10.18), and Kahn focuses on the word 'cow' in this line, which is its only use as a verb in Shakespeare and which probably derives from the Old Norse term 'kuga', meaning 'to oppress'. It is, Kahn suggests, 'a fitting irony' that 'Macduff's bond with the feminine ... triumphs over Macbeth's manly valour, ... cows him into his first cowardly refusal to fight'. Moreover, 'the cow as the most common milk-giving animal suggests the milk of human kindness' and, more generally, 'all those representations of nurturant tenderness' that Macbeth, and Lady Macbeth, tried to reject, and, 'simply as a female animal', the cow implies that Macbeth 'has been feminized' – he initially refuses to fight and is only provoked to again when Macduff calls him a 'coward' and conjures up the prospect of public humiliation.[12] Kahn concludes that Macbeth has 'murdered his deepest self in the attempt to become a man' and 'has accomplished nothing'.[13]

Kahn's interpretation is fascinating, though it sometimes shows signs of strain – for example, the word 'cow' is rather heavily milked for meaning – and, compared to the readings that we considered in the previous chapter, it is rather conservative, both in its method and its underlying assumptions. Although Kahn claims, in the introduction to *Man's Estate*, that she is 'not trying to psychoanalyze individual characters, but to discover dilemmas of masculine selfhood in [Shakespeare's] works as a whole',[14] some of her commentary does sound like an analysis, in terms of ego psychology, of Macbeth and other characters as if they were real people with psyches; and although she sometimes draws attention to the historical shaping of ideas about masculinity and femininity – for example, when she refers to 'the natural (in terms of the social order as Shakespeare knew it) dependency of women on men'[15] – she more generally implies a transcendent norm of what constitutes proper manliness and womanliness. This norm is suggested by a remark that we have already quoted: that Macbeth's 'barrenness' is 'a metaphor for his unfinished, not fully individuated, manly identity'.[16] Such a remark implies that it is possible, as indeed ego psychology would claim, to achieve a completed, fully individuated, manly and womanly identity, and this is the premise with which Kahn works – a premise strongly challenged by the post-structuralist and deconstructionist accounts discussed in the previous chapter. For Kahn, as much as for Lady Macbeth, Macbeth is not a man, though for different reasons. Marilyn French also challenges the version of manhood which Macbeth adopts, but she relates it more to the values of the 'heroic' culture of which he is a part. French provided the second important feminist account of *Macbeth* to appear in the 1980s, but psychoanalysis is not central to her argument.

MARILYN FRENCH

In *Shakespeare's Division of Experience* (1982), Marilyn French affirms that the subject of the tragedy of *Macbeth* is the suppression of the feminine principle that occurs in a 'heroic' culture – one that appears to be always at war – in which 'women must become as men' and in which 'manhood is equated with the ability to kill'.[17] Like Alan Sinfield, French cites Ross's lines about Macbeth carving his way through to Macdonald and unseaming him from the nave to th' chops (1.2.17–23), and she points out the potentially shocking quality of the violence they evoke. Coppélia Kahn had also observed that the 'vicious stroke' which ends the combat is 'described so viscerally as to make us shudder, and at least momentarily question the value conferred on such brutality',[18] but French presses that question more strongly to challenge the division between the 'good' and 'bad' Macbeth that the play, and many of its critics, have made. Though Malcolm condemns Macbeth as a 'butcher' in the closing lines (5.11.35), he is, French asserts, 'no more a butcher at the end than he is at the beginning. Macbeth lives in a culture that values butchery ... Macbeth's crime is not that he is a murderer: he is praised and rewarded for being a murderer. His crime is a failure to make the distinction his culture expects among the objects of his slaughter.'[19]

According to French, a violent culture of the kind that *Macbeth* portrays must, in order to function, define sectors – the home, the family, the state – in which violence is not supposed to occur, and those who belong to that culture must abide by those definitions if they are to remain acceptable members of it. When Macbeth kills Macdonald, his violence is acceptable because it occurs in a situation where it is permissible, indeed praiseworthy; when Macbeth kills Duncan, his violence is unacceptable because it occurs in a sector from which it has supposedly been excluded and because it has been performed by a figure who should have respected that exclusion. Its unacceptability is increased insofar as he has been driven to do it by his wife – for the play strongly suggests that, left to himself, he might not have done it. '[W]ithin the feminine/masculine polarity of morals and roles in Shakespeare's division of experience, it is Lady Macbeth's function to dissuade him' from killing Duncan and by performing the opposite function she 'violates her social role', 'fails to uphold the feminine principle' and thus becomes more evil, in the moral scheme of the play, than Macbeth – if Malcolm, at the end, condemns Macbeth as a 'butcher', he calls Lady Macbeth, who has committed no violent acts herself, 'fiend-like' (5.11.35).

French suggests that the imagery of *Macbeth* falls into masculine and feminine categories. On the masculine side, blood and royal robes symbolize 'male prowess, authority and legitimacy'; on the feminine side, babies, children, the female breast and milk symbolize procreation and nourishment. In steeling herself and her husband to kill Duncan, Lady Macbeth invokes the feminine imagery only to reject its implications – for example, when she judges her husband 'too full o'th' milk of human kindness', asks the 'murd'ring ministers' to 'come to my woman's breasts, / And take my milk for gall' (1.5.15, 45–6) or claims that she would, if necessary, dash out the brains of 'the babe that milks me' (1.7.55). Both the Macbeths value manliness above all, but Lady Macbeth's idea of manliness excludes feminine values such as caring. When this idea of manliness comes to prevail with Macbeth and he kills Duncan, the feminine principle is defeated by the masculine principle; but this defeat empties life of meaning for the Macbeths since there is no sector in which the feminine principle can operate: 'home becomes part of the war zone'.[20]

Duncan might seem to embody a fusion of masculine and feminine principles, in view of his combination of power and saintliness, his graciousness, and his nurturing concern – as when he says to Macbeth 'I have begun to plant thee, and will labour / To make thee full of growing' (1.5.28–9). Macbeth himself could appear to reinforce this androgynous view of Duncan when, in the 'Pity, like a naked new-born babe' speech, he uses both masculine and feminine images in his vision of the outrage that killing the supposedly meek and blameless king would provoke. But, French argues, Duncan partakes of the cultural bias which favours masculine values; his praise for the killing which preserves his power dips him in the blood that has been shed by Macbeth and his fellow-warriors. 'Like Macbeth, Duncan is destroyed by the principle to which he grants priority.'

With the 'empty victory' of the masculine principle that the killing of Duncan represents, the world of the play becomes insanely unbalanced. As French puts it, in a metaphor that recalls Jan Kott's linking of *Macbeth* with 'the Auschwitz experience': 'Murder follows murder until the entire country becomes a death camp'.[21] But the feminine principle, though scorned and suppressed, does not disappear: French states in the first chapter of *Shakespeare's Division of Experience* that the most extreme form of the masculine principle is the ability to kill and the most extreme form of the feminine principle is the ability to give birth, and it is through characters and images linked to birth and procreation that the feminine principle reasserts itself in *Macbeth*: for example, the children of Banquo and Macduff, and the two babes and the line of Banquo's descendants, stretching out 'to th' crack of doom' (4.1.33) whom the witches conjure up. The 'moral climax' of the play, the starkest opposition of masculine and feminine principles, is the attack on Lady Macduff and the onstage killing of her son. But this is also 'its moral turning point'. For French, however, this does not mean that the rest of the play shows the rise of the feminine principle, or its harmonious integration with the masculine one.

Like Kahn, French focuses on Macduff's response, after he has heard of the murder of his wife and children, to Malcolm's call to 'Dispute it like a man'. When Macduff replies 'But I must also feel it as a man' (4.3.221–3), French claims that 'for the first time in the play', this 'expands the meaning of the word *man*'. But in contrast to Kahn, French does not see this as the moment when Macduff is able to integrate courage and pity and emerge as a defender of family values and of procreation; despite his expanded definition of manliness to incorporate emotion, the masculine principle remains, in French's view, almost as dominant at the end of the play as it did at the start. French is much more critical than Kahn of old Siward's response to his son's death and sees the father as 'a touchstone of manhood' only in a stereotypical sense, remarking that he 'should have been played by John Wayne'. She points out that Malcolm dissents from old Siward's truncation of grief, saying 'He's worth more sorrow / And that I'll spend for him' (5.11.16–17), and observes that the tone of the dialogue in the closing scene of the play is more subdued than it was in the violently exuberant account of the victory at the beginning. It remains the case, however, that Siward 'has the last word' in the exchange with Malcolm – 'He's worth no more' (5.11.17); French feels that '[h]is mother might not agree'. In the world that *Macbeth* portrays, 'sons exist to go to war, and women exist to give birth to sons who are born to kill or be killed in battle. The language remains the same right to the end of the play'. While Kahn sees *Macbeth* as ending with the triumph of a proper manhood, embodied in Macduff, which uses its manly strength and courage to defend an ongoing form of human life that incorporates such feminine elements as procreation, nurturance and pity, French finds that the conclusion of the play leaves intact a structure of values in which the masculine principle dominates the feminine. All that is restored is the division which prevailed at the beginning, between the sectors of society where violence is permitted and praised and those where it is forbidden and condemned. In French's view, this merely reasserts 'moral schizophrenia'.[22] Shakespeare may have felt this was inescapable, but he shows, in *Macbeth*, the danger of a culture in which the masculine principle has priority and may seek to override other values.

French's approach, then, is cultural rather than psychoanalytical; the implication is that a different culture, in which the masculine principle did not have priority, might produce different values and different behaviour. A third key feminist interpretation of the later twentieth century, by Janet Adelman, sometimes converges with French's account, but is informed throughout by psychoanalysis, resulting in a reading that has significant links with Kahn's interpretation but also important divergences from it – for example, in its account of Macduff.

JANET ADELMAN

In *Suffocating Mothers: Fantasies of Maternal Origin in Shakespeare's Plays, Hamlet to The Tempest* (1992), Janet Adelman's central claim is that *Macbeth* 'represents in very powerful form both the fantasy of a virtually absolute and destructive maternal power and the fantasy of absolute escape from this power'.[23] The fantasy of escape could initially seem to be embodied in Duncan, who might appear to provide both a substitute for and a refuge from feminine maternal power by combining fathering and mothering functions; but his feminine aspects also threaten to subvert his masculinity, making him weak, over-trusting, vulnerable, reliant on 'real men' like Macbeth for his safety and insecurely ruling a kingdom already invaded by malign maternal forces in the shape of the witches. As Duncan's death approaches, his feminization increases; it is evident, Adelman suggests, in the lines in which Macbeth personifies himself as the figure of Murder moving 'With Tarquin's ravishing strides, towards his design' (2.1.55) and thus, by comparing himself to Tarquin, turns murder into rape and Duncan into Lucrece, the female victim of Tarquin's sexual aggression. When Macduff, after the murder, describes the dead Duncan as 'a new Gorgon' (2.3.68), he also turns the father into a female figure and thus perhaps implies that death has revealed him to be feminine all along, a failed patriarch, a female man.

The death of Duncan the father, dubiously masculine though he may be, gives greater scope to the destructive maternal forces which already dominate Macbeth. They are represented by the malign mother-figures of the witches and Lady Macbeth, who are linked in a range of ways. Both disturb gender divisions – the witches' beards prevent Banquo from interpreting them as women, and Lady Macbeth tries to unsex herself and perhaps to obstruct, not only her gentler emotions, but also her capacity to reproduce (in gynaecological treatises of Shakespeare's time, the term 'visitings of nature' refers to menstruation, and 'passage' was used for the neck of the womb (1.5.42–3)).[24] Adelman contends that the horror of Lady Macbeth's lines lies not only in their manifest content – their rejection of remorse, compunction and benign maternity – but also in their latent concentration of the contemporary cultural fear of the diseases and evil influences that the nursing mother could transmit to her child. When Lady Macbeth asks the 'murdering ministers' to 'take my milk for gall' (1.5.46), most editors interpret 'take my milk for gall to mean 'take my milk in exchange for gall', but Adelman suggests that it could mean 'take my milk *as* gall', so that her milk would be the poison that feeds the evil spirits. She would thus take on one of the functions attributed, in Shakespeare's time, to witches: the 'nursing of devil-imps'.[25] This is one example of the ways in which Lady Macbeth takes on some of the more alarming functions of witches as they were represented in contemporary accounts and becomes a more frightening figure, in Shakespeare's play, than the weird sisters themselves, whom Adelman regards as 'an odd mixture of the terrifying and near-comic'.[26] The attribution of these alarming functions to Lady Macbeth rather than to the witches suggests, for Adelman, 'the firmly domestic and psychological basis of Shakespeare's imagination'.[27]

Adelman locates the source of Lady Macbeth's power over her husband partly in her ability to arouse his fear of becoming her vulnerable child if he does not behave in a way that accords with her definition of masculinity. The 'babe' whose brains she would dash out if necessary is, in a sense, the dependent infant, subject to the potentially destructive power of the mother, who Macbeth himself will turn into, if he does not become a man in his wife's terms. To avoid this alarming regression, he is ready to murder Duncan, which, in effect, means turning the victim into the vulnerable infant which the murderer could have become; as Macbeth prepares to perform this act, he also tries to escape from his vulnerability to women by engaging in a fantasy in which Lady Macbeth becomes almost an all-male mother, a 'metal' mother armoured (clad in 'mail') like a man: 'Bring forth men-children only, / For thy undaunted mettle should compose / Nothing but males' (1.7.72–4). The logic of this fantasy is that 'only the child of an all-male mother is safe';[28] and in the rest of the play, it is a logic that manifests itself in another fantasy, in which women, even masculinized women, are completely cut out of the source that brings forth males: the fantasy epitomized in the idea of the 'man not born of woman'. Of course, *Macbeth* does, on one level, show this to be a fantasy; the man not born of woman turns out to be born of woman after all, and his apparent independence of a female source is revealed to be a result of the equivocation that is associated with the female figures of the witches. Nonetheless, Adelman argues, 'the play curiously enacts the fantasy that it seems to deny: punishing Macbeth for his participation in a fantasy of escape from the maternal matrix, it nonetheless allows the audience the satisfaction of a partial equivalent to it'.[29]

Adelman sees this fantasy of escaping from the maternal matrix as active at the start of the play and as not belonging only to Macbeth; rather, it spreads across the male figures of whom, initially, Macbeth is the most vigorous representative. We saw that both Harry Berger Jr, in Chapter 5, and Malcolm Evans, in Chapter 6, indicated the blurring of the distinction between characters and categories which occurs in Ross's account of the fight between Macbeth and Macdonald; Adelman points to a further aspect of this blurring, though in this case it also works to sharpen a definition: the partial feminization of Macdonald which strengthens the masculine identity of Macbeth. Initially clearly identified as '[t]he merciless Macdonald' (1.2.9), the rebel becomes intertwined with the female figure of fortune, who is at first introduced as the 'rebel's whore', smiling on 'his [i.e. Macdonald's] damned quarry [or, in many editions, "quarrel" ']' (1.2.14), but then seems partly to fuse with Macdonald, to become the object of Macbeth's disdain, in the lines: 'For brave Macbeth – well he deserves that name! – / Disdaining fortune' (1.2.16–17). Through this semi-fusion, Macdonald becomes partly female, while Macbeth, as the 'minion' of the masculine figure of valour (1.2.19), is wholly male. Adelman suggests that Macbeth's final unseaming of the apparently androgynous Macdonald-male/fortune-female from the nave to the chops performs, with one stroke, a castration and a caesarean section that turns his body into a wholly female one and confirms the suspicions already raised by his liaison with fortune: that he was a woman already. So Macbeth's killing of Macdonald is, on a fantasy level, a defeat of female power in which his fellow-warriors and his king, a male community, can share; it is an assertion of independence from women.

This fantasy is partly counteracted by the female power of the witches and Lady Macbeth, and by Macduff, with his more inclusive definition of manhood as incorporating 'feminine' and familial emotion and his revelation that he was born of woman after all. But as the play proceeds, the witches disappear – Macbeth never mentions them again after the apparition scene in 4.1 – and Lady Macbeth is increasingly disempowered, no longer capable, after the banquet, of conscious and forceful action, reduced to fragments of a figure of conventional feminine remorse and wifely concern, and despatched offstage with a cry of women. Lady Macduff might seem to embody another kind of female power in her forceful denunciation of her husband's 'unnatural departure', but she is physically defenceless without him and, as Adelman puts it, 'exists only to disappear'.[30]

Macduff himself is, for Adelman, an ambivalent figure, and some of the reasons for this have been suggested earlier in this Guide; he deserts his family and never explains why; it is the death of his family, rather than its survival, that makes him fully a family man; and his revelation that he was indeed born of woman is combined with the assertion that he was untimely ripped from his mother's womb, thus 'sustain[ing] the sense that violent separation from the mother is the mark of the successful male'.[31] Finally, his mortal combat with Macbeth confirms the power of the man who has been successfully torn away from women and has no wife or children over the man who had a wife and who was driven towards death by malign maternal domination.

The ambivalence of Macduff is echoed by the ambivalence of the play's ending, which restores an order from which women are excluded. We have already seen how the female figures diminish or disappear; Adelman also highlights the way in which the movement of the trees of Birnam Wood – seen by Wilson Knight, for example, as a reassertion of 'creative nature'[32] – in fact reconstructs an almost woman-free nature, a family tree without daughters and with little reference to mothers. The trees obscure not only the soldiers but also the march of male power behind the leafy screens which supposedly represent nature. They reinforce the fantasy of female-free generation.

Adelman suggests one further dimension on to which the fantasy of a female-free zone is mapped: that of England. Scotland is the realm of the malign mother and England of the benign father, and the strength of this opposition is indicated by the fact that Macduff can only move from one to the other by deserting his wife and family; Lady Macduff is a good mother but she still cannot keep him in the diseased womb of his native land. Even at the start of the play, when Duncan still reigns in Scotland, Adelman sees him, as we have already discussed, as a partly feminized father whose kingdom is the haunt of witches, and whose death makes him wholly female and marks the ascendancy of Lady Macbeth and of a destructive maternal power: Ross tells Macduff that Scotland 'cannot / Be called our mother, but our grave' (4.3.166–7). By contrast, England is the place of the benign father-king, whose holy healing power opposes the witches' devilish force, and whose surrogate son Malcolm, who is 'unknown to woman' (4.3.127), counterbalances Macbeth, the 'son' of the bad mother, and finally returns to Scotland to reassert patriarchal power. So the fantasy of a self-generating, self-perpetuating community of men without women persists at the end of the play.

Adelman's interpretation of *Macbeth* is ingenious and enriching, moving between a close attention to textual detail, a sense of the structural and dramatic patterns in the play, and a grasp of relevant psychoanalytical concepts which are intelligently applied. It both complicates and deepens the previous feminist readings of Coppélia Kahn and Marilyn French, and the historical, political, post-structuralist and deconstructionist accounts of Berger, Hawkins, Stallybrass, Sinfield, Belsey, Eagleton and Evans. But it may also seem to focus too much on a significant but not all-embracing aspect of a play which is, arguably, about other things besides gender and fantasy and which is a text, and a set of possibilities for performance, rather than a psyche. And considering *Macbeth* as a set of possibilities for performance brings us back to the witches and their significance, and to two key essays of the 1990s which focus on these spectacular, ambivalent figures. The first, by Stephen Greenblatt, considers the portrayal of the witches in *Macbeth* in relation to the broader discourses of witchcraft which were circulating in Shakespeare's era.

STEPHEN GREENBLATT

In 'Shakespeare Bewitched' (1993), Stephen Greenblatt rehearses a provocative list of possible charges against *Macbeth*, charges which are supported, he suggests, by the respective analyses of Peter Stallybrass and Janet Adelman. Greenblatt proposes that *Macbeth*, like the *Malleus maleficarum* [*The Hammer of Witches*], if with much greater literary power, could be indicted with using misogyny for political purposes, with undermining rather than strengthening the scepticism about witchcraft that could spread into a scepticism about royal authority, and with reinforcing, indirectly but potently, popular panics about demons and aiding and abetting the state harassment and execution of vulnerable, marginal women. Concluding his opening statement for the prosecution, Greenblatt asks: 'Why shouldn't we say that this play about evil is evil?'[33]

His vivid summation of the charges, however, then gives way to a case for the defence which offers five 'important and cogent reasons' for rejecting them. First, Macbeth 'is a self-conscious work of theatrical fiction', an entertainment which does not demand that it be taken for reality. Second, although the acting company known as the 'King's Men' presented it, this did not give the play the status of a royal pronouncement: the 'King's Men' spoke on behalf of no institution 'except the marginal ... institution of the theatre' which was 'somewhat disreputable ... precisely because it was the acknowledged house of fantasies'. Third, the play offers no advice about how to deal with witches on an official and legal level; it provides no approval of prosecution or execution, in contrast to, for example, Shakespeare's own 1 Henry VI, or The Witch of Edmonton (probably first performed 1621, published 1658) by Thomas Dekker (?1570–1632), John Ford (1586–after 1639), William Rowley (?1585–1626) and, possibly, John Webster (about 1578–about 1632). For instance, at the end of Macbeth, Malcolm does not announce that he will purge the nation of witches, although presumably it would have been easy enough to supply him with words to this effect. The witches 'simply disappear'. Fourth, the 'significance and power' of the witches in the play is deeply ambiguous; for instance, they are not essential to making things happen; the action of the play might have unfolded without them (a point made, as we saw in Chapter 3 of this Guide, by A. C. Bradley). Fifth, even if it could be shown – and this would be very difficult – that Macbeth added fuel to the flames of witch persecution, the play could not be blamed for it, any more than The Satanic Verses (1988) by Salman Rushdie can be blamed for the deaths in the riots that its publication provoked.

Greenblatt's exculpation of Macbeth leads him to a larger affirmation: it is 'important, in the interest of preserving the small breathing space of the imagination, to resist the recent tendency to conflate, or even to collapse into one another, aesthetics, ethics and politics'. But for Greenblatt, this does not mean that Macbeth – or any other text – has no social power, or that its only social power is the production of a particular kind of pleasure: while Macbeth could indeed be said to produce a particular kind of pleasure, this involves a 'representation of witches' that 'was only possible in and through a particularly fraught cultural negotiation with theological and political discourses that had a direct effect on the lives of men and women'. While the play cannot be reduced to its 'political and ethical consequences', it inevitably has consequences, even if they cannot easily be identified. The topic of witches – their nature, their power, their very existence – was a hotly contested one which affected public policy; the representation of witches on the public stage was necessarily part of that contest.

Greenblatt argues that witchcraft 'provided Shakespeare with a rich source of imaginative energy, a collective disturbance upon which he could draw to achieve powerful theatrical effects' But, according to classical and Renaissance literary theorists, such effects could only be achieved if this energy were combined with 'what Aristotle called *energeia*, the liveliness that comes when metaphors are set in action, when things are put vividly before the mind's eye, when language achieves visibility'. And this is what Shakespeare does in *Macbeth*. Early in the play, the problems that the topic of witchcraft posed in Shakespeare's time are set in action, put vividly before the mind's eye (and, in the theatre, the body's eye) in Banquo's questions and comments when he and Macbeth first meet the witches. Banquo initially asks 'What are these / So wither'd and so wild in their attire, / That look not like th' inhabitants o'th'earth, / And yet are on't?' (1.3.37–40), and Macbeth puts the question of their identity to them directly: 'Speak if you can. What are you?' (1.3.45), only to receive his own name in reply: 'All hail, Macbeth!' (1.3.46). Banquo then interrogates the witches directly himself: 'I'th'name of truth, / Are ye fantastical, or that indeed / Which outwardly ye show?' (1.3.50–2) – a question which, Greenblatt suggests, could sound 'slightly odd' since the 'outward show' of the witches has already seemed 'fantastical', as his earlier words show: 'You should be women, / And yet your beards forbid me to interpret / That you are so' (1.3.43–5). Greenblatt argues, however, that 'fantastical' refers here, not to the doubt about gender which is raised by the witches' 'equivocal appearance', but to a deeper doubt about whether they have an objective existence, outside the imaginings of the mind, and about what kind of existence that is, natural or supernatural.[34] Banquo tries to comprehend the witches in natural terms which would explain their appearance and disappearance – 'The earth hath bubbles, as the water has, / And these are of them' (1.3.77–8) – but this hardly settles the matter, and the issue of whether they are natural is raised again by Macbeth's words when they vanish: 'What seemed corporal [corporeal] [is] / Melted as breath into the wind' (1.3.79–80).

The uncertainties of this scene are also the uncertainties of theatre. *Macbeth* implicitly recognizes that both theatre and witchcraft inhabit 'the boundary between fantasy and reality, the border or membrane where the imagination and the corporeal world, figure and actuality, psychic disturbance and objective truth meet', and where the means by which they are supposedly policed – 'speech and sight' – are themselves ambiguous. These uncertainties are echoed and amplified in the rest of the play, which moves on that 'border between fantasy and reality', in 'a sickening betwixt-and-between' – Greenblatt echoes here L. C. Knights's phrase 'a sickening see-saw' – 'where a mental "image" has the uncanny power to produce bodily effects "against the use of nature", where Macbeth's "thought, whose murther yet is but fantastical" can so shake his being that "function / Is smother'd in surmise, and nothing is / But what is not" (1.3.138–41), where one mind is present to the innermost fantasies of another, where manhood threatens to vanish and murdered men walk, and blood cannot be washed off'. But the uncertainty about the nature and very existence of the witches means that they can neither be held responsible for these crossovers between fantasy and reality nor simply dismissed as fantastical or fraudulent: *Macbeth* 'achieves the remarkable effect of a nebulous infection, a bleeding of the demonic into the secular and the secular into the demonic'.

The most famous example of this 'bleeding' is Lady Macbeth's apparent attempt to summon the 'spirits / That tend on mortal thoughts' (1.3.37–8). In this soliloquy, she seems to regard demonic forces as real entities – 'substances' – and asks them to produce changes in her body: 'unsex me', 'fill me from the crown to the toe top-full / Of direst cruelty', 'Make thick my blood', 'take my milk for gall' (1.3.39–46). These substantial entities are also, however, 'sightless' – that is, invisible – and this differentiates them from the witches, who certainly seem to have some kind of visible earthly existence, even if its precise nature is difficult to determine. To call these spirits 'sightless', deny them corporeal visibility, is to link them with the metaphorical use of 'spirits' in the preceding soliloquy, where Lady Macbeth wishes to 'pour [her] spirits' into Macbeth's ear – and where she is talking, not about demonic spirits, but about the words she will use to persuade Macbeth to kill Duncan in order to win the throne. But the boundaries between a metaphorical and literal use of the term 'spirits' remain blurred: 'all her expressions of will and passion … strain towards bodily realization, even as they convey a psychic and hence invisible inwardness'. Although Lady Macbeth speaks metaphorically when she says that she will pour her spirits into her husband's ear, the play can convey an uncanny sense that she has done so literally; the influence she has gained over Macbeth can look as if her 'spirits' have invaded him. So a metaphorical term can take on an almost literal dimension. And the same can happen in reverse: the literal 'sightless substances' that Lady Macbeth invokes can also seem to be a metaphor for her desires.

To try to grasp 'the means by which Shakespeare achieves … "bleeding" – the mutual contamination of the secular and the demonic' – Greenblatt refers to a passage from what he sees as 'the greatest English contribution to the sceptical critique of witchcraft' – *The Discovery of Witchcraft* (1584) by Reginald Scot (about 1538–99), in which Scot mocks the supposedly marvellous powers of witches which are evoked by the ancient Roman poet Ovid (43 B.C.–A.D. 17/18). One of those marvellous powers is, as Scot puts it, the ability to 'go in and out at auger holes'[35] and the term 'auger hole' occurs in *Macbeth*, though it is not applied to the witches, but used by Donalbain when, after Duncan's murder, he speaks to Malcolm of the danger of their situation: 'What should be spoken here, where our fate / Hid in an auger-hole [in a cranny; in ambush], may rush and seize us?/ Let's away' (2.4.117–19). Here, Greenblatt contends, the 'auger hole has ceased to be an actual passageway, uncannily small and hence virtually invisible, for witches to pass through and has become a figure for the fear that lurks every-where in Macbeth's castle', and 'the Weird Sisters, of whose existence Malcolm and Donalbain are entirely unaware, have been translated into the abstraction to which their name is etymologically linked – fate'. This exemplifies an important general claim which Greenblatt makes:

■ The phantasmagorical horror of witchcraft, ridiculed by Scot, is redis-tributed by Shakespeare across the field of the play, shaping the repre-sentation of the state, of marriage, and, above all, of the psyche. When Lady Macbeth calls upon the 'spirits / That tend on mortal thoughts' to unsex her, when she directs the 'murdering ministers' to take her milk for gall, the terrifying intensity of her psychological malignity depends upon Shakespeare's deployment or – to borrow a term from [*The Art of English Poesy* (1589) by George Puttenham (1529–90)] – his 'translac-ing' of the ragged, filthy materials of inquisitorial credulity.[36]

Translacing is a mode of rhetorical redistribution in which the initial verbal elements remain partially visible even as they are woven into something new. Hence Lady Macbeth is not revealed to be a witch, yet the witches subsist as a tenebrous filament to which Lady Macbeth is obscurely but palpably linked.[37] □

It is this translacing that makes it impossible, in *Macbeth*, to separate the secular and the demonic, that works to suggest both that the witches may still be present even when they are not visible and that even when they are visible they may still be illusions. *Macbeth* seems to provide 'visible proof of the demonic in action' but this proof is 'maddeningly equivocal'. 'The "wayward" witches appear and disappear, and the language of the play subverts the illusory certainties of sight. The ambi-guities of demonic agency are never resolved, and its horror spreads like a mist through a murky landscape.'

Reginald Scot's sceptical approach to witchcraft involved firmly defining it as theatrical illusion, as fiction, as unequivocally imaginary. He believed that if it were understood in this way, it would lose its power over people's minds and free them to turn towards God. *Macbeth* also dramatizes the view that witchcraft may be a theatrical illusion; 'a self-conscious theatricality tinges all of the witches' appearances', and their prophecies to Macbeth can be seen as bad jokes. But the play does not use this theatricality to support an unequivocally sceptical approach to witchcraft; witchcraft is theatre, but this does not rob it of social power or mean that it is necessarily untrue. After all, 'Shakespeare was part of a profession that made its money manipulating images and playing with the double and doubtful senses of words'. It is only in Macbeth's most despairing moment that he sees the theatrical illusion as pathetically empty and as an image of the emptiness of life itself: 'Life's but a walking shadow, a poor player / That struts and frets his hour upon the stage, / And then is heard no more' (5.5.23–5):

■ The closing moments of the play invite us to recoil from this black hole just as they invite us to recoil from too confident and simple a celebration of the triumph of grace. For Shakespeare the presence of the theatrical in the demonic, as in every other realm of life, only intensifies the sense of an equivocal betwixt-and-between, for his theatre is the space where the fantastic and the bodily, *energia* and *energeia* touch. To conjure up such a theatre places Shakespeare in the position neither of the witchmonger nor the skeptic. It places him in the position of the witch.[38] □

Shakespeare, in *Macbeth*, thus performs witchcraft to conjure up – with a little help from another, probably Thomas Middleton – the witches who figure so largely in the play; and it is on those witches that Stephen Orgel's essay focuses.

STEPHEN ORGEL

In his lively, provocative essay '*Macbeth* and the Antic Round' (1999), Stephen Orgel points out that this is the only Shakespeare play in which 'witches and witchcraft are such an integral element of the plot'[39] and asks 'What is the relation between tragedy and the antic quality of the witches? Why does that antic quality keep increasing in size and importance in the stage history of the play from the seventeenth through the nineteenth century'.[40] Like Terry Eagleton, Orgel stresses the 'unsettling quality of the witches', not only in terms of gender, but also in the way in which they upset 'that sense of the deference Macbeth feels he owes to Duncan' and thus perhaps release into the play 'something [which it] both overtly denies and implicitly articulates: that there is no basis whatever for the values asserted on Duncan's behalf; that the primary characteristic of his rule, perhaps of any rule in the world of the play, is not order but rebellion'.[41]

Orgel also discusses the riddles, 'those verbal incarnations of the imperfect speakers the witches',[42] giving particular attention to the prophecy that 'none of woman born / Shall harm Macbeth' (4.1.95–7) and suggesting that Macbeth is an imperfect interpreter who takes the key word to be 'woman' – 'None of *woman* born / Shall harm Macbeth' (4.1.96–7) – whereas the crucial term is in fact 'born' – 'No man of woman *born* shall harm Macbeth'. Orgel suggests that the underlying assumption here is that 'a Caesarian section does not constitute birth' and contends that this is historically significant; whereas 'a vaginal birth would have been handled by women ... with no men present', 'surgery was a male prerogative': Macduff's 'surgical birth ... thus means, in Renaissance terms, that Macduff was brought to life by men, not women: carried by a woman, but made viable only through masculine intervention. Such a birth, all but invariably, involved the mother's death'.

Orgel relates this riddle to the more general question of the place of women in the world of *Macbeth* and the way in which they are represented as disruptive. For example, it seems significant that Malcolm offers, as the first of the qualities that make him a potentially better ruler than Macbeth, his virginity: 'I am yet / Unknown to woman' (4.3.126–7); this makes him free of feminine interference. And Lady Macduff, the one 'good' woman in the play, constitutes a threat to her husband's project of overturning Macbeth from which he has to rip himself by deserting her and his children. Macduff implicitly affirms the claims of masculine fraternity. As Orgel provocatively asks: 'Is the answer to Malcolm's question about why Macduff left his family, "Because it's *you* I really love"?'

In this 'claustrophobic', 'astonishingly male-oriented and misogynistic play', the witches' scenes 'open up ... a subversive and paradoxical space' for women. Paradoxes are also embodied in Lady Macbeth, in her desire to 'unsex' herself, in her apparent readiness to dash out her baby's brains and, above all, in her dominance over her husband. This dominance is exercised within a marriage which is, in Orgel's view, 'one of the scariest things' in *Macbeth*,[43] but is also, 'as Shakespearian marriages go ... a good one: intense, intimate, loving'.[44] Orgel finds that 'probably the most frightening thing in the play is the genuine power of Lady Macbeth's mind – not just her powers of analysis and persuasion, but her intimate apprehension of her husband's deepest desires, her perfect understanding of what combination of arguments will prove irresistible to the masculine ego: "Be a man," and "If you really loved me you'd do it"'. But when he stops being, in her terms, a child and becomes a 'man', she loses her power over him and her own potency. 'Her own power was only her power over the child, the child she was willing to destroy to gain the power of a man'.[45]

Published almost at the end of the twentieth century, Orgel's essay demonstrates the irreverent, challenging approach to *Macbeth* – and to Shakespeare more generally – which had developed since the 1960s.

Whereas the critics of the early and mid-twentieth century had, with varying degrees of subtlety, interpreted the play in terms of its dominant antitheses, as a drama in which evil was pitted against good, the critics we have considered in this chapter and in Chapters 5 and 6 have, in their different ways, interrogated those antitheses, and suggested how they are called into question by the language and action of the play itself and by an awareness of its historical contexts. As the world moved into the twenty-first century, *Macbeth*, unseamed from the nave to the chops, could never look quite the same again.

Conclusion: The Twenty-first Century and Future Directions

In this Guide, we have explored key examples of essential criticism of *Macbeth* from the seventeenth century to the end of the twentieth century. We have examined interpretations which approach the play from a wide variety of angles – for example, character, tragedy, imagery, philosophy, history, politics, psychology, psychoanalysis and feminism – and we have seen that each of these approaches has yielded insights, intriguing suggestions and topics for further debate. Most critics today see criticism as fruitfully interminable – it can never come to an end, never deliver the complete, final and definitive interpretation of a text – and criticism of Shakespeare seems an especially vivid demonstration of this. We know there is much more to say about *Macbeth*. In what directions might *Macbeth* criticism develop in the early twenty-first century?

It looks likely that the awareness of the contradictions and ambivalences of the play which emerged in the 1980s will persist for some time, and will continue to generate interpretations, as the earlier twentieth-century view of the play as a poetic whole did. This raises the question of whether it is possible – or desirable – to try to put *Macbeth* together again; it would be interesting, at the very least, to aim to produce readings of the play which took full account of its contradictions and ambivalences, and of the fact that it is probably not wholly by Shakespeare, but which nonetheless sought to show that it did form a unity which is greater than its many tendencies to fracture and fissure. Such readings could not simply return to Wilson Knight or L. C. Knights, though they may well draw on their insights; but any plausible case for the unity of *Macbeth* would have to find new terms and perspectives.

The historical and 'new historicist' approaches to *Macbeth* which emerged and became strongly influential later in the twentieth century, and which are often linked with an awareness of the contradictions and ambivalences of the play, are also likely to endure. The historical approach – exemplified in this Guide by Michael Hawkins – aims to relate the play to what historical research, based on primary sources, can tell us about aspects of Shakespeare's time – the way people thought about politics, for instance. The 'new historicist' approach, associated above all with Stephen Greenblatt, rejects the positivist assumption that there are 'facts' of history which can be ascertained and related to literary texts – since historical facts, and the relationships between historical facts and literary texts are after all, like literary texts themselves, only debatable interpretations – and links the literary texts, in ways that can be surprising, to a range of sometimes unexpected historical details and documents which occasionally seem to be selected for the interpretive opportunities they offer rather than in accordance with any more rigorous criteria of relevance. This provocative approach has produced many rewarding results but has also licensed speculation which has sometimes ranged a little too freely; it seems possible that a stronger sense of responsibility to historical evidence and a greater sense of criteria of relevance will now grow, which acknowledges that such evidence is never simply 'there' and never simply 'reflected' in the play, but which nevertheless scrupulously tries to assess its validity and reliability and the extent and nature of its possible relationships to Macbeth. Such a development is likely to be accompanied by a renewed sense of the distinctiveness of literary texts; as we saw in the final chapter of this Guide, Greenblatt himself does not think that Macbeth is a text like any other but holds that it can have effects that other texts cannot produce and cannot simply be indicted in the court of political correctness.

A sense of the political dimensions of the play, in relation both to the Jacobean era and to our own, is also likely to continue – the Introduction to this Guide suggested how it resonates with some of the urgent political issues of the early twenty-first century. But it is important to mark the difference between the political readings of the play, such as Alan Sinfield's, which surfaced provocatively in the 1980s, and those which might emerge today. Critics such as Sinfield challenged a dominant interpretative consensus which ignored politics or took implicitly, and sometimes explicitly, conservative positions; now left-wing political readings of Macbeth have become dominant. There is therefore scope for new readings which would take a different political position, without merely reiterating older interpretations. One prototype of such a reading occurs in Robert Headlam Wells's account of Macbeth in Shakespeare on Masculinity (2000); Wells takes issue with the interpretations of Terry Eagleton and Alan Sinfield and argues that '[l]ike Virgil's Aeneid, Macbeth presents an agonistic vision that shows 'the paradox of men defending civilized principles with heroic action'. Wells calls this vision 'cultural pluralism', taking the term from John Gray's study of the philosopher Isaiah Berlin (1909–97). The 'cultural pluralist' view is that 'human value systems ... are inherently conflictual';[1] they conflict, not only with one another, but also within themselves, and some of these conflicts cannot be resolved because they are incommensurable – the same standard of judgement cannot be applied to them and one value may contradict another. Wells concludes that 'a sense of human values as inherently conflictual ... seems to be one of the fundamental ordering principles of Shakespeare's plays' and that

Macbeth is 'neither a defence nor an "arraignment" of James's rule', but – again like Virgil's *Aeneid* – 'an anatomy of heroic values that offers no solution to the conundrum it dramatizes'.[2]

Wells's interpretation of *Macbeth* moves in the zone in which politics merges into, and sometimes clashes with, philosophy. The philosophical aspect of the play is one which merits more critical attention and which could provide a further fruitful source for twenty-first century criticism. *Macbeth* is not as obviously 'philosophical' a play as *Hamlet*, but it clearly poses, in dramatic form, key philosophical questions about, for example, the nature of human agency, free will and determinism, the meaning and purpose of human existence, and epistemology – how we know and what we can know. There is certainly room for future readings which would relate *Macbeth* to those abstract philosophical questions without sacrificing either the particularity of the dramatic text or the rigour of philosophical thought. Another way of approaching the philosophical aspect of the play would be to relate it to the concepts and writings of particular thinkers. Simon Palfrey, for example, adopts this approach in 'Macbeth and Kierkegaard' in *Shakespeare Survey 57*; this essay treats the Danish existentialist philosopher Søren Kierkegaard (1813–55), and the Macbeth whose character we may infer from Shakespeare's play, as 'mutual illuminators' who shed light on each other in a complex and constantly shifting interplay of ideas and images.[3]

There is, then, much scope for future criticism of *Macbeth*, but it will always return – and, to ensure continued critical vitality, it should always return – to the power, the pace, of the play itself – without forgetting that the 'play itself' is never a pure essence, and is always multiply mediated. It is a play which sweeps reader or audience into a vortex of toil and trouble, of bravery and brutality, of strangely compelling witches and wives, of naked new born babes and old men with so much blood in them, of sleep-murder and nightmare, of bloody instructions and daggers sheathed with gore, of yesterdays that light our ways to death and brief candles that flicker out, of walking woods and men not born of women, and of a time of freedom that is marked by a severed head; a play which always leaves us with enigmas which we must try to understand – this is where criticism begins – but which can never be fully resolved.

Notes

INTRODUCTION

1 See A. C. Bradley, *Shakespearean Tragedy: Lectures on* Hamlet, Othello, King Lear, Macbeth, St Martin's Library (London: Macmillan, 1957), p. 278: *Macbeth* 'is the most vehement, the most concentrated, perhaps we may say the most tremendous, of the tragedies'; S. T. Coleridge, *Lectures and Notes on Shakespeare and Other Dramatists* (London: Oxford University Press, 1931), p. 205: 'the movement throughout is the most rapid of all Shakespeare's plays ... there is an entire absence of comedy'; Stephen Greenblatt (ed.), *The Norton Shakespeare Based on the Oxford Edition: Tragedies* (New York and London: W. W. Norton, 1997), p. 784: 'Of all Shakespeare's tragedies, *Macbeth* has always seemed the most topical'; David Scott Kastan, *Shakespeare After Theory* (London and New York: Routledge, 1999), p. 165: '*Macbeth* is at once the most violent of the major tragedies and the one whose violence has been most securely recuperated by criticism'.

CHAPTER ONE

1 Stanley Wells and Gary Taylor (eds), William Shakespeare, *The Complete Works: Compact Edition* (Oxford: Clarendon Press, 1990), p. 975.
2 Kenneth Muir (ed.), William Shakespeare, *Macbeth* (London and New York: Routledge, 1987), p. xx.
3 Stephen Greenblatt (ed.), *The Norton Shakespeare, Based on the Oxford Edition: Tragedies* (London and New York: Norton, 1997), p. 1066.
4 Muir (1987), pp. xv, xvii.
5 Muir (1987), p. 172.
6 Muir (1987), p. xix.
7 Muir (1987), p. xv.
8 Muir (1987), p. xvi.
9 Muir (1987), p. xvi.
10 Muir (1987), p. xvi.
11 Kathleen McCluskie, 'Humane Statute and the Gentle Weal: Historical Reading and Historical Allegory', in Peter Holland (ed.), *Shakespeare Survey: An Annual Survey of Shakespeare Studies and Production: 57: 'Macbeth' and Its Afterlife* (Cambridge: Cambridge University Press, 2004), p. 5.
12 McCluskie (2004), p. 6.
13 Brian Vickers (ed.), *Shakespeare: The Critical Heritage: Volume I: 1623–1692* (London and Boston: Routledge and Kegan Paul, 1974), p. 5. Hereafter referred to as 'Vickers 1'.
14 Peter Thomson, 'English Renaissance and Restoration Theatre', in John Russell Brown (ed.), *The Oxford Illustrated History of the Theatre* (Oxford and New York: Oxford University Press, 1995), pp. 203–4.
15 Phyllis Hartnoll, *The Theatre: A Concise History*, 3rd edn updated by Enoch Brater (London: Thames and Hudson, 1998), p. 114.
16 Vickers 1, p. 5.
17 Ian Ousby (ed.), *The Wordsworth Companion to Literature in English* (Ware, Herts: Wordsworth, 1992), p. 230.

18 Christopher Spencer (ed.), *Davenant's Macbeth from the Yale Manuscript: An Edition, with a Discussion of the Relation of Davenant's Text to Shakespeare's* (New Haven: Yale University Press, 1961), p. 94.

19 Spencer (1961), p. 93.

20 Spencer (1961), pp. 113–14.

21 Spencer (1961), p. 89.

22 Spencer (1961), p. 106.

23 Spencer (1961), p. 111.

24 Spencer (1961), p. 120.

25 Spencer (1961), p. 120.

26 Spencer (1961), p. 129.

27 Spencer (1961), p. 132.

28 Spencer (1961), p. 132.

29 Spencer (1961), p. 145.

30 Nicholas Rowe, 'Some Account of the Life of Mr William Shakespeare', in D. Nichol Smith (ed.), *Shakespeare Criticism: A Selection 1623–1740*, World's Classics Series (London: Oxford University Press, 1958), p. 32.

31 Rowe (1958), p. 31.

32 Rowe (1958), p. 32.

33 Rowe (1958), p. 36.

34 Rowe (1958), p. 37.

35 Bertrand H. Bronson and Jean O'Meara (eds), *Selections from Johnson on Shakespeare* (New Haven and London: Yale University Press, 1986), p. 275.

36 Bronson and O'Meara (1986), pp. 254–5.

37 Bronson and O'Meara (1986), p. 258.

38 Bronson and O'Meara (1986), p. 270.

39 Bronson and O'Meara (1986), p. 273.

40 Bronson and O'Meara (1986), p. 270.

41 Bronson and O'Meara (1986), pp. 263–4.

42 Bronson and O'Meara (1986), p. 264.

43 Bronson and O'Meara (1986), p. 267.

44 William Richardson, *A Philosophical Analysis and Illustration of Some of Shakespeare's Remarkable Characters* (London: J. Murray; Edinburgh: W. Creech, 1774), p. 42.

45 Richardson (1774), p. 39.

46 Richardson (1774), p. 41.

47 Richardson (1774), p. 47.

48 Richardson (1774), p. 48.

49 Richardson (1774), p. 58.

50 Richardson (1774), pp. 72–3.

51 Richardson (1774), p. 76.

52 Richardson (1774), p. 80.

53 Richardson (1774), p. 85.

54 Richardson (1774), pp. 87–8.

55 Richardson (1774), p. 43.

56 Whately, Thomas, *Remarks on Some of the Characters of Shakespeare* (London: Frank Cass, 1970), p. 25.

57 Whately (1970), pp. 18–19.

58 Whately (1970), pp. 25, 27.

59 Whately (1970), p. 28.

60 Whately (1970), pp. 119–20.

61 Whately (1970), p. 89.

62 Whately (1970), p. 54.

63 Whately (1970), pp. 56, 57.

64 Whately (1970), p. 67.

65 Whately (1970), pp. 102–3.

66 Brian Vickers (ed.), *Shakespeare: The Critical Heritage: Volume 6: 1774–1801* (London, Boston and Henley: Routledge and Kegan Paul, 1981), p. 430. Hereafter referred to as 'Vickers 6'.

67 Vickers 6, p. 431.

68 Vickers 6, p. 435.

69 Vickers 6, p. 435.

70 Vickers 6, p. 448.

71 Vickers 6, p. 448.

72 Vickers 6, p. 449.

73 Vickers 6, p. 449.

74 Vickers 6, p. 451.

75 Vickers 6, p. 454.

CHAPTER TWO

1 For Pope's 'Preface', see Brian Vickers (ed.), *Shakespeare: The Critical Heritage: Volume 2: 1693–1733* (London and Boston: Routledge and Kegan Paul, 1974), pp. 403–15. Hazlitt quotes the third and fourth paragraphs of Pope's 'Preface'.

2 William Hazlitt, *Characters of Shakespeare's Plays* (London: Oxford University Press, 1939), p. xxviii.

3 Hazlitt (1939), p. xxxvii.

4 Hazlitt (1939), p. 13.

5 Hazlitt (1939), pp. 13–14.

6 Hazlitt (1939), p. 14.

7 Hazlitt (1939), p. 15.

8 Hazlitt (1939), p. 15.

9 Hazlitt (1939), p. 17.

10 Hazlitt (1939), p. 17.

11 Hazlitt (1939), p. 17.

12 Terry Eagleton, *William Shakespeare* (Oxford: Blackwell, 1986), p. 2.

13 Hazlitt (1939), p. 19.

14 G. Wilson Knight, *The Imperial Theme: Further Interpretations of Shakespeare's Tragedies Including the Roman Plays* (London: Methuen, 1961), p. 125.

15 Hazlitt (1939), p. 20.

16 Samuel Taylor Coleridge, *Lectures and Notes on Shakespeare and Other Dramatists* (London: Oxford University Press, 1931), p. 205.

17 Coleridge (1931), p. 205.

18 Coleridge (1931), p. 205.

19 Coleridge (1931), p. 215.

20 Coleridge (1931), p. 216.

21 Coleridge (1931), pp. 205–6.

22 Oscar James Campbell, 'Shakespeare and the "New Critics" ', in James G. McManaway, Giles E. Dawson, Edwin E. Willoughby (eds), *Joseph Quincy Adams:* Memorial Studies (Washington: The Folger Shakespeare Library, 1948), p. 227.

23 Coleridge (1931), p. 206.

24 Coleridge (1931), pp. 213–14.

25 Coleridge (1931), p. 207.

26 Thomas de Quincey, 'On the Knocking at the Gate in *Macbeth*', in D. Nichol Smith (ed.), *Shakespeare Criticism: A Selection 1623–1740* (London: Oxford University Press, 1958), p. 331.

27 De Quincey (1958), p. 334.

28 De Quincey (1958), pp. 334–5.

29 De Quincey (1958), p. 335.
30 Smith (1958), pp. 335–6.
31 Smith (1958), p. 334, note 1.
32 Anna Jameson, *Characteristics of Women, Moral, Poetical, and Historical* (London: Saunders and Otley, 1833), vol. 2, pp. 300–1.
33 Jameson (1833), p. 302.
34 Jameson (1833), p. 303.
35 Jameson (1833), p. 304.
36 Jameson (1833), p. 305.
37 Jameson (1833), p. 303.
38 Jameson (1833), p. 309.
39 Jameson (1833), p. 313.
40 Jameson (1833), p. 315.
41 Jameson (1833), p. 316.
42 W. E. Channing, 'Remarks on the Character and Writings of John Milton', in *People's Edition of the Entire Works of W. E. Channing, D.D.*, 2 vols, published under the care of the Rev. R.E.B., MacLellan (London: Simms and McIntyre, 1849), vol. 2, p. 8. In this edition, 'not' is in standard type rather than italics.
43 Jameson (1833), p. 320.
44 Jameson (1833), p. 322.
45 Jameson (1833), p. 324.
46 Jameson (1833), pp. 324–5.
47 Edward Dowden, *Shakspere: A Critical Study of His Mind and Art* (London: Kegan Paul, Trench, Trübner, reprint, about 1918, of 3rd edn of 1877), p. 224.
48 Dowden (1918), p. 226.
49 Dowden (1918), p. 227.
50 Dowden (1918), p. 245.
51 Dowden (1918), p. 246.
52 Hazlitt (1939), p. 17.
53 Coleridge (1931), p. 207.
54 Dowden (1918), p. 247.
55 Dowden (1918), p. 250.
56 Dowden (1918), p. 251.
57 Dowden (1918), p. 252.
58 Dowden (1918), p. 254.
59 Dowden (1918), p. 255.
60 Dowden (1918), p. 256.

CHAPTER THREE

1 A. C. Bradley, *Shakespearean Tragedy: Lectures on* Hamlet, Othello, King Lear, Macbeth, St Martin's Library (London: Macmillan, 1957), p. 3.
2 Bradley (1957), p. 3.
3 Bradley (1957), p. 6.
4 Bradley (1957), p. 7.
5 Bradley (1957), p. 8.
6 Bradley (1957), p. 16.
7 Bradley (1957), p. 24.
8 Bradley (1957), p. 25.
9 Bradley (1957), pp. 27–8.
10 Bradley (1957), p. 29.
11 Bradley (1957), p. 278.

12   Bradley (1957), p. 281.
13   Bradley (1957), p. 295.
14   Bradley (1957), p. 299.
15   Bradley (1957), p. 296.
16   Bradley (1957), pp. 296–7.
17   Sigmund Freud, *The Interpretation of Dreams*, The Pelican Freud Library vol. 4 (Harmondsworth: Penguin, 1977), p. 368.
18   Sigmund Freud, 'Some Character-Types Met With in Psycho-Analytical Work', in John Strachey and Anna Freud (eds) *The Complete Psychological Works of Sigmund Freud*, vol. 14, 1914–1916 (London: The Hogarth Press and the Institute of Psycho-Analysis, 1957), p. 320.
19   Freud (1957), p. 321.
20   Freud (1957), p. 319.
21   Freud (1957), p. 320.
22   Freud (1957), p. 322.
23   Freud (1957), p. 321.
24   Freud (1957), p. 323.
25   Freud (1957), pp. 322–3.
26   Freud (1957), p. 323.
27   Freud (1957), p. 323.
28   Wain (1974), p. 137.
29   G. Wilson Knight, *The Imperial Theme: Further Interpretations of Shakespeare's Tragedies Including the Roman Plays* (London: Methuen, 1961), p. 130.
30   Caroline F. E. Spurgeon, *Shakespeare's Imagery and What It Tells Us* (Cambridge: Cambridge University Press, 1952), p. 326.
31   Spurgeon (1952), p. 332.
32   G. Wilson Knight, *The Wheel of Fire: Interpretations of Shakespearean Tragedy With Three New Essays*, University Paperbacks series (Methuen: London, 1960), p. 1.
33   Knight (1960), p. 14.
34   Knight (1960), p. 140.
35   Knight (1960), p. 144.
36   Knight (1961), p. 125.
37   Knight (1961), p. 126.
38   Knight (1961), p. 141.
39   Knight (1961), p. 142.
40   Knight (1961), p. 145.
41   Knight (1961), p. 153.
42   Bradley (1957), p. 422.
43   Brian Vickers (ed.), *Shakespeare: The Critical Heritage: Volume 6: 1774–1801* (London, Boston and Henley: Routledge and Kegan Paul, 1981), p. 409.
44   L. C. Knights, 'How Many Children Had Lady Macbeth? An Essay in the Theory and Practice of Shakespearean Criticism?', in *Explorations: Essays in Criticism Mainly on the Literature of the Seventeenth Century* (Harmondsworth: Penguin Books in association with Chatto and Windus, 1964), p. 13.
45   Knights (1964), p. 16.
46   Knights (1964), p. 22.
47   Knights (1964), p. 28.
48   Knights (1964), p. 25.
49   Knights (1964), p. 30.
50   Knights (1964), p. 32.
51   Knights (1964), p. 33.
52   Knights (1964), p. 33.
53   Knights (1964), p. 40.

54   Knight (1961), p. 145.
55   William Empson, *Seven Types of Ambiguity* (Harmondsworth: Penguin Books in association with Chatto and Windus, 1965), p. 18.
56   Empson (1965), pp. 19–20.
57   Empson (1965), p. 20, note 1.
58   Empson (1965), p. 48.
59   Empson (1965), pp. 49–50.
60   Empson (1965), p. 201.
61   Empson (1965), p. 201.

CHAPTER FOUR

1   E. M. W. Tillyard, *Shakespeare's History Plays* (London: Chatto and Windus, 1944), p. 315.
2   Tillyard (1944), p. 316.
3   Tillyard (1944), p. 317.
4   Henry N. Paul, *The Royal Play of Macbeth: When, Why and How It Was Written by Shakespeare* (New York: Macmillan, 1950), p. 41.
5   Quoted Paul (1950), p. 136.
6   Paul (1950), p. 149.
7   Paul (1950), p. 195.
8   Kenneth Muir (ed.), *Macbeth* (London and New York: Routledge, 1987), p. xxvii.
9   Eugene M. Waith, 'Manhood and Valor in Two Shakespearean Tragedies', *ELH: A Journal of English Literary History*, vol. 17, no. 4 (December 1950), p. 263.
10   Waith (1950), p. 262.
11   Waith (1950), p. 266.
12   Waith (1950), p. 268.
13   Cleanth Brooks, 'The Naked Babe and the Cloak of Manliness', in *The Well Wrought Urn: Studies in the Structure of Poetry* (London: Dennis Dobson, 1949), pp. 45–6.
14   Brooks (1949), p. 37.
15   Brooks (1949), p. 27.
16   Oscar James Campbell, 'Shakespeare and the "New Critics"', in James G. McManaway, Giles E. Dawson and Edwin E. Willoughby (eds), *Joseph Quincy Adams Memorial Studies* (Washington: The Folger Shakespeaer Library, 1948), p. 90.
17   Brooks (1949), p. 42.
18   Brooks (1949), p. 43.
19   Brooks (1949), p. 43.
20   Brooks (1949), p. 38.
21   Brooks (1949), p. 37.
22   Brooks (1949), p. 42.
23   Brooks (1949), p. 38.
24   Brooks (1949), p. 42.
25   Caroline F. E. Spurgeon, *Shakespeare's Imagery and What It Tells Us* (Cambridge: Cambridge University Press, 1952), p. 326.
26   Brooks (1949), p. 32.
27   Brooks (1949), p. 33.
28   Brooks (1949), p. 36.
29   Brooks (1949), p. 43.
30   See G. Wilson Knight, *The Imperial Theme: Further Interpretations of Shakespeare's Tragedies Including the Roman Plays* (London: Methuen, 1961), p. 141; L. C. Knights, 'How Many Children Had Lady Macbeth? An Essay in the Theory and Practice of Shakespearean Criticism', in *Explorations: Essays in Criticism Mainly on the Literature of the*

Seventeenth Century (Harmondsworth: Penguin Books in association with Chatto and Windus, 1964), p. 33.

31   Brooks (1949), p. 43.
32   Brooks (1949), p. 44.
33   Campbell (1948), p. 85.
34   Campbell (1948), p. 88.
35   Campbell (1948), pp. 89–90.
36   Campbell (1948), p. 89.
37   Campbell (1948), p. 90.
38   Campbell (1948), p. 91.
39   Helen Gardner, *The Business of Criticism* (Oxford: Clarendon Press,1974), p. 53.
40   Brooks (1947), p. 27.
41   Gardner (1959), pp. 59–60.
42   Gardner (1959), p. 61.
43   L. C. Knights, *Some Shakespearean Themes* (London: Chatto and Windus, 1959), p. 17.
44   Knights (1959), p. 18.
45   Knights (1959), p. 18.
46   Knights (1959), p. 19.
47   Knights (1959), p. 19.
48   Knights (1964), p. 29.
49   Knights (1959), p. 120.
50   Knights (1959), p. 133.
51   Knights (1959), p. 134.
52   Knights (1959), p. 136.
53   Knights (1959), pp. 139, 140.
54   Knights (1959), p. 138.
55   Knights (1959), p. 141.
56   Jan Kott, *Shakespeare Our Contemporary*, trans. Boleslaw Taborski (London: Methuen, 1965), p. 74.
57   Kott (1965), p. 74.
58   Kott (1965), p. 76.
59   Bradley (1957), p. 301.
60   Knights (1959), p. 141.
61   Kott (1965), pp. 71, 72.
62   Wilbur Sanders, *The Dramatist and the Received Idea: Studies in the Plays of Marlowe and Shakespeare* (Cambridge: Cambridge University Press, 1968), p. 254.
63   Quoted Sanders (1968), p. 253.
64   Sanders (1968), p. 293.
65   Sanders (1968), p. 290.
66   Sanders (1968), p. 291.
67   Sanders (1968), p. 292.
68   Bradley (1957), p. 303.
69   Sanders (1968), p. 292.
70   Sanders (1968), p. 293.
71   Sanders (1968), p. 294.
72   Knights (1959), p. 136.
73   Sanders (1968), p. 295.
74   Sanders (1968), p. 296.
75   Sanders (1968), p. 305.
76   Sanders (1968), p. 306.
77   Sanders (1968), p. 307.
78   Knights (1964), p. 22.

CHAPTER FIVE

1 Harry Berger Jr, 'The Early Scenes of *Macbeth*: Preface to a New Interpretation', in Peter Erikson (ed.), *Making Trifles of Terrors: Redistributing Complicities in Shakespeare* (Stanford: Stanford University Press, 1997), p. 72.

2 Berger (1997), p. 75.

3 Berger (1997), p. 74.

4 Berger (1997), p. 77.

5 Roy Walker, *The Time Is Free* (London: Andrew Dakers, 1949), pp. 31–2.

6 Berger (1997), p. 78.

7 Walker (1949), pp. 34–5.

8 Berger (1997), p. 81.

9 Berger (1997), p. 82.

10 Berger (1997), p. 89.

11 Berger (1997), p. 90.

12 Berger (1997), p. 92.

13 [Berger's Note:] Marcel Mauss, *The Gift: Forms and Functions of Exchange*, trans. Ian Cunnison (New York: Norton, 1972), p. 72.

14 Berger (1997), p. 93.

15 Berger (1997), p. 96.

16 Michael Hawkins, 'History, Politics and *Macbeth*', in John Russell Brown (ed.), *Focus on Macbeth* (London, Boston and Henley: Routledge and Kegan Paul, 1982), p. 164.

17 Hawkins (1982), p. 164.

18 Hawkins (1982), p. 165.

19 Hawkins (1982), p. 168.

20 Hawkins (1982), p. 165.

21 Hawkins (1982), p. 165.

22 Hawkins (1982), pp. 165–6.

23 Wilbur Sanders, *The Dramatist and the Received Idea: Studies in the Plays of Marlowe and Shakespeare* (Cambridge: Cambridge University Press, 1968), p. 295.

24 Malcolm Evans, *Signifying Nothing: Truth's True Contents in Shakespeare's Text*, 2nd edn (New York, London, Toronto, Sydney, Tokyo: Harvester Wheatsheaf, 1989), p. 122.

25 Hawkins (1982), p. 175.

26 Walker (1949), p. 39.

27 Hawkins (1982), p. 177.

28 E. M. W. Tillyard, *Shakespeare's History Plays* (London: Chatto and Windus, 1944), p. 317.

29 Kenneth Muir (ed.), *Macbeth*, (London and New York: Routledge, 1987), p. 173.

30 Muir (1987), p. 171.

31 Muir (1987), pp. 171–2.

32 Peter Stallybrass, '*Macbeth* and Witchcraft', in John Russell Brown (ed.) *Focus on Macbeth* (London, Boston and Henley: Routledge and Kegan Paul, 1982), p. 195.

33 Stallybrass (1982), p. 198.

34 Stallybrass (1982), p. 198.

35 Stallybrass (1982), p. 199.

36 Stallybrass (1982), p. 202.

37 Stallybrass (1982), p. 205.

38 Stephen Booth, *King Lear, Macbeth, Indefinition, and Tragedy* (New Haven and London: Yale University Press, 1983).

39 Booth (1983), p. 86.

40 Booth (1983), p. 91.

41 Booth (1983), p. 97.

42 Booth (1983), p. 97.

43 Booth (1983), p. 98.

44 Booth (1983), p. 105.

45   Booth (1983), p. 106.
46   Booth (1983), p. 106.
47   Booth (1983), p. 106.
48   Booth (1983), p. 107.
49   Booth (1983), p. 112.
50   Booth (1983), p. 115.
51   Booth (1983), p. 117.
52   James L. Calderwood, *If It Were Done:* Macbeth *and Tragic Action* (Amherst: University of Massachusetts Press, 1986), p. ix.
53   Calderwood (1986), p. x.
54   Calderwood (1986), p. 4.
55   Calderwood (1986), p. 7.
56   Calderwood (1986), p. 11.
57   Calderwood (1986), p. 12.
58   Calderwood (1986), p. 19.
59   Calderwood (1986), p. 26.
60   Calderwood (1986), p. 27.
61   Calderwood (1986), p. 29.
62   Calderwood (1986), p. 43.
63   Calderwood (1986), p. 44.
64   Calderwood (1986), p. 45.
65   Calderwood (1986), p. 142, note 8.
66   Calderwood (1986), p. 98.
67   Calderwood (1986), p. 100.
68   Calderwood (1986), p. 103.
69   Alan Sinfield, *Faultlines: Cultural Materialism and the Politics of Dissident Reading* (Oxford: Clarendon Press, 1992), p. 95.
70   Walker (1949), p. 11.
71   G. K. Hunter (ed.), *Macbeth* (Harmondsworth: Penguin, 1967), pp. 9–10.
72   Sinfield (1992), p. 98.
73   Sinfield (1992), p. 98.
74   Sinfield (1992), p. 99.
75   Sinfield (1992), p. 106.
76   Sinfield (1992), p. 108.

CHAPTER SIX

1   Catherine Belsey, *Critical Practice* (London: Methuen, 1980), p. 89.
2   Belsey (1980), p. 89.
3   Catherine Belsey, *The Subject of Tragedy: Identity and Difference in Renaissance Drama* (London and New York: Methuen, 1985), pp. 47–8.
4   Terence Eagleton, *Shakespeare and Society: Critical Studies in Shakespearean Drama* (London: Chatto and Windus, 1967), p. 137.
5   Eagleton (1967), p. 134.
6   Eagleton (1967), pp. 137–8.
7   Eagleton (1967), p. 138.
8   Terry Eagleton, *William Shakespeare*, Rereading Literature series (Oxford: Blackwell, 1986), p. 2.
9   Eagleton (1986), p. 2.
10   Eagleton (1986), p. 4.
11   Eagleton (1986), p. 6.
12   Eagleton (1986), p. 4.
13   Eagleton (1986), p. 7.

14   Malcolm Evans, *Signifying Nothing: Truth's True Contents in Shakespeare's Texts*, 2nd edn (New York, London, Toronto, Sydney, Tokyo: Harvester Wheatsheaf, 1989), p. 114.
15   Kenneth Muir (ed.), *Macbeth* (London and New York: Routledge, 1987), p. 7, note 20.
16   Evans (1989), p. 117.
17   L. C. Knights, *Explorations: Essays in Criticism, Mainly on the Literature of the Seventeenth Century* (Harmondsworth: Penguin Books in association with Chatto and Windus, 1964), p. 32.

CHAPTER SEVEN

1   Coppélia Kahn, *Man's Estate: Masculine Identity in Shakespeare* (Berkeley, Los Angeles, London: University of California Press, 1981), p. 184, note 32.
2   Kahn (1981), p. 179.
3   Kahn (1981), p. 176.
4   Kahn (1981), p. 182.
5   Kahn (1981), p. 182.
6   Kahn (1981), p. 183.
7   Kahn (1981), p. 185.
8   Kahn (1981), p. 186.
9   Kahn (1981), p. 187.
10   Kahn (1981), p. 188.
11   Kahn (1981), p. 190.
12   Kahn (1981), p. 191.
13   Kahn (1981), p. 192.
14   Kahn (1981), p. 2.
15   Kahn (1981), p. 189.
16   Kahn (1981), p. 184, note 32.
17   Marilyn French, *Shakespeare's Division of Experience* (London: Cape, 1982), p. 243.
18   Kahn (1981), p. 175.
19   French (1982), p. 243.
20   French (1982), p. 247.
21   French (1982), p. 248.
22   French (1982), p. 250.
23   Janet Adelman, *Suffocating Mothers: Fantasies of Maternal Origin in Shakespeare's Plays, Hamlet to* The Tempest (New York and London: Routledge, 1992), p. 131.
24   Adelman (1992), pp. 135, 315–16, note 11.
25   Adelman (1992), p. 135.
26   Adelman (1992), p. 136.
27   Adelman (1992), p. 137.
28   Adelman (1992), p. 139.
29   Adelman (1992), p. 140.
30   Adelman (1982), p. 145.
31   Adelman (1982), p. 144.
32   G. Wilson Knight, *The Imperial Theme: Further Interpretations of Shakespeare's Tragedies Including the Roman Plays* (London: Methuen, 1961), p. 145.
33   Stephen Greenblatt, 'Shakespeare Bewitched', in Jeffrey N. Cox and Larry J. Reynolds (eds), *New Historical Literary Study: Essays on Reproducing Texts, Representing History* (Princeton, New Jersey: Princeton University Press, 1993), p. 111.
34   Greenblatt (1993), p. 123.
35   Quoted Greenblatt (1993), p. 117.
36   [*Greenblatt's Note:*] Puttenham introduces the term in an account of the rhetorical figure of 'Traductio, or the Translacer', 'which is when ye turn and tranlace [sic] a word

into many sundry shapes as the Tailor doth his garment, & after that sort do play with him in your dittie', *Art of English Poetry* (Menston: Scolar Press Facsimile, 1968), p. 170.

37   Greenblatt (1993), p. 125.

38   Greenblatt (1993), p. 127.

39   Stephen Orgel, 'Macbeth and the Antic Round', in Stanley Wells (ed.), *Shakespeare Survey: An Annual Survey of Shakespeare Studies and Production: 52: Shakespeare and the Globe* (Cambridge: Cambridge University Press, 1999), p. 145.

40   Orgel (1999), p. 149.

41   Orgel (1999), p. 146.

42   Orgel (1999), p. 149.

43   Orgel (1999), p. 150.

44   Orgel (1999), p. 353.

45   Orgel (1999), p. 151.

CONCLUSION

1   Robert Headlam Wells, *Shakespeare on Masculinity* (Cambridge: Cambridge University Press, 2000), p. 137.

2   Wells (2000), p. 143.

3   Simon Palfrey. 'Macbeth and Kierkegaard', in Peter Holland (ed.) *Shakespeare Survey: An Annual Survey of Shakespearean Studies and Production 57,* Macbeth *and Its Afterlife* (Cambridge: Cambridge University Press, 2004), p. 96.

Select Bibliography

EDITIONS OF SHAKESPEARE

Greenblatt, Stephen (ed.). *The Norton Shakespeare, Based on the Oxford Edition: Tragedies*. New York and London: W. W. Norton, 1997.

Wells, Stanley and Taylor, Gary (eds). *The Complete Works: Compact Edition*. Oxford: Clarendon Press, 1990.

EDITIONS OF *MACBETH*

Barnet, Sylvan (ed.). *The Tragedy of Macbeth*. Signet Classic Shakespeare. New York and Toronto: New American Library; London: New English Library, 1963.

Braunmuller, A. R. (ed.). *Macbeth*. The New Cambridge Shakespeare. Cambridge: Cambridge University Press, 1997.

Brooke, Nicholas (ed.). *Macbeth*. Oxford World's Classics series. Oxford: Oxford University Press, 1998.

Miola, Robert S. (ed.). *Macbeth*. Norton Critical Edition. New York and London: W. W. Norton, 2004.

Muir, Kenneth (ed.). *Macbeth*. The Arden Shakespeare, Second Series. London and New York: Routledge, 1987.

D'AVENANT'S MACBETH

Spencer, Christopher (ed.). *Davenant's Macbeth from the Yale Manuscript: An Edition, with a Discussion of the Relation of Davenant's Text to Shakespeare's*. New Haven: Yale University Press, 1961.

SEVENTEENTH AND EIGHTEENTH-CENTURY CRITICISM

Richardson, William. *A Philosophical Analysis and Illustration of Some of Shakespeare's Remarkable Characters*. London: J. Murray; Edinburgh: W. Creech, 1774.

Rowe, Nicholas. 'Some Account of the Life of Mr William Shakespeare', in D. Nichol Smith (ed.) Shakespeare Criticism: A Selection 1623–1740, World's Classics series. London: Oxford University Press, 1958, pp. 27–37.

Vickers, Brian (ed.). *Shakespeare: The Critical Heritage*: Volume 1: 1623–1692. London and Boston: Routledge and Kegan Paul, 1974.

——. *Shakespeare: The Critical Heritage*: Volume 2: 1693–1733. London and Boston: Routledge and Kegan Paul, 1974.

——. *Shakespeare: The Critical Heritage*: Volume 3: 1733–1752. London and Boston: Routledge and Kegan Paul, 1975.

——. *Shakespeare: The Critical Heritage*: Volume 4: 1753–1765. London, Henley and Boston: Routledge and Kegan Paul, 1976.

——. *Shakespeare: The Critical Heritage*: Volume 5: 1765–1774. London, Henley and Boston: Routledge and Kegan Paul, 1976.

——. *Shakespeare: The Critical Heritage*: Volume 6: 1774–1801. London, Boston and Henley: Routledge and Kegan Paul, 1981.

NINETEENTH-CENTURY CRITICISM

Coleridge, Samuel Taylor. *Lectures and Notes on Shakespeare and Other Dramatists*. London: Oxford University Press, 1931.

De Quincey, Thomas. 'On the Knocking at the Gate in *Macbeth*', in D. Nichol Smith (ed.) *Shakespeare Criticism: A Selection 1623–1740*. World's Classics series. London: Oxford University Press, 1958, pp. 331–36.

Dowden, Edward. *Shakspere: A Critical Study of His Mind and Art*. London: Kegan Paul, Trench, Trübner, reprint, about 1918, of 3rd edn of 1877.

Hazlitt, William. *Characters of Shakespeare's Plays*. World's Classics series. London: Oxford University Press, 1939.

Jameson, Anna. *Characteristics of Women, Moral, Poetical, and Historical* London: Saunders and Otley, 1833, 2 vols.

EARLY TWENTIETH-CENTURY CRITICISM

Bradley, A. C. *Shakespearean Tragedy: Essays on* Hamlet, Othello, King Lear, Macbeth. St Martin's Library. London: Macmillan, 1957.

Empson, William. *Seven Types of Ambiguity*. Harmondsworth: Penguin Books in association with Chatto and Windus, 1965.

Freud, Sigmund. 'Some Character-Types Met With in Psycho-Analytical Work', in John Strachey and Anna Freud (eds) *The Complete Psychological Works of Sigmund Freud, vol. 14, 1914–1916*. London: The Hogarth Press and the Institute of Psycho-Analysis, 1957, pp. 311–33.

Knight, G. Wilson. *The Wheel of Fire: Interpretations of Shakespearean Tragedy with Three New Essays*. University Paperbacks series. Methuen: London, 1960.

———. *The Imperial Theme: Further Interpretations of Shakespeare's Tragedies Including the Roman Plays*. London: Methuen, 1961.

Knights, L. C. 'How Many Children had Lady Macbeth? An Essay in the Theory and Practice of Shakespearean Criticism?', in *Explorations: Essays in Criticism Mainly on the Literature of the Seventeenth Century*. Harmondsworth: Penguin Books in association with Chatto and Windus, 1964, pp. 13–50.

Spurgeon, Caroline F. E. *Shakespeare's Imagery and What It Tells Us*. Cambridge: Cambridge University Press, 1952.

MID-TWENTIETH-CENTURY CRITICISM

Campbell, Oscar James. 'Shakespeare and the "New Critics" ', in James G. McManaway, Giles E. Dawson and Edwin E. Willoughby (eds) *Joseph Quincy Adams: Memorial Studies*. Washington: The Folger Shakespeare Library, 1948, pp. 81–96.

Gardner, Helen. *The Business of Criticism*. Oxford: Clarendon Press, 1959.

Kott, Jan. *Shakespeare Our Contemporary*, trans. Boleslaw Taborski. London: Methuen, 1965.

Sanders, Wilbur. *The Dramatist and the Received Idea: Studies in the Plays of Marlowe and Shakespeare*. Cambridge: Cambridge University Press, 1968.

Tillyard, E. M. W. *Shakespeare's History Plays*. London: Chatto and Windus, 1944.

Waith, Eugene M. 'Manhood and Valor in Two Shakespearean Tragedies'. *ELH: A Journal of English Literary History*, vol. 17, no. 4 (December 1950), pp. 262–73.

Walker, Roy. *The Time is Free*. London: Andrew Dakers, 1949.

LATER TWENTIETH AND EARLY TWENTY-FIRST CENTURY CRITICISM

Adelman, Janet. *Suffocating Mothers: Fantasies of Maternal Origin in Shakespeare's Plays, Hamlet to The Tempest*. New York and London: Routledge, 1992.

Belsey, Catherine. *Critical Practice*. New Accents series. London: Methuen, 1980.

Belsey, Catherine. *The Subject of Tragedy: Identity and Difference in Renaissance Drama*. London and New York: Methuen, 1985.

Berger, Harry, Jr. 'The Early Scenes of *Macbeth*: Preface to a New Interpretation', in Peter Erikson (ed.) *Making Trifles of Terrors: Redistributing Complicities in Shakespeare*. Stanford: Stanford University Press, 1997, pp. 70–97.

Booth, Stephen. King Lear, Macbeth, *Indefinition, And Tragedy*. New Haven and London: Yale University Press, 1983.

Brown, John Russell (ed.). *Focus on* Macbeth. London, Boston and Henley: Routledge and Kegan Paul, 1982.

Calderwood, James L. *If It Were Done*: Macbeth *and Tragic Action*. Amherst: University of Massachusetts Press, 1986.

Eagleton, Terence. *Shakespeare and Society: Critical Studies in Shakespearean Drama*. London: Chatto and Windus, 1967.

Eagleton, Terry. *William Shakespeare*. Oxford: Blackwell, 1986.

French, Marilyn. *Shakespeare's Division of Experience*. London: Jonathan Cape, 1982.

Greenblatt, Stephen. 'Shakespeare Bewitched', in Jeffrey N. Cox and Larry J. Reynolds (eds) *New Historical Literary Study: Essays on Reproducing Texts, Representing History*. Princeton, New Jersey: Princeton University Press, 1993, pp. 108–35.

Hawkins, Michael. 'History, politics and *Macbeth*', in John Russell Brown (ed.) *Focus on* Macbeth. London, Boston and Herley: Routeledge and Kegan Paul, 1982, pp. 155–88.

Holland, Peter (ed.). *Shakespeare Survey: An Annual Survey of Shakespeare Studies and Production: 57:* Macbeth *and its Afterlife*. Cambridge: Cambridge University Press, 2004.

Kahn, Coppélia. *Man's Estate: Masculine Identity in Shakespeare*. Berkeley, Los Angeles, London: University of California Press, 1981.

Kastan, David Scott. *Shakespeare After Theory*. London and New York: Routledge, 1999.

Orgel, Stephen. '*Macbeth* and the Antic Round', in Stanley Wells (ed.) *Shakespeare Survey: An Annual Survey of Shakespeare Studies and Production: 52: Shakespeare and the Globe*. Cambridge: Cambridge University Press, 1999, pp. 143–53.

Palfrey, Simon. 'Macbeth and Kierkegaard', in *Shakespeare Survey* 57 (2004), pp. 96–111.

Sinfield, Alan. '*Macbeth*: History, Ideology, and Intellectuals', in *Faultlines: Cultural Materialism and the Politics of Dissident Reading*. Oxford: Clarendon Press, 1992, pp. 95–108.

Stallybrass, Peter. '*Macbeth* and Witchcraft', in John Russell Brown (ed.) *Focus on* Macbeth. London, Boston and Henley: Routledge and Kegan Paul, 1982.

Wells, Robert Headlam. *Shakespeare on Masculinity*. Cambridge: Cambridge University Press, 2000.

Select Filmography

Macbeth (1948). 89 minutes. Black and white. USA. Republic/Mercury.

Director: Orson Welles
Writer: Orson Welles
Cast: Orson Welles: Macbeth
      Jeanette Nolan: Lady Macbeth
      Edgar Barrier: Banquo
      Dan O'Herhily: Macduff
      Erskine Sandford: Duncan
      Roddy McDowall: Malcolm

Welles himself called this version, shot on a tight budget in twenty-three days, 'a violently sketched charcoal drawing of a great play'. It aroused largely hostile responses – for example, the *New York Times* said that Welles 'deploys himself and his actors so that they move and strike the attitudes of tortured grotesques and half-mad zealots in a Black Mass or an ancient ritual' (Rothwell and Melzer, 1990, pp. 150, 151) – but Kenneth Rothwell (Rothwell, 1999, p. 77) affirms that 'the sheer nerve and energy of the movie in probing for the devil-driven horror at the soul of its tragic hero makes it impossible to ignore'.

Macbeth (1972). 140 minutes. Colour. Great Britain. Playboy/ Caliban.

Director: Roman Polanski.
Writers: Roman Polanski, Kenneth Tynan
Cast: John Finch: Macbeth
      Francesca Annis: Lady Macbeth
      Martin Shaw: Banquo
      Terence Bayler: Macduff
      Nicholas Selby: Duncan
      Stephan Chase: Malcolm

The most sensational film of *Macbeth*, notable for showing naked witches, Lady Macbeth sleepwalking in the nude and for its graphic blood and violence, which provoked questionable comparisons with the brutal murder of Polanski's pregnant wife, Sharon Tate, by the Charles Manson 'family' in 1971. It is a very 1960s film in many ways, as Deanne Williams points out, and opinion differs as to its current stature: A. R. Braunmuller, in the New Cambridge Shakespeare *Macbeth* (1997, p. 86) calls it 'the most distinguished cinematic version of the play', but Peter Holland (2004, p. 375) finds it 'oddly timid' in its conventional realism.

Macbeth (1997) 129 minutes. Colour. Scotland. CIP/Cromwell/Lamancha/Grampian

Director: Jeremy Freeston
Writers: Bob Carruthers, Jeremy Freeston
Cast: Jason Connery: Macbeth
    Helen Baxendale: Lady Macbeth
    Kenny Bryans: Macduff
    Graham McTavish: Banquo
    John Corvie: Duncan
    Ross Dunmore: Malcolm

Made on a comparatively low budget, this stays fairly close to the text, and was praised in *Total Film* as 'honest, faithful Shakespeare dialogue in a historically accurate setting' (Sammons, 2000, p. 74). But Peter Holland (2004, p. 358) observes that its 'visual style ... is ... heavily dependent on the twin conventions of film costume drama and nineteenth-century theatre spectacle' and is 'locked into a set of conventions that it never questions or extends, but only absorbs'.

ADAPTATIONS WHICH USE SOME ELEMENTS OF *MACBETH* BUT TRANSPOSE THEM INTO A DIFFERENT TIME AND PLACE

Joe Macbeth (1955). 91 minutes. Black and white. Great Britain. Columbia.

Director: Ken Hughes. Philip Shipway
Writer: Philip Yordan (possibly a 'front' for blacklisted writers)
Cast: Paul Douglas: Joe Macbeth
    Ruth Roman: Lili Macbeth
    Sidney James: Banky
    Gregoire Aslan: Duncan the Duke

A *film noir* set in gangland Chicago. A review in *America* called it 'a comic-book version of an immortal piece of literature' and the *National Parent Teacher* felt that 'the sordid gangsters, realistically treated, are no parallels for Shakespeare's exalted personages, whose characters are illuminated by great poetry' (quoted Holland, 2004, p. 361), but Holland himself (2004, p. 364), while finding it 'often poorly acted and weakly shot', commends 'the cleverness of some of its thinking'.

Kumonuso-Jo (1957) [*Throne of Blood* – but Braunmuller (1997, p. 84) suggests that a more accurate and revealing translation is: *The Castle of the Spider's Web*]. 110 minutes. Black and white. Japan. Toto.

Director: Akira Kurosawa
Cast: Toshiro Mifune: Taketoi Washizu [the Macbeth figure]
    Isuzu Yamada: Asaji [the Lady Macbeth figure]
    Minoru Chiaki: Yosiaki Miki [the Banquo figure]
    Takashi Shimura: Kuniharu Tsuzuki [the Duncan figure]

A remarkable and rewarding Japanese version of *Macbeth* by one of the world's leading art-cinema directors. Graham Holderness (1994, pp. 213–14) points out that 'the film's visual style ... is largely structured by the conventions of Japanese Noh drama' and praises the way in which it works in an 'epic' rather than 'tragic mode', making social problems and contradictions visible in a distanced historical setting, and thus alerting us to the 'epic' aspect of Shakespeare's *Macbeth*.

Men of Respect (1990). 113 minutes. Colour. USA. Central Film City/Arthur Goldblatt Productions.

Director and writer: William Riley
Cast: John Turturro: Mike Battaglia [Italian for 'Battle']
    Katherine Borowitz: Ruth Battaglia
    Dennis Farina: Bankie Como
    Peter Boyle: Duffy
    Stanley Tucci: Mal
    Rod Steiger: Charlie D'Amico [the Duncan figure]

Like *Joe Macbeth*, this is set in the United States, but this time, trading on the success of the *Godfather* trilogy, among Mafia families in New York. The idiomatic dialogue often recalls Shakespeare's lines – for example, 'If it were done when 'tis done, then 'twere well / It were done quickly' (1.7.1–2) becomes 'If it's gonna get done, it better get done quick'. Peter Holland claims that *Men of Respect* 'deserves full-scale examination for its often brilliant re-imaginings of Shakespeare's play'.

Scotland, PA. (2001). 144 minutes. Colour. USA Abandon Pictures; Paddy Wagon Productions; Veto Chip Productions.

Director: Billy Morrisette
Cast: James LeGros: 'Joe 'Mac' McBeth
    Maura Tierney: Pat McBeth
    Christopher Walken: Lieutenant McDuff
    Kevin Corrigan: Anthony 'Banko' Banconi
    James Rebhorn: Norm Duncan
    Tom Guiry: Malcolm Duncan

Like *Joe Macbeth* and *Men of Respect*, Billy Morisette's first feature film is set in the United States, but this time not in the big city but in a roadside fast-food restaurant in rural Pennsylvania in the 1970s. Peter Holland calls it 'a parodic displacement of *Macbeth* into a bleakly and blackly comic tale of ambition', while Lauren Shohet (2004, p. 186) finds that it 'offers a surprisingly detailed and nuanced set of ways to think about identity and agency in both *Macbeth* and the 1970s'.

REFERENCES AND FURTHER READING

Holderness, Graham. 'Radical Potentiality and Institutional Closure: Shakespeare in Film and Television', in Jonathan Dollimore and Alan Sinfield (eds). *Political Shakespeare: Essays in Cultural Materialism*. 2nd edn. Manchester: Manchester University Press, 1994, pp. 206–25.

Holland, Peter. ' "Stands Scotland Where It Did?": The Location of *Macbeth* on Film', in Robert S. Miola (ed.). *Macbeth*. Norton Critical Edition. New York and London: W.W. Norton, 2004, pp. 357–80.

Rosenthal, Daniel. *Shakespeare on Screen*. London: Hamlyn, 2000.

Rothwell, Kenneth S. *A History of Shakespeare on Screen: A Century of Film and Television*. Cambridge: Cambridge University Press, 1999.

Rothwell, Kenneth S. and Melzer, Annabelle Henkin. *Shakespeare on Screen: An International Filmography and Videography*. New York: Neal-Schuman, 1990.

Sammons, Eddie. *Shakespeare: A Hundred Years on Film*. London: Shepheard-Walwyn, 2000.

Shaughnessy, Robert (ed.). *Shakespeare on Film*. New Casebooks series. Basingstoke and London: Macmillan 1998.

Shohet, Lauren. 'The Banquet of Scotland (PA)', in *Shakespeare Survey 57* (2004), pp. 186–95.

Williams, Deanne. 'Mick Jagger Macbeth', in *Shakespeare Survey 57* (2004), pp. 145–58.

INDEX